Creative Urbanity

CONTEMPORARY ETHNOGRAPHY

Kirin Narayan and Alma Gottlieb, Series Editors

A complete list of books in the series is available from the publisher.

Creative Urbanity

*An Italian Middle Class in
the Shade of Revitalization*

Emanuela Guano

PENN

UNIVERSITY OF PENNSYLVANIA PRESS

PHILADELPHIA

Published by
University of Pennsylvania Press
Philadelphia, Pennsylvania 19104-4112
www.upenn.edu/pennpress

Printed in the United States of America
on acid-free paper

10 9 8 7 6 5 4 3 2 1

A Cataloging-in-Publication record is available from the Library of Congress

ISBN 978-0-8122-4878-4

Contents

Introduction

> Cities are a combination of many things: memory, desires, signs of a
> language: they are sites of exchange, as any textbook of economic
> history will tell you—only, these exchanges are not just trade-in
> goods, they also involve words, desires, and memories.
> —Italo Calvino (1972)

Clad in a bright green suit, Beatrice, a tall woman in her forties, is leading
a walking tour entitled "I misteri di Genova," Genoa's mysteries. Her group
comprises eleven people, all of whom are local; the setting is this city's
centro storico (historic center). For the occasion, the medieval neighborhood is bathed in a sallow moonlight. Through the evocative power of
Beatrice's words and the suggestiveness of the built environment, we
encounter sinful nuns, murderous aristocrats, and medieval mass burials.
The highlight of Beatrice's tour, however, is one of Genoa's most recent
ghosts: the *vecchina* (little elderly lady) who haunts Via Ravecca, wandering
about with a lost expression on her face on her quest for an ancient *vicolo*
(alley) that no longer exists. Beatrice informs us: "The vecchina began man-
ifesting in 1989. Those who saw her claim that the elderly woman would
ask passersby for directions to Vico dei Librai, and then she would vanish.
Vico dei Librai no longer exists: it was razed to the ground during the
project that destroyed part of the centro storico in the late 1960s to build
the Centro dei Liguri complex."

Widely publicized by local newspapers, the ghost's appearances immediately struck a chord with Genoese publics: as a phantom presence that
transmits affect through the materialities it haunts (Navaro-Yashin 2012),

the vecchina posited an implicit denunciation of the alienation of modern-ist architecture and of what had been ruined by industrial progress (Benson 2005; Johnson 2013). Yet the ghost's timing also presaged an urban re-enchantment process (Ritzer 2010) and an aestheticization of the cityscape that were meant to foster this city's visitability (Dicks 2004) as an alterna-tive to its declining industrial economy. Celebrated in books and websites, the vecchina has now become a staple in local lore. During this walking tour, her presence is effectively channeled through Beatrice: the adept enchantress who, using her personal talents and professional expertise, mediates access to an esoteric facet of urban experience.

Drawing on her evocative words as well as the suggestive settings of the tour, Beatrice allows glimpses of a long-gone Genoa to emerge within the imagination of her audiences, thus conjuring the hidden out of the familiar. Yet Beatrice's tales are not just commodities. Instead, they are also the cre-ative results of her own scholarly interests (she is a published author of urban history books) as well as her passion for the occult. A few days after the tour, Beatrice will be walking around Genoa's centro storico with a subtle energy sensor in her hands. A tremor of her biotensor will indicate a ghastly presence; Beatrice's task, then, will be to use her spells to bring it to the fore. As it leaves its hideout, the ghost may become a story in Beatrice's rich repertoire as a professional teller of tales about all that Genoa hides. Original though her craft may be, Beatrice is hardly alone in her endeavor of shaping new experiences for urban publics eager to view their city through new eyes. Working along with her in revitalized Genoa are scores of fellow walking-tour guides, artisans, shopkeepers, festival organiz-ers, artists, and poets who, since the early 1990s, have contributed to what is now Genoa's culture industry. This book explores how, working in the shade of Genoa's revitalization process, creative individuals like Beatrice have turned their education, interests, and sensibilities into a source of income, thus helping craft urban imaginaries (Cinar and Bender 2007) that reflect their own experiences as passionate explorers of the urban everyday.

The Explorer of the Urban Everyday

The most popular trope in the scholarly analysis of urban experience and the leisurely exploration of a city's social, cultural, and material landscape is that of the *flâneur* (Kramer and Short 2011). First celebrated by nineteenth-century French poet Charles Baudelaire, the flâneur was the prototypical urbanite: the painter of modern life and the man of the crowd (1964). His passion and his profession were

> to become one flesh with the crowd. For the perfect *flâneur*, for the passionate spectator, it is an immense joy to set up house in the heart of the multitude, amid the ebb and flow of the movement, in the midst of the fugitive and the infinite . . . thus the lover of universal life enters into the crowd as though it were an immense reservoir of electrical energy. Or we might liken him to a mirror as vast as the crowd itself; or to a kaleidoscope gifted with consciousness, responding to each one of its movements and reproducing the multiplicity of life and the flickering grace of all the elements of life. (1964: 9)

As a malleable allegory for the description and analysis of urban experience, the image and the experience of the flâneur were soon to become objects of intense critical debate (Kramer and Short 2011). Writing in the early twentieth century, German philosopher Walter Benjamin deprecated how the commercial phantasmagorias of consumer capitalism had transformed the flâneur into the *badaud*: the gaper as a passive consumer of images whose observation skills had gone stagnant (Benjamin 1973). Benjamin's critique became immensely influential for urban studies across disciplinary boundaries. Resonating with the Marxist suspicion of consumption as well as with the elitist disdain for the tastes of the masses and the masculinist contempt for shopping as a female practice (Featherstone 1998; Morris 1993), in the late twentieth century the condemnation of the intensely aesthetic commercial enchantment of the contemporary "voodoo" or "fantasy" city (Dicks 2004; Hannigan 1998; Harvey 1988; Ritzer 2010; Zukin 1996) became synonymous with the allegedly mindless "enjoyment without consequences" (Welsch 1998: 3) of the crowds. While ranging considerably in disciplinary paradigm, methodological approach, and level of empiricism, these studies share a critical focus on the all-powerful role of corporate capitals in shaping the urban everyday. Their core argument is that what ensues from the commercial aestheticization of the urban experience disempowers city dwellers, seducing them into surrendering to the material and ideological might of corporate capitals.

Yet, while much of North Atlantic scholarship indicts consumer capitalism for the loss of truly democratic public space (Mitchell 2003; Harvey 1991; Zukin 1991, 1996), it bears remembering that not all revitalized cityscapes around the world are organized along the lines of the same social, spatial, and above all capitalist criteria as U.S. cities (Soja 1996; Featherstone 1998). In distancing herself from the political economy paradigm that has long been hegemonic in the study of cities, Aihwa Ong (2011: 2) recently argued that the attempt to posit global capitalism as the singular causality of all urban dynamics worldwide inevitably reduces remarkably different cities to the role of manifestations of the same, and globally homogeneous, economic template. Drawing on Michel de Certeau (1984: 159), one may also argue that such analyses are at least partly concocted through an observation of the "concept city": a view from "above" that is enabled by focusing on a "finite number of stable, isolatable, and interconnecting properties" while neglecting the intricacies of the city's everyday. The view from "down below" (de Certeau 1984: 158), instead, allows for an ethnographically inflected approach to the varieties of urban practice that can help produce more nuanced analyses of how urban worlds are made *both* through the top-down intervention of states and capitals *and* through the bottom-up creative practice of city dwellers. The latter, as this book suggests, may use their skills not only to navigate and consume the city (Richards 2011: 1229), but also to shape the kind of experiences that punctuate its quotidian. Instead of reducing urban aestheticization to a crass consumerist spectacle engineered by corporations, here I seek to offer a more nuanced exploration of forms of production of highly symbolic and experiential goods that are both material and intangible (Featherstone 1998: 916), and that are designed and commodified by the very same city dwellers who are also adept at consuming them in the first place. As the "artist who doesn't paint" and the "writer who will one day write a book" (Featherstone 1998: 913), Baudelaire's flâneur limited himself to a close exploration of urban life that was fundamentally unproductive; soon enough he became a gaper trapped in a commercialized urban space (Benjamin 1973). Even though they are themselves adept at consuming various aspects of city life, the protagonists of this book, instead, are neither idle voyeurs nor are they passive gapers. Rather, they are both purposeful explorers of the urban experience and creators of a range of material and immaterial cultural goods and services capable of enacting an aestheticization of the city that is largely independent from corporate dynamics.

Urban Anthropology and the Middle Classes

The contemporary, purposeful, and creative flâneuses and flâneurs portrayed in this book are mostly members of the urban middle classes whom social scientists have consistently classified as the predominant consumers of revitalized cityscapes and of their cultural products (Richards 2006: 266; Smith 1996; Zukin 1989, 1996). As such, they are uneasy subjects of anthropological inquiry. On the basis of the implicit division of scholarly labor that assigned the study of modernity to sociologists and the investigation of traditional cultures to anthropologists (Wolf 1982: 12–13), for a long time the latter eschewed the issue of class. When they began expanding their horizons to urban societies, most anthropologists still limited themselves to studying down, thus focusing their attention exclusively on the marginal and the downtrodden. It is only in recent years that anthropologists have overcome the "Marxist 'embarrassment' of the middle class" (Wright 1989: 3, in Heiman, Liechty, and Freeman 2010: 11) to pay an increasing attention to these social groups. Recent ethnographies of middle-class life range from the former Soviet Union (Patico 2008; Richardson 2008) to India (Dickey 2012; Srivastava 2014) and Nepal (Liechty 2003); from Vietnam (Leshkowich 2014) to China (Hoffman 2010; Zhang 2010); from the United States (Heiman 2015; Low 2003; Newman 1999; Ortner 2003) to Italy (Cole 1997; Molé 2011; Muehlebach 2012) and Egypt (de Koning 2009), and from Barbados (Freeman 2000, 2014) to Brazil (Caldeira 2001; O'Dougherty 2002) and Argentina (Guano 2002, 2003a, 2003b, 2004). And yet, influenced by the Marxist paradigm (Ong 2011) as well as by anthropology's traditional emphasis on the "other," the vast majority of ethnographies with an explicitly urban agenda still focus on the plight of the poor and the disenfranchised. While such scholarship has the merit of shedding light on dynamics of downright oppression and resistance, it also reiterates the anthropological invisibility of the middle classes—almost as if, as Nick Dines (2012: 18) put it, these often remarkably large social groups "did not require investigation or were simply not anthropologically interesting."

While it would be incorrect to claim that urban anthropologists have consistently disregarded the role of the middle classes in the production of urban space worldwide (see, e.g., Low 2003; Caldeira 2001; Guano 2002, 2007; de Koning 2009; Richardson 2008), several of the exceptions zero in on these social groups' known urge to reinforce social boundaries (Bourdieu

1984; Liechty 2003; Ortner 2006), thus highlighting middle-class contributions to the spatialization of prejudice and social fear (Caldeira 2001; Guano 2003a, 2003b; Heiman 2015; Low 2003; Srivastava 2014).[1] Taking a somewhat germane stance, geographic scholarship portrays the middle classes as agents of gentrification and the displacement of urban working classes. Even though they may differ on whether the urban middle classes operate on the basis of culture and taste or whether they are simply the dupes of top-down capitalist dynamics, such approaches classify these social groups along a continuum that ranges from the limited agency of marginal gentrifiers (Beauregard 1986; Rose 1984) and the contradictions intrinsic to liberal middle-class subjectivities (Ley 1996) to the downright racist and classist revanchism of yuppies (Smith 1996).

Suggesting a strikingly different perspective, in 2002 urban theorist Richard Florida targeted an audience of urban administrators and policy-makers with his argument that cities experience growth only when they are successful in attracting highly educated and creative people—a feat at which they can only succeed by fostering an atmosphere of diversity and tolerance set against the backdrop of easily available advanced technology. Florida's thesis drew a considerable amount of criticism for its hyperbolic advocacy (Peck 2005: 741) as well as for its elitism (Gornostaeva and Campbell 2012) and its tendency to obscure the potential implication of the "creative class" in exclusionary forms of urbanism (Markusen 2006; Peck 2005). On the other hand, a cautious reading of Florida's work calls for a reflection on the urban life of social groups that have often been neglected by anthropological inquiry. Utilized as an analytical category rather than as a tool for social engineering, Florida's notion of the "creative class" helps sharpen the focus on the role of middle-class individuals not just as consumers, but rather and above all as producers and marketers of goods and services (see also Freeman 2014; Hoffman 2010; Leshkowich 2014). As such, it invites a reflection on how mid-level processes of cultural production participate in urban revitalization by intervening at a capillary level in a city's everyday. This agency is precisely what, in recent years, anthropologists have called "poiesis" (Calhoun, Sennett, and Shapira 2013) or "worlding" (Ong 2011) as ways of making the city through a quotidian practice that may unfold against the backdrop of large-scale interventions on the cityscape.

Placing an explicitly Marxist emphasis on class struggle, anthropological analyses have frequently cast the dichotomy of structure and agency as one of domination and resistance (Ortner 2006: 137), thus forgetting that opposition is only one out of many possible forms of agency (Ahearn 2001: 115; Mahmood 2005: 155). This is part of the reason why the agency of those social groups that may at least in part benefit from neoliberalization has rarely been addressed (Brash 2011).[2] Along these lines, the agency of the creative middle-class individuals described in this book does not arise as a form of downright opposition to urban revitalization: a "system" (to co-opt sociological terminology) that, while controlled by the local administration as well as by private capitals, is usually experienced by the subjects of this ethnography as a potential source of opportunities rather than as exclusively oppressive. While certainly not devoid of the challenges and the frustrations that characterize the encounter with the public administration and its bureaucracies (Guano 2010a) and of the anxieties brought about by an increasingly stifling corporate presence, the "system" of Genoa's revitalization can still, in some cases, be navigated in a fairly fruitful manner by those who have sufficient cultural capital and initiative to do so. Hence, the latter's agency manifests in its most basic form as a "socio-culturally mediated capacity to act" (Ahearn 2001: 112; Rotenberg 2014: 36), and as a form of "action and control" (Cassaniti 2012: 297) that tweaks and modifies existing circumstances in order to carve productive niches at their margins. The arena and medium of their practice is a rich public urban sphere where experiences are formed along a continuum of sociability, sensoriality, and consumption whereby city dwellers strive to define their relationship to each other through the spaces they share (Moretti 2015: 7).

Italian Urbanity: Sociability and Sensuousness

"Each time you walk into the piazza, you find yourself in the middle of a dialogue," wrote Italian novelist Italo Calvino (1972: 37), thus implicitly underscoring how, in the face of a suburbanization that has segregated North American cityscapes, the piazzas of Italian cities have retained their role as stages for an intense practice of relating to others, often through nonverbal performative means (Del Negro 2004; Guano 2007). It is in these piazzas that one is constantly confronted with the physical presence of others—and, along with it, their experiences and subjectivities (Moretti 2008, 2015).[3] Yet Calvino was hardly the only writer to comment in the public life of Italian piazzas. Walter Benjamin, too, expressed his amazement at how, in Italian cities, private life keeps bursting out of the domestic sphere to be negotiated publicly. In this environment, Benjamin argued, houses are "less the refuge into which people retreat than the inexhaustible reservoir from which they flood out" (1986: 171). "Place of promenades, encounters, intrigues, diplomacy, trade and negotiations, theatricalizing itself" as well as a "vast setting where . . . rituals, codes and relations become visible and acted out": thus Henri Lefebvre (1996: 236–237) described the intense public sociability of towns and cities all over the peninsula. Out of the multiple practices conducted in the piazzas of Italian cities, one in particular attracted scholarly attention: the *passeggiata*, or urban stroll (Del Negro 2004; Moretti 2015; Pitkin 1993). As an only approximate translation of flânerie, the Italian passeggiata entails an exploration of the urban everyday that is not just visual but multisensory, as well as a performance of one's own classed and gendered identity, in a practice where walking is purposeful (Richardson 2008: 148) and being seen is just as important—and socially foundational—as seeing others (Del Negro 2004; Guano 2007; Moretti 2015). Yet, as a form of "being together of strangers" (Young 1990: 234, 256), the passeggiata also opens up the possibility for affective dimensions of this public practice. The proximity with other bodies can trigger responses ranging from repulsion to fear, from mistrust to pleasure, and from curiosity to a desire (Hall 1966) that Calvino thus epitomizes (1972: 24): "The people who pass by each other on the street do not know each other. As they see each other, they imagine a thousand things: the encounters that could take place between them, the conversations, the surprises, the caresses, the bites. Yet nobody acknowledges anybody else, the gazes cross paths for a moment and then they escape each other, seeking out other gazes, they never stop."[4] Calvino's description of the erotic potential fostered by infinite possibilities of city life highlights an Italian urban sensorium that involves not just sight, but also touch, hearing, and taste as essential components in communication (Howes 2003; Jackson 2007).[5] This multisensory communication, I suggest, involves not just the encounter with fellow urbanites but rather also that with the built environment and the materialities of commerce.

Writing about the corridor streets of Italy's Renaissance cities and their role in framing social practice, James Holston (1989) observed that, in relatively narrow streets where architectural solids prevail over voids, ornate façades may be visually organized in the likeness of both an aristocratic interior and a stage for the performance of elitist spectacles of identity whereby, as Guy Debord put it, "a part of the world represents itself in front of the [rest of the] world, and as superior to it" (1984: 21). Hence, according to Holston, the publicness and openness of the corridor street provides only a fiction of participation. As a fundamental form of public sociability in Italian cities, the downtown urban stroll may well have originated as the practice through which local aristocrats showcased their privilege to each other as well as the commoners (Pitkin 1993). Yet, since Italy's economic miracle of the 1960s and the rise of the local middle classes, the competent performance of taste and appropriate behavior during a democratized version of the urban stroll has become a means to claim one's participation in the relatively more inclusive local and national collective imaginaries that materialize against the backdrop of the city (Del Negro 2004). Indeed, in the 1960s the popularization of the passeggiata went along with the increased wealth available to Italy's new middle classes as well as their willingness to consume the plethora of goods displayed in shop windows. Much ink has been poured to describe the badaud mall-goer who, immersed in a pleasurable substitution of reality (Friedberg 1993: 122) and bedazzled and overwhelmed by its cloistered commercial phantasmagorias, "purchases the part for the whole" (Baudrillard 2001: 33, in Friedberg 1993: 116). Yet, if such claims obviously fail to exhaust the actual range of possible practices in U.S. suburban shopping malls such as walking, people-watching, and socializing, they are all the more inadequate to define the experience of Italian urban strollers. Immersed in a complex street environment that little resembles the sanitized seclusion of malls, the latter constantly juggle multiple tasks. These range from the performative enactment of one's own classed and gendered identities (Del Negro 2004; Guano 2007; Moretti 2015; Pipyrou 2014; see also Liechty 2003: 23) to the competent evaluation other people's performances; from assessing one's own safety in the midst of a heterogeneous crowd to navigating an often challenging physical environment and an unruly traffic; and from appraising the goods on display in the shop windows to running necessary errands. The Italian passeggiata may, indeed, encompass the experiences of both the flâneur and the badaud; however, it also and most certainly exceeds them. The Genoese urban stroll is no exception.

Genoa's Middle Classes and the City

Like most Italian cities, Genoa, too, has been a traditional haven for the intricate—and formerly elitist—pleasures of the Italian passeggiata. Writing about his travels through Europe in 1867, Mark Twain (2010: 103) observed that "the gentlemen and ladies of Genoa have a pleasant fashion of promenading in a large park on top of a hill in the centre of the city, from six till nine in the evening, and then eating ices in a neighbouring garden an hour or two longer." Twain's "gentlemen and ladies" were members of Genoa's oligarchy: a class that, in the early 1800s, had emerged out of the assimilation of entrepreneurial families with the local aristocracy (Garibbo 2000: 38). With the complicity of Italy's economic boom, however, a century later the practice of the urban stroll extended to a larger segment of the local population: the middle classes that emerged in the 1960s as a result of Genoa's industrialization and the tertiarization of segments of the local workforce (Arvati 1988).[6]

Middling sectors come into being not only through relations of production, but also and just as importantly from economies of discourse and practice that mold the ever-shifting boundaries with the lower and the upper classes (Bourdieu 1984; Freeman 2000, 2014; Heiman 2015; Hoffman 2010; Leshkowich 2014; Liechty 2003; Ortner 2006). Their identities are predicated upon, among others things, taste (Bourdieu 1984), affect (Freeman 2014), and the competent use of things and places (Guano 2002, 2004; Heiman 2015; Zhang 2010); however, they also draw on cultural capital both in the form of educational credentials and as proficiency in socially hallowed forms of cultural consumption (Bourdieu 1984; Bourdieu and Passeron 1990). Fostered by the relative democratization of the public education system but also by the expansion of the administrative sector subsidiary to their city's industries, Genoa's new middle classes mainly comprised white-collar employees and small business owners. Their aspirational models were not just the local elites, but also the professionals and the high-ranking administrators who had enjoyed a life of relative privilege at least since the mid-1800s (Garibbo 2000: 41). Cultural consumption and educational credentials quickly became fundamental markers of middle-class status. Children of upper- to middle-class families often pursued an education in the classics—preferably at the prestigious Liceo Classico Andrea D'Oria, a rigorous public school where they would rub elbows with the children of the local elite.[7] As they did so, they also complied with the still-prevalent belief that a knowledge of Latin and ancient Greek language and literature is the prerequisite for a superior mind. The prestige attached to classicist education helped drive a wedge between *Genova bene* (well-to-do) offspring who could spend their time pondering issues of Aristotelian metaphysics in preparation for a brilliant career as physicians, lawyers, or administrators, on one hand, and the lower-middle-class and working-class youth who had to learn a practical trade, on the other hand. The propensity for a highbrow style of cultural consumption was not the only aspirational characteristic of Genoa's middle classes, though. Genoa's aristocracy had been known for its reluctance to flaunt its wealth publicly, preferring instead to cultivate subtler tastes that, during the second half of the twenti-eth century, came to be compared to those of the British gentry. A middle-class lifestyle emerged in Genoa that was characterized by sobriety and by a fondness for quality consumer goods that withstood the test of time. This preference pitted the sober consumption practices of Genoa's middle classes against the fashion-conscious flamboyance of their Milanese coun-terparts (Moretti 2015) as well as the stigmatized styles of the local working classes.[8] In a city that, more than others, had known the ravages of war,[9] frugality and chicness became mutually compatible, and the discrimination and poise required to select and wear even plain clothes with debonair elegance came to be appreciated as much as the possibility of shopping at expensive stores. As a skill that in fact "classifies the classifier" (Bourdieu 1984: 6), taste was thus somewhat democratized.

In the 1960s, with a rise in blue- and white-collar employment rates as well as in consumption standards, more and more Genoese became eager to participate in the formerly aristocratic ritual of the urban stroll during which they would perform their proper personas while enjoying the sen-sory, social, cultural, and commercial stimuli provided by fellow passersby, the cityscape, and local businesses. Strolling practices were established that are still popular today. During the warm season, the seaside promenades of bourgeois Corso Italia and Nervi began to brim with smartly dressed crowds enjoying the view and the sea breeze as well as the sight of their fellow Genoese while eating gelato or sipping a soda. In fall and winter, much of the passeggiata practice was—and still is—conducted downtown, especially in the very central (and conveniently porched) Via Venti Settem-bre, where the windows of some of the city's trendiest stores provide addi-tional entertainment, and the coffee shops delight the crowds with the aromas of espresso and fresh pastry. Lurking under the porches like papa-razzi in Federico Fellini's 1960 film *La Dolce Vita*, in those years profes-sional photographers used to take flattering shots of passersby who would then purchase the photos as mementos of their apt urbanity. Local slang emerged defining the passeggiata as *fare le vasche*—literally, to "do laps" by

Figure 1. Passeggiata in downtown Genoa, circa 1962. Photo by Cineclair.

walking back and forth from one end of the street to the other—as well as *fare lo struscio*, "to do the rub," a phrase that hints at the sensuous experience of bodies fleetingly feeling each other in a casual mutual acknowledgment. The popularity of this practice went along with the rapid tertiarization of Genoa's workforce and the rise of its middle class.

Deindustrialization and the Rise of a New Sensibility

Tastefully clad and equipped with a newly found knack for proper forms of consumption as well as, in most cases, a working knowledge of high culture, in the 1960s Genoa's middle classes were poised to enjoy their city the way local elites had done before them. Yet the arena where they could see and be seen even as they pursued their urban pleasures was somewhat sketchy. Their sensuous fruition of their city was limited on one hand by the lingering ravages of World War II bombardments and a considerably degraded centro storico, and on the other by the prioritization of industrial production and the modernist rationalization of urban space (Avila 2014; Lefebvre 1978) that had been conducted for much of the twentieth century at the expense of residents' needs and their quality of life (Gazzola, Prampolini, and Rimondi 2014). As Genoa's mechanical industries, its port, and its steelworks continued to expand, forms of pollution emerged that ranged from toxic fumes and sludge to coal dust and airborne particulates. Yet, while its nefarious effects were naturalized as an inevitable part of life in a modern city (Mirzoeff 2014), the distribution of industrial discomfort was hardly class-blind. Most of the problems caused by Genoa's metropolitan expansion and its industrialization were concentrated in the working-class peripheries. While bourgeois Albaro and Castelletto remained pristine, the city's western outskirts were forced to host the factories, the port, the airport, the city's garbage dump, and a highway—Genoa's first—built right between rows of apartment complexes. The destructive effects of Genoa's modernization extended to its downtown, too—though there they only affected the historic center that had been progressively abandoned since the nineteenth century. In the 1950s, a first swath of the centro storico had been bulldozed to give way to Piccapietra, a commercial and administrative district. In 1965, an unsightly junction known as *sopraelevata* was installed between Genoa's historic center and the port, thus finalizing the disconnection between this sparsely populated working-class neighborhood and an already barely visible sea. Between the late 1960s and the early 1970s, the area of the centro storico known as Via Madre di Dio was razed to the ground and replaced with a modernist conglomerate of office buildings known as Centro dei Liguri. Immediately populated by pushers and heroin addicts, the adjacent park was dubbed "Giardini di plastica" (Plastic Gardens) and proactively avoided by everybody else. The early 1970s was also a negative turning point for Genoa: the steep decline of its port as well as its steelworks and mechanical industries ensuing the rise of global competition and the energy crisis of 1973 brought about the demise of thousands of jobs. The rise of hopelessness went along with a steep increase in drug abuse and crime as well as politically motivated violence even as protests and strikes lacerated the city's quotidian. Angry, dangerous, and ravaged by an ailing industrialism, Genoa became a "ghost city" (Ginsborg 2003: 17) where the leisurely fruition of public urban space had to yield in the face of a rapid decline, and an everyday life often marked by fear and despondency began to erode the urban pleasures of the Genoese.

In the 1980s, a rising critical stance vis-à-vis the logic of industrialism and its consequences for the environment and the lives of people spread all over Europe (Beck 1997: 38). This sentiment rose in Genoa, too, going along with a more reflexive stance toward an urban environment that, as the revitalization process began to take its first steps, intensified its role as not only an object of sensuous, material, and cultural consumption, but also as an arena and a tool for the creation of self-narratives involving lifestyle choices (Giddens 1991). During the late twentieth century, cities in Europe and North America developed an increasing focus on leisure and consumable experiences that blended high culture with the popular and the spectacular (Featherstone 2007: 94). In Genoa, too, this process drew on urban consumers' growing hunger for experiences, their desire for self-development, and the appeal of skilled consumption and self-expression (Richards 2011: 1229) to further shape the middle-class habitus of exploring and enjoying the city purposefully. The latter began to unfold along an experiential continuum that ranges from the pursuit of leisure and sensuous fruition to aesthetic and historical appreciation (Richardson 2008: 148). Driven by the desire to replace this city's ailing industries with a new economy of tourism, the partial reversal of some of the projects carried out in the name of industrial modernization and the recovery of Genoa's premodern architecture began in the late 1980s. By then, the Italian media had begun to describe tourism as an "industry without chimneys," thus pitting it against a faltering industrialism for its allegedly low environmental impact and its high economic potential. Furthermore, in the late 1970s and throughout the 1980s, internal tourism to Italy's cities of art (Florence, Venice, and Rome) had grown exponentially, fueled by the rising educational standards and the newly found cultural tastes of Italy's middle classes (La Francesca 2003). A new urban habitus (Bourdieu 1977) emerged as a set of dispositions, tastes, and sensibilities that further honed middle-class subjectivities increasingly keen on assembling reflexive self-narratives (Giddens 1991: 54). With place being integral to the very structure and possibility of experience (Malpas 1999: 31), the city became not just the canvas on which people live their lives (Rotenberg 2014: 29), but also a privileged arena for the negotiation of their self-narratives (Richardson 2008: 167).

With the rise of cultural tourism in the 1980s, many Genoese, too, became more eager to exercise their own urbanity in novel ways. They became willing to look at their own city through new eyes, consuming it the way they had learned to consume the sites and sights of Florence, Venice, and Rome. As the nexus of place, memory, and self-identity (Malpas 1999: 176–181) became more prevalent, many of them sought out new ways to enjoy their city. What drove them was not just the pursuit of leisure, but also the pride they had long been denied as residents of an "ugly" industrial town as well as the keen curiosity for their own cultural and historical "roots." Yet even though the new urban model introduced in Genoa pivoted on the production of visitability as a source of revenues (Dicks 2004), its material benefits were not limited to the municipal coffers, the deep pockets of developers, and those of the administrators who earned kickbacks in return for lucrative contracts. Instead, they were also reaped by considerably smaller, and largely middle-class, players. The purpose of this book is to explore the lives and experiences of those middle-class Genoese who, seeking to escape consistently high unemployment rates, invented self-employment venues for themselves: the walking-tour guides, the street antique dealers, the artisans, the small businesses owners, and the festival organizers and participants who creatively established ways of making a living in the shade of a broader revitalization process.

Genoa's Creative Class

Succumbing to the global fascination with Richard Florida's tenets, in recent years Genoa's administration utilized his measurements to quantify intangibles such as "talent," "innovation," "diversity," and "tolerance toward homosexuals." The municipality thus classified its city's "creative index" at "23.99%," claiming that Genoa is the "second-most creative city in Italy after Rome."[10] Yet what the municipality failed to mention is that the differences between Genoa's "creative class" and its U.S. counterparts as prospected by Florida are remarkable. First and foremost, in spite of its newly found cultural vibrancy—its symposia, its festivals, its theaters, and its public events—Genoa is not a city to proactively attract or nurture a highly qualified, talented, and creative workforce. As a matter of fact, for much of the twentieth and the early twenty-first centuries, Genoa has suffered a deep demographic decrease: though, in 1971, Genoa's population peaked at over 800,000 and was expected to reach one million in a matter of years, by 2012 it had shrunk back to 580,000: that is, its 1920s level.[11] This change was largely due to a steep decline in birth rates as well as to an emigration that often takes the form of a brain drain. While early twentieth-century Genoese emigrants usually belonged to the peasantry and the proletariat, over the last forty years educated individuals have become much more likely to move to other Italian cities or even abroad in order to find a job that matches their qualifications (see also Gabaccia 2000). This is largely due to the limited opportunities locally available in the university, the scientific and high-tech sector, museums, the arts, and the media, where the few jobs available are frequently co-opted through the clientelistic logics of political parties as well as through the nepotism and the cronyism of powerful individuals and families. Hence, what I explore in this book is a creative class that is in many ways residual, in that it frequently consists of those individuals who, often for lack of better prospects, engage in creative practices as a way to support themselves through forms of self-employment that may require a considerable cultural capital but only a shoestring budget. In spite of the professional gratifications (and in some cases the prestige) afforded to them by their entrepreneurship, the majority of the individuals featured in this ethnography live hand to mouth.[12] Many—though certainly not all of them—are women: a social category that is traditionally marginal to Italy's job market. Put at a disadvantage by patriarchal gender politics, women often have to think creatively in order to find ways to earn a living; their flexibility and their aesthetic and affective expertise make them ideally suited for participation in a neoliberal economy of experience (Freeman 2014). Yet Genoa's creative sector is also a product of the precarity (Butler 2009) that began in the early 1970s, hurling many of

Genoa's blue- and white-collar (and mostly male) workers into a state of redundancy and vulnerability. Additionally, as I argue in Chapter 1, Genoa's creative sector is a child of deeply ingrained social inequities that, with their corollary of cronyism, nepotism, and clientelism, curtail the professional hopes of highly educated and talented individuals. Last but not least, it is also a close relative of the precariousness that, with the labor reforms of 2003, maximized the flexibility of a large share of the Italian workforce while minimizing its rights (Molé 2011; Muehlebach 2013), leading some to envision self-employment as preferable to the vagaries of contract work. Yet, as a frequent middle- and working-class strategy in the face of unemployment, the small-scale entrepreneurship of the creative class described in this book is not new, either. The industrial crisis of the 1970s induced many a Genoese to start a diminutive business to make ends meet. Laid-off workers would open hole-in-the wall stores, often subsidizing them with their severance package: the layoffs and the high unemployment rates that began in the 1970s brought about a proliferation of newsstands, dairy and coffee shops, tobacconists, and the like. If many Genoese always regarded self-employment as the last resort, however, what has changed since the late 1980s is the nature of their businesses. What stands in stark contrast is the profusion of tangible though highly symbolic cultural goods and the intangible and equally symbolic experiences that are being sold in contemporary Genoa—from handmade pottery to ghost tours. Not only does such production fulfill the requirements of a global hierarchy of value (Herzfeld 2004) where more and more Italian cities occupy a peculiar place as objects of cultural consumption, but it also follows the increasingly pervasive substitution of wage labor with a constellation of immaterial labor practices spawned by the commodification of heritage (Comaroff and Comaroff 2009: 144). It also responds to the skills, experiences, and sensibilities of individuals who are themselves adept consumers of urban cultures, and who, in producing and selling symbolic goods and experiences, are exercising their agency in shaping the urban experience of their publics.

A Confession and the Plan of the Book

Just like Baudelaire's flâneur, I, too, cherish losing myself in the crowd, soaking in the impressions of the urban everyday even as I seek to track the experiences of those around me. I do this for pleasure, and I do this as a professional ethnographer. This passion of mine accounts for the itinerant, multi-sited (Marcus 1998; Peterson 2010) quality of this book, with several of its chapters presenting a different creative community through their experiences and the kind of urban imaginaries they seek to shape. While this ethnography does not claim to exhaust the range of creative individuals and communities commercializing aesthetic and cultural experiences in Genoa, it seeks to offer a few glimpses into this city's nature as a fluid assemblage coming into being through the work of a variety of actors as well as a plethora of events (Farías 2010: 15). The temporal depth and the emergent quality of several of the ethnographies in this book stem from my own biography as a diasporic Italian. Genoa is not only my field site; it is also my hometown. Like many fellow Genoese, I left Genoa in 1991 to pursue an academic career from which I would have otherwise been precluded. This is why my account of the transformations in how middle-class Genoese experienced their city initially unfolds against the backdrop of my own formative years as a local. As the narration approaches the decade of the 1990s, however, my attention to Genoa's urban processes becomes a diasporic gaze whose discontinuity kindles a keen curiosity for the transformations at work not just in Genoa's cityscape, but also and above all the everyday of its residents. This is where the "ethnographic I" begins to blend with the "ethnographic eye" (Ellis 2004): it is only in 2002 that this curiosity is formalized as an ethnographic project, one that renews itself on a yearly basis with each trip home.[13] My continuing connections with Genoese society set the tempo of my research, allowing for an enhanced awareness of its diachronic dimension.

Ethnographies are usually based on the conventional one- to two-year field projects that, once the ethnographer returns home and begins the write-up process, may allow for the crafting of truth claims that are frozen in time. Geographical distance becomes temporal remoteness, thus immobilizing a culture, a society, and a country in the authoritative meshes of the ethnographic present (Fabian 2002). Being ensconced in a thick web of relationships that preexisted my ethnography, and returning to Genoa several times a year, year after year, for a range of purposes that include, but also exceed, scholarship, I never had the luxury of regarding my ethnographic research as a completed project. In fact, at times the dynamics and conditions I was observing kept shifting so fast that the attempt to write about them generated anxieties. I often started tackling a topic only to realize that the realities I was analyzing were no longer quite as current, and something new had already entered the scene. My way of overcoming this impasse was to destabilize the ethnographic present by incorporating temporal depth whenever possible.

Furthermore, given my own identity as a diasporic Genoese who has lived and worked in the United States for more than twenty years, mine was not quite the "going back to the field" that characterizes the work of many anthropologists who "leave home" to go "elsewhere" (Reed-Danahay 1997). Instead, it was a form of circulatory migration whereby "home" was, more than anything else, an ever-shifting center (Baldassar 2001: 6–11): a modus vivendi based on shuttling back and forth between two countries while never really leaving either home or the elsewhere behind. As time went by, my ethnographic research both unraveled and intensified multiple affective threads, which in turn opened up new areas of investigation before my eyes where the personal was never divorced from the anthropological. As several of my friends became my informants, many of my informants became my friends: I started intellectual collaborations with some of them and volunteered to help others with their businesses, sharing their enthusiasms and their worries as they sought to preserve their livelihood in the face of a fluctuating economy. In all of this, Genoa always loomed large as the city that never ceased to intrigue, charm, and disappoint me. It tantalized me with memories of my youth and with the changes it superimposed on them; it also tormented me with its imperviousness, and, most importantly, it marked my personal life through its refusal to host my future and its simultaneous unwillingness to let fully go of me. My decision to conduct this project in Genoa was a way of deepening my connection to this city even as I looked for answers whose relevance was both anthropological and personal. Hence, this book is the labor of love: a contrasted love where an intermittent distance intensifies both longing and disappointment, and whose bitter breakups are often followed by the temporary pleasures of a renewed romance.

In this vein, the first chapter of this book is a semi-historical excursus set against the backdrop of my own experience. Moderately autoethnographic, this chapter is steeped in the assumption that our own stories are more than just personal experiences (Ellis 2004: 37), and that my own narrative has received its words from other voices (Bakhtin 1982: 202): those of the family members, friends, acquaintances, and mentors who contributed to my formative years, who walked with me through innumerable experiences, who helped me process them, and the many more who, in recent years, volunteered to take on the role of ethnographic informants.

My stories are never fully mine, in that they are also implicitly interwoven with the voices of all those who provided me with critical perspectives even as they helped me shape my own (Bourguignon 1996). The latter category includes the historians, the sociologists, the anthropologists, but also the writers whose musings provided a springboard for this work. Due to the hybrid quality of the story I set out to tell, I opted for replacing the sanitized, objective, historical contextualization that is required of any book-length ethnography with a chapter where I provide chronotopic perspectives on the urban everyday starting with the 1970s—that is, the decade when Genoa's deindustrialization process and its decline began. Drawing on formal histories and personal stories, on my own memories and those of people I met and interviewed, but also of those with whom I grew up and grew older, as well as on the works of local poets, novelists, and songwriters, Chapter 1 explores how, in the 1980s, the promises of neoliberalism led many a Genoese to hope for a better future. These promises hinged among others on the gradual but radical process that, by the end of the decade, had begun transforming Genoa's cityscape, flashing glimpses of optimism for what had become a ghost city—or, in the words of local novelist of national renown Maurizio Maggiani (2007), a city of shattered mirrors. Unfortunately, even these promises were destined to be broken as—with the complicity of the recession that began in 2008 and deepened in 2011—Genoa's newly found tourist vocation failed to provide the deliverance for which many had hoped.

Chapter 2 interrupts the narrative of local middle-class urbanity to present a different kind of aestheticization of the city: one that, unlike the other ethnographies in this book, does not emerge from the residents' creative practice but rather from the transformation of Genoa into a stage for the performance of a global political drama in which the state played a paramount role. The Genoa that hosted the 2001 Group of Eight summit was one in a series of great events meant to contribute to Genoa's revitalization by, among others, showcasing the city to global audiences. Yet in spite of the promise it allegedly held, this event was characterized by the exclusion of the local population through a top-down intervention on the cityscape at the hands of state representatives as well as by the ensuing backlash by a resistive multitude. As it shows what may happen when mutually antagonistic social groups lay a symbolic as well as a material claim to a cityscape, this chapter is a reminder of the potentially highly contested nature of urban revitalization—even when what is at stake is neither the commercialization of public space nor corporate profit per se, but rather the very same role of the urban as an arena for political performance. Just as importantly, this chapter outlines the contours of a collective trauma that marred the collective hope in the face of a state violence that had no antecedents in post–World War II Western history.

Written against the grain of political economy scholarship, Chapter 3 is an ethnographic analysis of the gentrification that has unfolded in Genoa's centro storico since the early 1990s, thus repopulating a neighborhood that had been largely abandoned in the nineteenth century. This, however, is not the same phenomenon as described by much Anglophone scholarship. To date, most scholarly approaches to gentrification have cast cities as playing fields of planetary capitalism (Farías 2011; Ong 2011; Roy 2011), thus engaging in a "sameing" process that not only disallows difference through the universalization of North Atlantic modernity (Blaser 2013), but that also reduces cities to arenas for the class struggle between globalized bourgeoisies and the poor (Ong 2011). While there is no doubt that the gentrification of Genoa's centro storico served the speculations of developers even as it increased the municipality's revenues, this chapter approaches this phenomenon as a more complex reality whereby capitalist dynamics are just one component of the story. More specifically, this chapter tackles gentrification as an assemblage of people, logics, and materialities (Farías 2010; Collier and Ong 2005): one whereby a nexus of neoliberal rationality, the built environment, and old and new neighborhood residents and users contribute to making a world whose emergent dynamics may at times unfold along the lines of the well-researched template of the capitalist "spatial fix" (Harvey 2001)—and yet, at other times they are considerably more complex. The protagonists of this chapter are marginal gentrifiers who, unlike the revanchist yuppies described by much Anglo-American literature, are neither part of a fleeting stage of gentrification nor upwardly mobile. Instead, they are residents and small business owners who, keen on consuming and producing culture on a budget, have found a modus vivendi with the local crime scene, and negotiate their daily lives along the increasingly thin line that separates them from poverty even as they seek to resist the crushing pressure of corporate commerce with its new spatialities.

Chapters 4 and 5 delve into the experiences of two social groups whose poiesis (Calhoun, Sennett, and Shapira 2013) has made substantial contributions to Genoa's public image as a "city of culture": street antique dealers and walking-tour guides. Chapter 4 describes how, since the mid-1990s, a proliferation of antique fairs have given chronically under- and unemployed middle-class women an opportunity for self-employment. This chapter explores how middle-class women antique dealers draw on their gendered and classed skills such as their aesthetic sensibility to stake out a place for themselves in an urban economy of culture, even though the domestic and decorative aura that at times surrounds women's endeavors may still undermine their efforts. Drawing on an ethnography of how Genoa's walking-tour guides describe and present the city as well as on the analysis of their professional histories and experiences, Chapter 5 suggests that these protagonists of Genoa's newly found tourist vocation are agentive cultural intermediaries who mediate between high and popular culture as they shape the urban experiences of their publics. Acting independently from the political and corporate entities that traditionally drive the transformation of postindustrial cities into consumption hubs, Genoa's walking-tour guides draw on their own creativity, their talents, and their educational background to generate venues of self-employment by spinning tales of concealment and discovery around the master narrative of Genoa's industrial decline and its tourist potential.

While Chapter 4 and 5 focus on the experiences and biographies of some of Genoa's creative individuals, Chapter 6 dwells on the kind of worlding practices that may emerge in the shade of revitalization. This chapter is an ethnography of the Suq (Souk): a multicultural festival held in Genoa every year under the supervision of two women who, since the late 1990s, have used their background in sociology, political science, and theater to further the cause of diversity in Genoa. Multicultural festivals have been frequently denounced as opportunities for the consumption of "other" cultures that are added as commoditized and politically irrelevant "spices" to the otherwise allegedly "bland" everyday life of mainstream groups (hooks 1992; Kirshenblatt-Gimblett 1991). Yet these critiques often fail to explore how such events articulate with sensuous modalities of constructing dominant identities. This chapter seeks to contextualize the Suq within the broader politics of representing and consuming selves and others in contemporary Italy, and it argues that the Suq's specific brand of strategic orientalism attempts to penetrate the Italian sensorium for the sake of challenging hegemonic representations of culture, identity, belonging, and roots. Just as importantly, this chapter suggests that, in a society where small businesses are a fundamental source of livelihood for both natives and immigrants, the Suq supports an alternative to forms of consumption increasingly shaped by the shopping malls and the big-box stores that, since

2000, have proliferated in Genoa's deindustrialized peripheries, bringing about blight in formerly thriving neighborhoods.

As an ethnographic analysis of those aspects of revitalization that often go neglected in urban studies literature, this book argues that tourist guides, small business owners, artisans, festival organizers, and street antique dealers have given, and continue to give, a fundamental contribution to the process of transforming Genoa into a city of culture. Yet, in seeking to explore facets of this revitalization that range from the ever-present voracity of corporate commerce to the poiesis of the self-employed, this book also acknowledges the impossibility of experiencing—and analyzing—the city in its totality (Cinar and Bender 2007: xii). Hence, neither does it attempt to represent the city as a bounded and stable entity (Farías 2010: 9), nor does it claim to exhaust the range of creative practices that unfold in the shade of revitalization. Instead, it approaches the city through the exploration of some of the subjectivities, practices, expectations, things, logics, and the built environment that contribute to its emergent formation: a process whereby neoliberalism is, I suggest, only one of the forces at work (Farías 2010; Ong 2011).

Chapter 1

Chronotopes of Hope

> It is useless to establish whether Zenobia should be classified as a
> happy or an unhappy city. It is not into these two species that one
> should divide the city; instead, one should ask whether it belongs to
> the category of those cities that continue to shape their wishes
> throughout the years, or to that of the cities that are erased by them.
> —Italo Calvino (1972)

> Genoa is the city of parting and oblivion. It is hard to stay, but it is
> even harder to leave and then return.
> —Maurizio Fantoni Minnella (2014)

By presenting a series of chronotopes (Bakhtin 1981) that offer an insight
into Genoa's ever-changing quotidian since the 1970s, this chapter begins
to investigate the tangle of place and hope that allows space to become
"charged and responsive to the movements of time, plot and history"
(Bakhtin 1981: 84). The chronotopes it outlines depict a specific dimension
of Genoa's time-space as an arena for the experiential modulation of economies of hope mediated by communist and capitalist political projects:
dreamworlds (Buck-Morss 2002) toward which the Genoese strove at different times in the history of their city, and that manifested through the
urban everyday and its spatialities (Harvey 2000; Lefebvre 1991). These
dreamworlds are not examined in their disembodied, ideal-typical form,
but rather as a plurality of communist and capitalist cultures (Yanagisako
2002) emerging in and through the quotidian through the friction between

globally traveling discourses and local circumstances (Tsing 2004). My purpose is to outline emergent forms of hope along with their blends of emanci-
patory qualities and mystifications (Bloch 1986). As Ernest Bloch (1998: 341)
suggested, hope dwells in a "region of the not-yet" that is characterized by
"enduring indeterminacy." Hope's dissatisfaction with the present and its orientation toward the future (Berlant 2011: 13), however, shape the "margin of
maneuvrability" and the "opening to experimenting" (Massumi 2002: 212)
through which this affect may foster initiative and the push for change
(Crapanzano 2003: 6). The hope I explore here is the kind of potentially
actionable affect that is driven by utopian dreams of modernization and the
promise of happiness (Buck-Morss 2002; Miyazaki 2006). As an orientation
toward the future that anticipates a happiness to come while simultaneously
signaling a critical occupation with the past and the present (Ahmed 2010:
181; 174), the hope I tackle in this chapter is more specifically a "plausible
narrative of progress" (Rorty 1999: 232): one that has the power of replicating
itself interdiscursively across ideological boundaries, both on the left and on
the right (Miyazaki 2004). This is the form of hope that drives the pursuit of
a better life—a notion that has its roots in Christianity as much as it draws
on the faith in progress promoted by the Enlightenment (Mayr 1992: 117).
In Genoa's case, hope includes first and foremost the possibility to make a
living and improve the circumstances of one's life.

In his ethnography of Zambia, James Ferguson (1999) provided a poi-
gnant analysis of the disconnection experienced by people when the modernization prospected by industrialization was suddenly derailed. In a
similar vein, writing about how young Ethiopian men lost hope as neoliberal reforms curtailed their employment opportunities, Daniel Mains
(2012) described the stagnation and despair that unfold when the narrative
of personal and collective progress is interrupted. While the African settings
of Ferguson's and Mains's ethnographies are quite different from the circumstances at hand in Genoa, the underlying collective narrative—the
promise of modernization, its interruption, and the ensuing stagnation and
despair—is remarkably similar. In Genoa, too, the relative prosperity and
stability brought about by twentieth-century industrialization found an
abrupt end in the 1970s. Blue-collar jobs that, up to then, had been readily
available to the point of attracting a considerable migration from the south
of the country became increasingly scanty. The tertiary sector that had been
experiencing steady growth due to the expansion of the public administration and the state-run industries also slowed down. In the face of rising

desperation, political parties and powerful individuals fastened their iron grip on the scarce employment opportunities, which they kept bartering in return for favors, cash, and power. It is in this context, I suggest, that the spread of north Atlantic neoliberal ideologies with their rhetoric of meritocracy brought about a new wave of hopefulness in the 1990s in the face of Genoa's continuing decline. The neoliberal hope that spanned the decades of the late 1980s, the 1990s, and the early 2000s pivoted on urban revitalization to prospect the possibility for change. This entailed in the first place the promise of employment and opportunities in the rising sector of tourism and cultural consumption; it also prospected a better quality of the urban everyday: one that entails, among others, increased safety from crime and violence and, with it, the fruition of a public sociability that, in much of Italy, is conceptualized as not just a desirable but also a necessary part of one's life in the city (Del Negro 2004; Guano 2007; Moretti 2015). Yet, embedded as it was in a capitalist dynamic whereby, as Laurent Berlant (2011: 171) put it, "if you're lucky you get to be exploited, and if you're lucky you can avoid one more day being the focus of a scene that hails and ejects you when it is your time to again become worthless," even this neoliberal version of hope was of the cruel kind, in that it, too, contained the seed of its own failure (Berlant 2011). I conclude this chapter with the discussion of how, by the early 2000s, even the hopefulness brought about by Genoa's revitalization became collateral damage to the dystopic, and equally neoliberal, rhetoric that "there is no alternative" (Harvey 2000: 17, 2007: 40). There is no alternative to the austerity measures imposed on all but the very wealthiest in the name of Italy's membership in the European Union, nor is there any alternative to the precarity of people whose disposability has become the only certainty in their lives (Butler 2006; Molé 2011).

The Beginning of the End

This story begins in the 1970s. As the seat of several of Italy's heavy industries and a vertex of the "industrial triangle" that had driven the country's economic miracle of the 1960s, Genoa by then had a longstanding industrial tradition, though one that had grown in the shade of the Italian state and its subsidies. The cityscape of those years bore witness to this industrialization as well as to the ravages of World War II: even the Carlo Felice opera theater was still a pile of rubble defacing Piazza de Ferrari, the heart

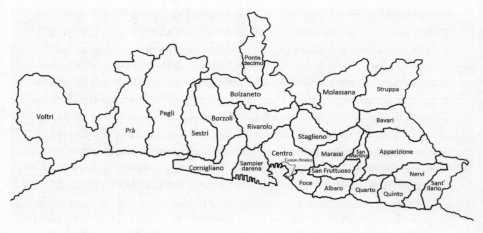

Figure 2. Genoa's neighborhoods. Map by Jessica M. Moss and Luciano Rosselli.

of Genoa's downtown. The imposing early twentieth-century city center was constantly grey with soot, and the bleak industrial peripheries had cannibalized previously pleasant maritime and rural villages. As a constant reminder that workers had had to choose between their life and their livelihood, until the early 2000s Cornigliano's steelworks kept spewing fumes that reeked of rot and spread cancer. In the meantime, a swath of the centro storico had been bulldozed and turned into the Centro dei Liguri administrative complex—yet another example of failed modernist architecture. Known as *sopraelevata*, a junction was built to connect the city center with the industrial peripheries; while aiding transit, it visually and physically separated the old city from the sea. Bourgeois neighborhoods such as Albaro continued to revel in their architectural and natural beauty, but the rationality of modernist urbanism did not contemplate issues of quality of life—let alone aesthetic pleasure—for working-class neighborhoods (Avila 2014; Lefebvre 1978: 77).

As to the centro storico, this is how, in 1974, popular Genoese singer and songwriter Fabrizio de Andrè described it in his *Città vecchia* (Old City) lyrics:

If you walk along the old docks
In that thick air loaded with salt and swollen with smell
There you will find the thieves the murderers and the strange guy
Who sold his mother to a midget for three thousand lire.

Back then, a considerable portion of the centro storico was still in shambles: piles of rubbles memorialized the wounds inflicted by allied bombs during World War II first, and, after that, by the continuing neglect exercised by local administrators. Many of its buildings were empty, deserted by all but the occasional drug addict, and infested by the hordes of rats that nested in the medieval sewage system and were said to outnumber residents seven to one. The viable apartment complexes were sparsely populated. Many of the ground floor spaces that had, in centuries bygone, hosted thriving businesses were now used for storage—and, when the first immigration waves from the Maghreb began in the 1970s, for cramming people in diminutive rooms in return for exorbitant rents. Floating above the dark, damp spaces of poverty, frequently empty frescoed apartments and penthouses with roof balconies suspended over a breathtaking view of the sea bore witness to the grandeur of the past, ready to spearhead the gentrification process that was to begin twenty years later. Back in the 1970s, however, the neighborhood catered predominantly to working-class families of mixed Genoese and Southern Italian provenance; elderly Genoese; hippie, anarchist, and Ultraleft communes; and a heterogeneous crowd of drug addicts, pushers, prostitutes, and smugglers.

In those years, many of the residents of Genoa's better-off neighborhoods such as Albaro would not have been caught dead in the *caruggi* (the alleys of the old city, as they are called in local dialect). "Too dangerous" was the general opinion. Following dynamics common to other South European cities (McDonogh 1987), for people from the lower-middle-class to upper-class uptown (*circonvallazione a monte*) who lived a short walking distance from the centro storico, a cautious excursion to this part of town had the prurient thrill of slumming or, better said, social tourism. After World War II, young men used to take walks through the centro storico to demonstrate their masculinity and bravado. Young women, instead, avoided it altogether, or took only quick trips to its well-known stores—but never alone. In the Genoa of those years, going to the centro storico had taken on the connotation of a "*discesa agli inferi*": a descent to the netherworld (Fusero et al. 1991: 86) that few were willing to undertake.

Drugs and the City

The Genoa of the 1950s, wrote sociologist Luciano Cavalli (1960), had been a "divided city" where neighborhood boundaries marked the separations between social classes as well as the intensification of the mistrust between the communist working classes from the peripheries and the Catholic bourgeoisie of better-off neighborhoods. In the late 1960s and early 1970s, the spread of Marxist ideas and the growing dissatisfaction with Italy's hierarchical and exclusionary society, its authoritarian and elitist education system, the exploitation of labor, dominant sexual and family mores, and even institutionalized communism (in the form of the Italian Communist Party) led to the emergence of youth movements all over the country, but especially in the industrial North (Balestrini and Moroni 1988). Like elsewhere in the Western world, hippies, anarchists, and other social movements often experimented with new social arrangements such as communes (Balestrini and Moroni 1988: 46; Ginsborg 1990: 298–309) where the youth could emancipate themselves from their family—though not from patriarchy per se (Ginsborg 1990: 306). In Genoa, such communes established themselves predominantly in the centro storico, where the youth known as *contestatori* (dissenters) made a home for themselves by squatting in rundown vacant buildings. Those were also the years of the spread of light drugs such as marijuana and hashish, initially sold by individuals who traveled back and forth from Great Britain or even India as part of their existential quest.

By the mid-1970s, however, the spirit of the movement had changed. As it faced the crisis of industrialism, the steep decline of employment, and an unrelenting censorship even at the hands of a parliamentary Left that was concerned about losing its legitimacy with mainstream voters, the optimistic rebelliousness of 1968 gave way to radical hopelessness (Balestrini and Moroni 1988: 369). Managed primarily by mafia cartels, heroin made its appearance, spreading especially among the youth; if, in 1976, there were approximately 10,000 heroin addicts, by 1978 this number had jumped to 70,000 (Balestrini and Moroni 1988: 385). In Genoa, heroin trafficking gained a foothold primarily in the centro storico.

Indeed, the dark, labyrinthine *vicoli* (alleys) were just as hospitable to *spacciatori* (dealers) as they were to *tossici* (short for *tossicodipendenti*, drug addicts). In the 1970s and the 1980s, seeing a man leaning idly against a wall, seemingly doing nothing, was sufficient for most passersby to take a detour. It was not the spacciatore per se that caused so much fear. The source of much concern, instead, was the predatory behavior of some of his customers: the "violent and destructive subjectivities" generated by the "structurally imposed everyday sufferings" (Bourgois and Schonberg 2009: 19) of those who had nothing to live for except their daily *dose* (fix). As many city residents proactively avoided the centro storico, tossici claimed large sectors for themselves. Among these were the Plastic Gardens: the product of the botched modernization project that, in the late 1960s, had led to bulldozing and redeveloping the ancient Via Madre di Dio area of the centro storico. Encased among tall walls and buildings and notorious for their modernist squalor, the Plastic Gardens were utilized exclusively by tossici. Everybody else carefully avoided them.

Well into the 1990s, a walk around the centro storico meant almost invariably coming across at least a few signs of the tossici's activities. At times, these would include mattresses strategically placed in less-trafficked corners; most often, however, the presence of tossici was signaled by their discarded syringes. It was not unusual to spot tossici, squatting against a wall, as they did their *buco* (injection). Just as often they could be seen as they waddled around with an easily recognizable gait, panhandling hesitant passersby. Back then, comedians and ruthless teenagers alike did not think much of mocking their characteristic way of asking, "*Scusa, ce l'hai cento lire?*"—"Excuse me, do you have 100 lire to spare?" Most people, however, felt at least somewhat anxious in their presence, fearing an attack or an unpredictable reaction from those who so blatantly defied bourgeois norms of sobriety and self-reliance.

In the 1970s and 1980s, Genoa ranked third in Italy for overall crime rate, but it came in first for juvenile crime (a ranking sociologists blamed squarely on addictions; see Arvati 1988: 49). Indeed, the 1970s were tense years in Genoa. Violent crime such as robberies in banks, restaurants, and post offices as well as kidnappings was on the rise, and so were burglaries and thefts. This is when the city earned a reputation as *capitale italiana degli scippi* (Italian capital of purse snatchings) that never went away. Whether they were committed by tossici, or whether the culprits were sober, able-bodied individuals, the majority of crimes in the old city were highly gendered purse- and jewelry-snatchings: young men riding a scooter or on foot would approach a woman, grab her purse or necklace, and vanish in the labyrinth of vicoli. Occasionally, the robbers would also shove their victim to the ground, dragging her if she resisted. Jewelry snatchings could be even more vicious, in that necklaces, bracelets, and watches were forcefully ripped off the victim's body, causing bruises and cuts. Injured and traumatized, victims of a *scippo* would go to the *carabinieri* precinct, only to be told that her chances of recovering the stolen goods were about nil. At times, however, the crimes attributed to tossici would be far more violent, often entailing stabbings and beatings administered for the sake of stealing enough cash for the next fix. "If you have to be the victim of a violent crime," people used to say, "pray that the robber is a professional and not a tossico." Professional criminals were allegedly more lucid in evaluating the ramifications of their actions. Tossici, instead, were the shadow cast by the supposedly rational life of an industrial city unable to handle its decline. As such, they served as the ideal folk devil in the Italian imaginary.

Ever since the beginning of the AIDS pandemic in the 1980s, tossici were accused of contributing to the spread of the disease. The moral panic that had been triggered by heroin addicts' casual needle-sharing practices extended to their habit of dumping their used syringes on sidewalks but also on city lawns, playgrounds, and beaches, thus exposing law-abiding citizens and their children to a possible source of contagion. In those years, Alessandra, a teacher at a local school and a centro storico resident, accidentally stepped on a syringe while walking to work. The needle penetrated her rubber boots and pierced her skin. Frightened, she immediately ran to the nearest hospital to request a tetanus shot and to undergo a series of HIV and hepatitis tests. The latter she had to repeat periodically for several months after the accident. Even though up to that point she had enjoyed her home in the not-yet-gentrified centro storico—so close to work but also theaters, museums, and shopping venues—only a few months later she moved out. That incident, she told me, had been pivotal in her decision to look for a home in a semi-rural neighborhood where, she said, "everybody knows everybody else and no one does drugs."

In those days, much of the social fear about tossici and their syringes converged upon the centro storico; however, the area behind my uptown apartment was carpeted with used needles, too, and so were urban parks and secluded corners in middle-class neighborhoods. At that time, the local newspaper frequently reported news of syringes buried needle-up on local beaches, planted behind train seats, and maliciously stuck in all sorts of places where unsuspecting citizens could be stung and potentially exposed to hepatitis and HIV contagion. Upon discovering the advantages of proactively performing the role of the villains that had been imposed on them anyway, some tossici took to using dirty syringes as weapons for their robberies: after all, demonized minorities are often empowered by the frightening auras built around them by concerned majorities (Appadurai 2006). Tossici's favorite targets were small business owners, especially in the centro storico, but at times they would attack passersby, too. Yet again, such incidents invariably struck a deep note with the local social imaginary, and were widely publicized in the media.

Then, in the early 1990s, heroin went out of fashion and was largely replaced by different drugs such as cocaine and designer drugs (Avico et al. 1992) In Genoa, the sight of heroin addicts dragging themselves through the centro storico and panhandling passersby became increasingly rare. As a social worker cynically put it in recent years, "By now most of the tossici from the 1970s and 1980s have died of an overdose, HIV or hepatitis. The few historical tossici who survived are so old and *malandati* (in bad shape) that they are getting ready to retire."[1]

The Years of Lead

Drugs were hardly the only scourge that afflicted Genoa in the 1970s. Named after a 1981 film by German director Margarethe von Trotta, Italy's 1970s went down in history as the "years of lead" (*gli anni di piombo*): a label that effectively reflects the somber atmosphere of that decade as a time in which violence, fear, and hopelessness permeated much of everyday life in most Italian cities.[2] As one of Italy's foremost industrial cities and the historical seat of a strong resistance to Mussolini's Fascist government and its German allies, Genoa had always been a stronghold of the Left: not just the Partito Socialista Italiano (Italian Socialist Party, or PSI), but also the Partito Comunista Italiano (Italian Communist Party, known as PCI; Arvati 1994). However, in the late 1960s the culture of older workers who had largely submitted to the PCI's line of command and its unions was increasingly challenged by a new type of worker: one that was both critical of official party lines and willing to explore new strategies of resistance. The contribution of Southern Italian immigrants to the emergence of new forms of dissent was fundamental: upon encountering the well-organized, but also regimented, communist culture of unionized Northern factory workers, they helped to shape novel forms of struggle that defied existing models (Dogliotti 2004: 1155; Balestrini and Moroni 1988: 67). Genoa thus became the hotbed for a plethora of movements known as *sinistra extraparlamentare* (extra-parliamentary Left) or *ultrasinistra* (Ultraleft), which were characterized by their radical opposition to a PCI they saw as too conservative, and by their eagerness to explore new forms of social struggle. Lotta Continua (Continuous Struggle), Autonomia Operaia (Workers' Autonomy), and XXII Ottobre (October 22) were some of the most visible groups active in the Genoa of those days. The latter, in particular, carried out the kidnapping of Sergio Gadolla (the heir of one of Genoa's foremost industrial families) as well as a robbery that caused the accidental death of a man. In 1974, magistrate Mario Sossi had all of the XXII Ottobre group members tried and convicted. Concerned with its own public legitimacy, the PCI dismissed XXII Ottobre members as criminals rather than freedom fighters; to some of the extra-parliamentary Left, instead, this trial became a turning point of sorts (Dogliotti 2004: 1661). Soon enough, the Red Brigades—Italy's foremost Ultraleft group—became active in Genoa (Dogliotti 2004: 1159). On April 18, 1974, a Red Brigades commando kidnapped Sossi, whom it set free only a month later. On June 8, 1976, Red Brigades members shot and killed Attorney General Francesco Coco and the two police officers who escorted him. If Sossi's kidnapping was a sign that the Red Brigades were taking aim at the state, the murder of Coco was their first politically motivated assassination (Dogliotti 2004: 1161). The attacks drove an even deeper wedge between the parliamentary Left and their extra-parliamentary interlocutors over the issue of violence as a tool of political struggle. The PCI recoiled at the violence, and Genoa's unions organized a protest against the assassination (Dogliotti 2004: 1163). The Red Brigades, however, were not deterred by the workers' dissent. Between 1975 and 1981, their Genoese branch carried out one robbery, injured sixteen people (often by knee-capping them), and committed nine public assassinations (Cavazza 2013). Their last victim was unionist Guido Rossa, whom they killed in 1978 for denouncing *brigatista* Francesco Berardi.

Being in a public place, in the Italy of those years, could be a risky proposition. Right-wing terrorists pursued their "strategy of tension" by carrying out indiscriminate bombings: they planted explosives in crowded piazzas, trains, and railway stations. Their goal was to terrorize the population in order to pave the way for a coup. The Ultraleft, instead, was more discriminating in selecting its targets. However, Red Brigades attacks still took place in the street, in broad daylight, and under the eyes of terrorized bystanders—a strategy that was utterly unsettling for the general population in that it further undermined increasingly obsolete assumptions about the safety of the urban everyday (see also Eyerman 2008); taking advantage of Genoa's convoluted map and its thick web of shortcuts (Dogliotti 2004: 1173), their commandos always managed to escape. Soon enough, Genoa became known as the "capital of the Red Brigades" (Dogliotti 2004: 1177).

The tension was so high that the sight of a five-pointed star (the symbol of the Red Brigades) spray-painted on a city wall would immediately trigger media coverage and a formal investigation. In turn, this general anxiety led to an escalation of repressive policing surveillance measures legitimized through the need to prevent terrorist acts. In those years, being searched by the police was a frequent occurrence, and long beards and parkas could trigger a frisking at any time. Very little ground was needed to obtain a formal warrant: my childhood home was once searched by the police on the basis of my father's visual likeness to a known terrorist.

Though the latter experience injected a degree of anxiety into my family life, as a child I usually found myself watching from the outside. Like many children my age, I normalized the violent world I grew up in because it was all I had ever known. At that time, people in my generation were too young to feel the full political and social import of the events; however, occasionally the angst of adult family members would filter through to us. Barely a pre-teen, on the day of Coco's murder I was on a city beach. When the management announced the terrorist attack on the loudspeaker, my mother stuffed my friends and me into her Fiat 500 and hurriedly took us all home. The news had frightened her, and she was worried about the possibility of unrest. And when, on the morning of March 16, 1976, Italy's President of the Council of Ministers Aldo Moro was kidnapped in Rome by a Red Brigades commando that slaughtered his escort only to kill him fifty-five days later, the middle school I attended immediately canceled all classes and sent the students home, where we would presumably be safer. Not only was this decision indicative of the role of the family as the ultimate bulwark of Italian society in the face of a weak state, but it also indexed the general astonishment at the news. Aldo Moro was an embodiment of the institutions, and the whole country was dumbfounded at the audacity of the terrorist group and the vulnerability of the state (Wagner-Pacifici 1986: 90). On that day, my father plunged into a deep anxiety from which he never recovered.

Violence and the threat thereof, those days, had become part of the quotidian. Going to the bank, the post office, or a restaurant could mean being held up in one of the robberies conducted to subsidize the Red Brigades and other extra-parliamentary groups. Going grocery shopping could get one caught between security and the dissenters seeking to carry out an *autoriduzione* (self-discount) event, and walking by a street protest could get you trapped in violent skirmishes between protesters and the police. For teenagers in my generation, violence was a constant possibility, especially in those high schools that had a consistent presence of either Ultraleft or Neo-fascist activists. Brawls and picketings were frequent occurrences. In discussing his fascination with the local Ultraleft as a precocious fourteen-year-old, Genoese novelist Roberto Demontis (born in 1964) wrote: "Living in a troubled world is very reassuring for a teenager, you feel better when you are surfing an earthquake than when you are caged in the nightmare of a life in which each day is the same. This is why, when you are young—or better, a teenager—you create so much trouble. At times you do it just to see what happens (*per vedere l'effetto che fa*) for the youth, living in troubled times is wonderful, because you can mirror yourself in the disquiet, you recognize yourself in it."[3] Perhaps the charm of the disquiet is one of the reasons why in those same years one of my childhood friends robbed a local branch of the Neofascist Movimento Sociale Italiano: after stealing a typewriter, he and his friends set the suite's door on fire. They were caught right away; they all earned the sobriquet of "*baby terroristi*," and my friend, the only one in the group who had barely turned eighteen, ended up in jail.

My high school was a little different in that it was a numerus clausus public *liceo linguistico* attended predominantly by academically ambitious girls (and a few boys) with little time for extracurricular activities.[4] Yet our school was not spared the violence, either, and we frequently had to evacuate due to bomb threats. Not that we were apolitical: on the contrary, we had an active *collettivo femminista*. On some level, many of us had developed the awareness that being driven young women in a Catholic country where not even the Ultraleft was interested in seriously supporting our struggles was a political challenge in its own right (Ginsborg 1990). Dressed in hippie garb, we would read feminist magazines such as *Effe* and *Noi donne,* eagerly discussing women's reproductive rights at every opportunity, penning feminist slogans in our journals, and yelling back in unison at anyone who tried to convince us that our place was going to be in the home. The price we had to pay for our own small-scale resistance, but above all for the successes in matters of family law, reproductive rights, and access to employment at the hands of women activists who were a decade older than us, was a backlash: a capillary symbolic and material violence that did not pursue a forthright exclusion, but rather a surveillance and policing mechanism that perpetuated women's subalternity by means of an incessant public harassment (Gardner 1995). Implicitly meant to remind women and especially vulnerable young girls that they did not belong in public, this harassment manifested as the barrage of slurs, insults, and even occasional physical attacks that could be meted out to us by men of all age groups in any public place: Genoa's streets and piazzas, but also its stores, churches, buses and trains, parks and beaches, workplaces and schools. In all cases, such aggressions were blamed on the victim's alleged breach of the unwritten rules of modesty (Guano 2007).

If Genoa's streets were a war zone for assorted class and gender struggles, my Genoese friends who are older than me still remember how the local university, too, was a political battlefield. Ultraleft activists had the power to shut down the university, canceling all classes, exam sessions, and thesis defenses at will. Some of the faculty and several of the students had close ties to the Ultraleft, and the tension was high. Students would often extract a "*18 politico*" ("political C-") from their professors: a passing grade granted to all students, regardless of performance. As to the local faculty, they positioned themselves on both sides of the barricade. In 1978, a Red Brigades commando kneecapped Christian Democratic law professor Fausto Cuocolo in front of his terrorized students. In 1979, Italian Literature professor Enrico Fenzi was arrested for being a member of the local Red Brigades branch.

The City of Shattered Mirrors

The last clamorous chapter in the history of Genoa's Red Brigades was the 1980 police raid of a *covo* (hideout) during which all the members of the local *colonna* (pillar) were killed. By then, the assassination of Guido Rossa had deprived the Red Brigades of much of the support they still enjoyed among the local working class and the intelligentsia: up to that point, they had been the *imprendibili* ("impregnable"; see Cavazza 2013) who eluded all police investigations and frightened bourgeoisie and state representatives alike. Yet with Rossa they had assassinated a worker, and this compromised the solidarity of even much of the most militant Ultraleft. Politically motivated violence did not disappear from Genoa—the kneecapping of Ansaldo Nucleare CEO Roberto Adinolfi was conducted as recently as May 2012 at the hands of an anarchist commando—but it dwindled to a barely noticeable level. In the meantime, increasingly deindustrialized Genoa had become what historian Paul Ginsborg called a "ghost city" (2003: 17): a city convulsed by strikes and protests, and whose residents had begun to leave in droves.

"Hopelessness," argued Ernest Bloch (1986: 5), "is itself in a temporal and factual sense, the most insupportable thing, downright intolerable to human needs." In describing the hopelessness that affected the Genoa of the early 1980s, Genoese novelist Maurizio Maggiani (2007: 84) wrote:

> I know that Genoa has been a city scattered with shattered mirrors. I remember them, the 1980s. . . . People walked in the streets with their heads hanging low, and they did not even feel like looking at themselves in the shop windows; it was a city of dirty glasses. Every millenarian city has had its plague, caught its infections. Sometimes it even dies of it. Genoa's latest plague was the disease of the iron. It had spread to the steel and had turned it into rusty mounds. The rust had spread and had smeared the whole city; people were leaving just like the exodus. The rust melted into the sea and started corrupting the port, and soon enough everything was falling apart. The plague comes when you need to purge your sins, Genoa's sin was the lethal sin of simplification.

The hopelessness that spread among the youth of the 1970s, inciting drug use and political violence, was in the first place the index of a larger crisis that affected Italian society as a whole (Ginsborg 1990), and Genoa more than other cities. The energy crisis of 1973 had delivered the first shock to Genoa's industries: the state-subsidized steelworks, the shipyards and the electromechanical sector that were increasingly struggling to compete in international markets even as they kept barely afloat at the national level (Arvati 1988). Genoa's single-handed investment in statalized heavy industries (its "sin of simplification") was backfiring. A decade later, the magnitude of the crisis was crushing the Genoese economy. The Ansaldo industrial conglomerate was languishing; the containerization of Genoa's port had made docks and workers redundant (Hillman 2008); Genoa's shipyards were suffering from the global demise of transatlantic passenger ships; and its steelworks were unable to keep up with the mounting foreign competition (Arvati 1988: 60–61). The negative trend seemed to have no end in sight. As jobs in traditionally masculine working-class sectors were on the wane (Arvati 1988; 1994), Genoese workers' struggles began displaying a peculiarly muscular feel.

Dissatisfied with the way their unions were conducting the negotiations, in 1980 Genoese steel and port workers began taking their grievances out of the factory and directly to the streets, with the intent of gaining the greatest visibility possible by disrupting the urban everyday. The sight of *cortei* (protest marches) slowly striding down Genoa's main thoroughfares with the explicit intent to bring traffic to a halt became a familiar one. Genoa's residents had to resign themselves to being stopped in their tracks when workers took to the streets. This trend intensified in January 1983, when street blockades evolved into the full-fledged occupation of one of Genoa's main railway stations, as well as its highway accesses, the airport, and the junction (*sopraelevata*) that connects downtown Genoa to its industrial peripheries, thus forcefully bringing the whole city to a chaotic standstill (Arvati 1988: 100).

Many middle-aged Genoese still remember the sight of the gigantic—and excruciatingly slow—machines that, operated by port workers, would irrupt into downtown Genoa. Carousing around its nineteenth-century piazzas, these mechanical giants would intentionally disrupt traffic, thus creating some of the worst congestions ever. What we were witnessing was a new type of strike: one that had moved out of factories and workplaces to claim the whole city as its arena. The old pattern in which workers stopped or slowed production to air their grievances to their employers had morphed into a type of protest in which causing discomfort to the citizenry as a whole became instrumental in forcing local and state-level politicians to intervene for the sake of preserving their own electoral bases (Pipan 1989). This tactic triggered ambivalent responses in those who were not directly affected by the layoffs. On one hand, many sympathized with the workers who were at risk of losing their livelihood for good. The centrality to Genoa's economy of the electromechanical sector as well as the shipyards and the steelworks also caused concerns about the future of the city as a whole. On the other hand, the workers' explicit intent to maximize the discomfort to the collectivity alienated many potential supporters by feeding into the old mythology of the "divided city" as well as the more recent representation of blue-collar workers as entitled, if anachronistic, bullies.[5]

Describing the society of the late 1950s, sociologist Cavalli (1960) had characterized Genoa as a divided city whose left-wing working classes residing in the western peripheries were "*arroccati*" (entrenched)—that is, refused any contact with the rest of society, a sizable portion of which was suffused with an exquisitely Catholic fear of communists. In the 1980s, the mythology of the divided city was deftly utilized by politicians keen on casting the workers' movements as fossilized and unrealistic (Arvati 1988:

101). The popularity of such stereotype ended up preventing the dialogue and exacerbating the conflict between the workers who sought to defend their employment on the one hand, and the politicians and entrepreneurs who supported "modernization" agendas entailing the privatization and the reorganization of what had been largely state-run industrial sectors on the other hand. According to those who pushed for "progress," workers were guilty of *continuismo* (Arvati 1988: 101): the inability to embrace inevitable change and to proactively adapt to new circumstances by accepting the much touted Thatcherite doctrine that "there is no alternative" to privatization and deindustrialization (Harvey 2000: 17). This narrative blamed the locally hegemonic Left for its unwillingness to shed the ailing state-subsidized industrial economy while embracing the "new": private ownership with its corollary of reorganization and downsizing. Indelibly etched in this chapter of Genoese history is former Socialist mayor Fulvio Cerofolini's 1984 refusal to allow Euro Disney to build a theme park in Genoa: "This is not a city of waiters," he notoriously said, voicing a proud workerist stance that synthetized the legitimate suspicion that the shift from industrial to service sector employment would hardly serve the interests of workers. Yet, to those who did not support his political views (mostly the private sector), this stance epitomized all that was wrong with a city that refused to move on. Three decades later, Cerofolini's sentence still haunts the collective memory of a largely deindustrialized Genoa that had to struggle to establish itself as a tourist destination.

Hope Is Elsewhere

While 1983 was the peak of the crisis, for much of Northern Italy the rebound was right around the corner (Ginsborg 2003: 32). By 1984, the Italian economy was already faring considerably better (Ginsborg 1990: 406–407). The restructuring and downsizing of Italy's main companies had increased profits, the stock market was on the rise, and the widely publicized new wave of young managers such as Raoul Gardini, Silvio Berlusconi, Carlo de Benedetti, and Luciano Benetton seemed to demonstrate that social mobility was, at long last, a possibility (Ginsborg 1990: 408). The neoliberal mythology of self-reliance (Ong 2006) made its appearance in a static society in which professions had often been (and continue to be) handed down from generation to generation (Guano 2010b; Yanagisako

2013; Zinn 2001). While Genoa's blue-collar workers were increasingly deprived of their hope, the educated middle classes saw neoliberal tropes of meritocracy and initiative (Ong 2006), along with the corollary of hedonism seeping in from the North Atlantic, as seemingly offering an alluringly modern alternative to all that had been wrong with Genoese society up to that point. This included complete reliance on the state, bureaucratism, aversion to change, the hegemony of political parties in all decision-making processes, and the cronyism, nepotism, and clientelism that had traditionally controlled the allocation of jobs and resources in a bloated public sector. In the private sector, thus went the rhetoric, initiative and talent were all that counted, and from then on the private sector had to be incentivized and privileged.

In order to better understand the success of this kind of right-wing utopia (Buck-Morss 2002; Harvey 2000) among young Italians of that time, it bears mentioning that the social upheavals of the late 1960s had brought about a profound transformation in the class politics of education—a transformation that was soon to be met with a decrease in the social value of recently democratized types of knowledge. Before then, working-class students had been encouraged to either leave school early or attend vocational institutes where they would learn a trade. Middle- and working-class women could at best expect to obtain some training to become elementary school teachers; lower- to middle-class men often attended professional schools where they acquired the skills they needed to become clerks (Barbagli 1969, 1974). Starting with the 1970s, however, more and more children of working-class and lower-middle-class families had begun pursuing college degrees, thus making inroads into a formerly bourgeois domain. They had several motivations. By then, access to sought-after stable employment in statalized industries and the public administration required a degree (Palumbo 1994: 937). Furthermore, the high unemployment rates among younger generations in a society where all occupational venues were taken by middle-aged men had also turned schools into outlets where the youth bode their time as they waited for opportunities to materialize (Palumbo 1994: 931). Unfortunately, as it often happens, the heightened hopes for social mobility brought about by increased educational achievements were to result in even bitterer disappointments (Mains 2012).

In spite of their degrees, many first-generation college graduates were still faced with a grim job market where all that mattered was a powerful patron's *raccomandazione* (intercession; see Zinn 2001). The latter would be issued in return for favors such as a sizable pool of electoral votes to be gathered among friends and family (Ferrera 1996), or, as happened to some of my friends, several months' worth of one's salary. It bears mentioning that, while widespread all over the country, in Genoa the practice of patronage was particularly acute due to how the local oligarchy had been exerting its hegemony even after Italy's unification. Local powerful families had traditionally wielded their financial prowess, their political clout, and their social prestige while controlling the city's political and economic life through cronyism and nepotism (Garibbo 2000: 306). This dynamic was further exacerbated by the prevalence of statalized employment both in the public administration and in the local industries, which had been colonized by political parties and their clientelistic logics. In a city where influence peddling was—and continues to be—the name of the game, whom you knew and what you were willing to do for them was considerably more important than any skills you could list on your resume.[6] Aside from stifling the hopes and thwarting the efforts of all those who could not count on a powerful patron, the practice of patronage promoted a self-referential managerial and administrative culture that was often criticized for valuing political networking more than professionalism and productivity, and for serving exclusively the interests of a rentier elite that was, and continues to be, averse to innovation and risk-taking (Castelli and Gozzi 1994; Palumbo 1994).

In the face of Genoa's dearth of opportunities, the neoliberal rhetoric of meritocracy that was being drilled into young students fostered a new type of hope: one that was steeped in the promise that, for the best and the brightest among them, the feudal immobility of yore would soon give way to a new world of opportunities (Signorelli 1990). Meritocracy may as well be, as Pierre Bourdieu and Jean Claude Passeron posited, a sham cast over the reproduction of privilege (1990); however, for generations of young Italians whom clientelism and nepotism had consistently barred from all professional outlets, meritocracy represented a break from social immobility as well as a hope for a "modern" future where all would have the same chances: the hope for fairness in the competition for securing jobs and resources had replaced the dream of social justice.[7]

By comparison with the intense political activism of the late 1960s and the 1970s, the Italian 1980s have been defined as an "age of [political] disenchantment" (Palumbo 1994: 984). Growing up in the shadow of the right- and left-wing terrorism and the violence that had tormented Italy for a whole decade, the youth of the 1980s increasingly associated the political activism of their teenage years with a stage in their life that, amounting to juvenile rebelliousness, had to be outgrown. On the other hand, people born in the mid- to late 1960s and early 1970s were also increasingly sensitive to the lure of the hedonism that had begun to seep into the country along with Thatcherite ideas about individualism and "freedom," and that was honed through the unprecedented proliferation of private television channels, several of which were owned by Silvio Berlusconi. Diverging from the predominantly educational purposes of Italy's public broadcasting stations and its Catholic mores, Berlusconi's television channels began to offer shows dominated by the crude objectification of women's bodies, by the display of unbridled wealth, and by an ethos of social ascent modeled after the American Dream (Ginsborg 2003). This was the model that Berlusconi himself sought to emulate as, in the early 1990s, he began positing himself as a "self-made man" who legitimized his claim to political power with his financial successes and his aversion to traditional politics (Ginsborg 2003). The spirit of the times was such that many young women in my generation hung up their hippie garbs and began donning stiletto heels as they made a beeline for the disco. Weekends were no longer devoted to political activism, but rather to going to the Riviera, in an increasingly collective hedonist frenzy that, weekend after weekend, trapped thousands of cars in endless traffic jams on their way to and from the beach. Internal tourism experienced a steep increase, too, and family vacations and school field trips were often devoted to visiting Italy's cities of art: Rome, Florence, and Venice. Although nearby Portofino and the Cinque Terre already enjoyed international visibility, at that time Genoa was not part of any tourist circuit worth mentioning.

Many hopeful young Italians were eager to break out of the mold of what they now regarded as sterile juvenile political rebelliousness by means of hard work and ambition, but societal change had been only skin-deep. The old privileges of the social, financial, and political elites—or what, in the parlance of the early 2000s, were to be defined as Italy's "castes"—remained largely untouched, and the eagerness of the new generations was to make the encounter with reality all the more disappointing. Even the upheavals of the late 1960s and the 1970s had done little to equalize the playing field of Italian society and prepare it for the meritocracy, the entrepreneurship, and the openness to change that were allegedly fundamental to the much-touted "new economy."

To make things worse, even though the economic climate in the rest of Northern Italy looked encouraging enough as to make younger generations hope for a brighter future, Genoa's decline seemed unstoppable. While Genoa's public industrial sector shrank considerably, large-scale private initiatives meant to boost the economy lagged behind. Blaming what they regarded as the entitlements and the combativeness of local workers, the local financial elites preferred to invest elsewhere or not to invest at all; as a result, unemployment rates remained higher than in the rest of the North, thus earning Genoa the title of "*meridione del nord*" (the underdeveloped South of Italy's developed North). Even as they were spurred to compete and be ready to claim their place in the sun, the generations of the late 1960s and the 1970s were implicitly being trained to become part of a large population of unemployed or underemployed but highly educated Genoese: an "intellectual capital" to whom a city focused on mourning the demise of its industrial sector had nothing to offer (Arvati 1988: 17). With few employment outlets other than the public administration or a rapidly shrinking school system, Genoa's intellectual capital languished. Many of the young and the hopeful left Genoa to make a living elsewhere—usually Milan, the thriving postindustrial metropolis that epitomized Italian modernity (Foot 2001). Those who stayed behind may have found ways to earn a living; however, this almost invariably entailed giving up some of their dreams: for many, this meant renouncing professional ambitions, settling for a lifetime of underemployment, postponing—or even renouncing—marriage and parenthood and keeping fertility rates well below replacement (Arvati n.d., 1994; Palumbo 1994).[8] While in 1971 Genoa had a population of well over 800,000, by 2001 it had dropped to 600,000.[9] I was one of those who left in the early 1990s, defeated by a lack of opportunities that translated as lack of hope.

The Rise of Affective Urbanism

The Genoa of the 1980s, wrote Maggiani, was a city of shattered mirrors. Another famous local novelist, Antonio Tabucchi, wrote about the "diffuse agony" of its centro storico as a "slow leprosy that has invaded walls and houses and whose rot is devious and unstoppable, like a sentence. The garbage collectors come by only rarely, like anyone else they also disdain the detritus of this lower humankind. At night, syringes sparkle in the vicoli, and so do plastic bags, along with the undecipherable mass of some rats that died in a corner where a phosphorescent pest control banner warns not to touch the poisonous copper green baits scattered on the pavement" (Tabucchi 1986: 11). As evinced from the renewal, regeneration, and gentrification processes ignited in the late twentieth century in postindustrial cities worldwide, this level of degradation in a strategically situated neighborhood had the potential to be palatable to investors. Soon enough this waste land shifted, in the words of local city assessor Bruno Gabrielli (1999), from being regarded as a "burden" to becoming an "opportunity." Even though in 1984 Mayor Cerofolini still thought that Genoa was not a city of waiters, the left-wing administrations' opposition to developing a tourist industry in Genoa did not last long. After all, the 1989 fall of the Berlin Wall had caused a profound identity crisis in the Italian Left (Kertzer 1998), which, ever since, had become increasingly sensitive to the lures of neoliberalism (Dines 2012).

All over Europe, administrations in cahoots with local elites were launching renewal projects that, while advertised as revitalization strategies, were, in fact, meant to bolster revenues for developers allied with the local political classes (Swyngedow, Moulaert, and Rodriguez 2002). Such transformations often took place through the organization of great events that bring in large amounts of governmental funding, and contributed to considerable interventions on the cityscapes (Mastropiero 2007). In Genoa, too, the conversion to cultural tourism unfolded through the organization of a series of great events—the Exposition of 1992; the Group of Eight summit of 2001, and Genoa's role as a Capital of European Culture in 2004—meant to showcase the city internationally.[10] As elsewhere, the transformation was presented to the residents as a positive impulse to the lagging economy (Swyngedow, Moulaert, and Rodriguez 2002); as elsewhere, it was welcomed by a citizenry that, tired of shattered mirrors, eagerly awaited a chance for change.

Just as in other postindustrial European cities, in Genoa hope started to materialize under the pressure of a new affective urbanism (Anderson and Holden 2008) whereby the planning of great events of international scope extensively used the media to build consensus and promote the vision of a bright urban future (Dines 2012: 42). Promoting hope as "infrastructural to urban change" (Anderson and Holden 2008: 144), affective urbanism flashes promises of "poverty alleviation, employment, better consumption practices (of images, experience), an improved material infrastructure of everyday life (environment, transport, etc.), and fewer 'incivilities' (liter, 'antisocial behavior')" (Anderson and Holden 2008: 152). Painting a utopian veneer of salvific promises (Comaroff and Comaroff 2000) onto a considerably grimmer reality, great events funnel considerable amount of local, national, and EU funding into creating a new, visitable urbanscape (Dicks 2004) that caters to tourists as well as locals. This is what happened in Genoa, too. Yet the pursuit of great events was hardly the only strategy in Genoa's revitalization.

In 1986, Genoa's city administration along with the port consortium and the urban planning department of the Liguria region put forth a strategic plan that sought to stop Genoa's decline by valorizing its centro storico and by converting its industrial areas to shopping centers (Hillman 2008: 306). The city administration elicited architectural proposals for the purpose of giving Genoa's old port a complete makeover in preparation for the Expo (Exposition) of 1992 with which Genoa celebrated Christopher Columbus's first voyage to the New World—its "discovery," as Italians unencumbered by extra-European perspectives liked to call it. The Italian government had committed 295 billion lire worth of funds for the project (Mastropiero 2007: 176). Among these proposals, a few stood out. American architect John Portman designed a 262-meter-tall tower built on an artificial island at the center of the old port. The tower would host restaurants and a gigantic hotel; built in its vicinity, an underwater aquarium would help attract visitors. The project was to be complemented by a "*sfoltimento*" (thinning out) of the centro storico: a selective destruction of buildings meant to provide the remaining ones with the space and the light they would need for a consistent property appreciation. Not only did many find serious flaws with the sfoltimento project, but Portman's plan triggered heated debates, too, and was eventually discarded due to the concern that his artificial island would deface what had been the core of Genoa's original port. Eventually, the bid was won by Renzo Piano, a Genoese architect of international renown who designed and saw to completion the waterfront now known as Porto Antico (Ancient Port). Installed on the premises of Genoa's earliest port, Porto Antico became a highly successful marina with a globalized feel endowed with restaurants, cinemas, museums, shops, a public library, a swimming pool, an outdoor theater, a panoramic elevator, a state-of-the-art aquarium, shopping facilities, and a large esplanade, later to be complemented by a swath of luxury housing units. In spite of all these efforts, however, the Exposition of 1992 was not a success. It failed to attract the international attention that the Genoese administration was hoping to elicit; the number of visitors was lower than expected, and so were the revenues it generated.

Overall, for much of Northern Italy the 1980s had been the years of the boom; the 1990s, instead, were marked by a contraction of the economy caused by a lack of planning at the hands of Italy's political and economic elites (Ginsborg 2003). The "years of lead" were over; yet the mafia assassinations of two prominent magistrates in Sicily and the bombings of historical and artistic sites in Rome, Florence, and Milan for the sake of bullying the state into submission periodically reminded Italy's publics that peace and stability were still a long way off.[11] The fall of the Berlin Wall in 1989 had eased the Cold War tension that had been particularly high in Italy, and the proclamation of the victory of Western capitalism had precipitated the identity crisis of the Italian Left (Kertzer 1998). Soon enough, however, Italy's other main parties ended up in a sea of troubles, too: the 1992 eruption of the *tangentopoli* (bribesville) corruption scandals led to the demise of Italy's Christian Democratic Party and the Socialist Party. For many, the political turmoil of the early 1990s raised hopes that the spoils system and the clientelistic infiltration of *partitocrazia* (partycracy) into all sectors of Italian society (Della Porta and Vannucci 1999) would finally come to an end. The dream of impending modernization was further intensified by the rise of the European Union, which in turn fed the hope that Italy was on its way to obtaining more nimble, transparent, and efficient state administration modeled after its North European counterparts (Koenig-Archibugi 2003). As Italians were to find out soon, none of these predictions was accurate: the parties that came down crumbling after the tangentopoli shakeup were promptly replaced by new—and possibly even more corrupt—ones, and, instead of simplifying Italy's abstruse bureaucracy, the European Union added new, and equally repressive, layers of red tape to people's everyday life.

For Genoa, the 1990s meant a further deterioration of its industrial sectors. Even though over the previous decade employment rates all over Northern Italy had increased by 10.6 percent, in Genoa they kept declining. By 1992, 13 percent of its population was unemployed (Castelli and Gozzi 1994: 890–894)—a number that did not take into account those who had surrendered to a "culture of resignation" (Palumbo 1994: 958) and were no longer even looking for a job. Yet Genoa as a whole did not give in to collective trauma (Castelli and Gozzi 1994: 885). In spite of all odds, for many a Genoese the 1990s were still characterized by a cautious optimism driven primarily by the affective impact of urban revitalization and the promise of a new and thriving postindustrial city.

As Ernest Bloch (1986: 10) observed, "The gulf between dream and reality is not harmful if only the dreamer seriously believes in his dream. . . . There only has to be some point of contact between dream and life for everything to be in the best order." For one, the dreams of many a Genoese were kindled by the promise of transforming Genoa into an all-Italian Silicon Valley (Castelli and Gozzi 1994: 995): a promise that pivoted on the creation of a science and technology park on the Erzelli hill where the local School of Engineering would spearhead the push for scientific research, technological innovation, and employment.[12] On a more immediate level—one that touched the everyday lives of many—change was under way in the cityscape itself: moving the School of Architecture to the centro storico brought new life to a formerly degraded and sparsely populated neighborhood. The thirteenth-century Palazzo Ducale, which had formerly been closed off to the general public and utilized for much of the twentieth century as a court, was restored to its original beauty and began hosting high-profile exhibitions that considerably increased Genoa's visibility and the number of visitors, thus generating revenues for local businesses. In discussing the spatial dimensions of neoliberal hope, David Harvey (2000: 181) pointed out how this entails the creation of a built environment meant to host commercial activities. This is certainly what happened in Genoa's centro storico—though on a considerably smaller scale than the corporate one surmised by Harvey. The municipal support (in the form of subsidized loans) for small businesses in the centro storico provided the "point of contact" between the dreamers' hope for a stable livelihood and a strategy meant to bring about a hike in property prices and tax revenues. Yet the proliferation of small businesses also contributed to somewhat alleviating this city's traditionally high unemployment rates, thus fostering hope that change was, after all, possible.

The attitudes of many a Genoese shifted, too, and the urban everyday gained back much of the sociability that had been disrupted in previous decades—with an added layer of hedonism fostered by the revitalization. All over the city, coffee shops installed *dehors* (small patios) on their premises, thus encouraging the habit of sitting outdoors while socializing over a cup of coffee. The *aperitivo* ritual became a common practice, and at 6 PM coffee shops and bars would start filling up with people sipping cocktails and sampling appetizers. In the mid-1990s, the first *mercatini dell'antiquari-ato* (street antique fairs) made their appearance in the courtyard of Palazzo Ducale, in the stylish nineteenth-century arcade known as Galleria Mazzini, and in the very central Via Cesarea, thus offering people a low-investment, low-cost opportunity to make a living even as they reinforced Genoa's halo as a city of culture. Rather than reducing the city to a consumable simula-crum, however, several of the transformations occurring under the auspices of Genoa's revitalization increased the symbolic sustenance and meaning-fulness that residents already drew from the spaces of their everyday life (Low 2000: 244). Overall, many Genoese were increasingly pleased with the changes that were taking place in their city, even as they kept hoping for more—more opportunities for work along with more opportunities for enjoying a city that they had long experienced as bleak, dangerous, and degraded. This hope was in line with the ethos of the time. The hedonistic education of the 1980s that had resulted from a mix of North Atlantic ideology on one hand and the very much local relief at the end of the terrorist era on the other had matured into the desire to consume "culture" as a blend of sensuous pleasures conveyed through the beauty of architec-tural and natural landscapes, the folklore of artisan production and petty commerce, a range of assorted public, free, and widely accessible urban activities ranging from street theater to concerts, from symposia to dance performances and museum events, and the ever-present pleasures of people-watching. Not only was the new Genoa more democratically enjoy-able, but it was also seemingly poised for a long overdue economic renais-sance as a tourist city.

With its partially renewed centro storico, the new waterfront, and the extremely popular exhibitions hosted in the newly restored Palazzo Ducale, the Genoa of the 1990s had already showed signs of change. More was on the horizon, though—namely, Genoa's role as the host of the Group of Eight summit of 2001 and its one-year tenure as European Cultural Capital in 2004. Massive injections of funds from the national government and the European Union subsidized the makeover of various areas of downtown Genoa. For a long time, much of the city was wrapped in scaffoldings. As one woman put it, "It's almost as if the city were pregnant. We [the Geno-ese] know it's going to take a while, and we are waiting to see what's going to be birthed." In a city whose residents are notorious for their pessimism, the late 1990s and the early 2000s were years of rising expectations and cautious optimism. For a while, even the most jaded Genoese held their breath and suspended judgment. The excitement of discovering what was to emerge from the construction sites is once again well captured by writer Maggiani:

Once the sin has been amended, the plague vanishes, the infections dry out and slowly heal. People go back to looking for a clean glass where to take a peek at themselves. I remember one day that could be memorialized as the morning of the mirrors. The morning when the canopy covers were torn down, the day after the San Lorenzo area was opened up to the city at the end of the restorations. After the years of the infection, [Genoa] had begun to clean the rot off. It had even found a way to project splendors. It was erecting constructions sites to incubate wonders worthy of glossy bilingual magazines. Yet, for the longest time the city continued to look askance at itself. It sought out its reflected image with the corner of the eye. Each time, one piece or the other was missing for it to be able to find itself whole, just like it had always been even in times of plenty. And something was found on that San Lorenzo morning. . . . That morning, the whole city was mirroring itself in San Lorenzo, the whole city had its nose turned up and was going "ah" and "oh." This was the city of those who were going to the post office, of those who needed to go buy some fish, of those who had gone out to get a cup of coffee, of those who wanted to get a new job or just find any job—all those who, for years, had walked through San Lorenzo with their head hanging, trying to avoid the traffic and seeking shelter in the shade of the dust clouds and the scaffoldings. And you could see that people were happy to love San Lorenzo, and everybody could see that San Lorenzo had started loving the city again. And that was something. (Maggiani 2007: 85)

What Maggiani describes as a renewed love affair between San Lorenzo and the Genoese only begins to highlight the importance of public space in Italian sociality, whereby a vibrant street life has long been part and parcel of everyday life in the city (Del Negro 2004; Moretti 2015). There is no question about the role of ornate corridor streets as markers of elitism that set the tone for an urban theater conducive to classist representations of selves and others (Holston 1989). On the other hand, the relative publicness

of such streets allows for a sociability and an enjoyment of the urban outdoors that is open to a broad range of activities: not just idle strolling and
hanging out, window shopping and seeing and being seen (Del Negro
2004), but also petty commerce, theater and art, panhandling, religious and
folkloric celebrations, political rallies and protests—to name a few. Genoa's
San Lorenzo area is a case in point. For the longest time, Via San Lorenzo—
the street that connects Palazzo Ducale to Genoa's gothic cathedral and the
waterfront—had been congested with loud traffic and smeared with smog.
Pedestrians had no choice but to negotiate the narrow sidewalks with
parked cars and scooters even as they filled their lungs with exhaust gases.
Once the renovation was completed in 2001, the newly pedestrianized Via
San Lorenzo became a haven for a plurality of practices at the hands of
locals (a category which includes both Genoese and immigrants) as well as
visitors.

On most days, the street hosts an intense foot traffic; some passersby
walk purposefully, seemingly intent on reaching a specific destination. Others, instead, wander aimlessly, taking it all in. Part of the street is lined up
with coffee shops and small stores selling antiques, books, prints and posters, ice cream, regional specialty foods, South Asian exotica, herbal prepara-
tions, pastry, eyeglasses, and cheap Chinese apparel. A smattering of
peddlers sell hand-made jewelry, crafts, and paintings from booths lined up
against the side of the San Lorenzo cathedral; street musicians perform for
passersby, and, on the first weekend of every month, the flea and antique
market hosted in the Palazzo Ducale spills into the San Lorenzo area, adding additional fodder for the visual and tactile pleasures of passersby. The
steps of the magnificent gothic cathedral provide popular accommodation
for tourists and locals alike, who often share them—though not without
discomfort—with the *punkabbestia*: anarchist-inspired homeless youth who
have selected this area as a hangout for themselves and their large-breed
dogs. Gypsy women and small groups of children blend in with the crowd,
panhandling visitors. The social life of San Lorenzo is punctuated by grand
public events, too. One of these is the yearly historical parade of San Giovanni Battista, during which the local Cardinal walks the ornate sixteenth-
century silver arc containing the local patron saint's ashes all the way to the
waterfront to bless the sea as the city's traditional source of livelihood. A
highly spectacular event that has been held for centuries for the sake of
fostering vertical solidarity and instilling both local pride and pious sentiments in the populace (Garibbo 2000: 67), the procession features medieval

Figure 3. Catholic procession in San Lorenzo. Photo by author.

and Renaissance costumes as well as the *portacristi*: members of Catholic confraternities who carry large and extremely heavy ancient crosses decorated with a profusion of silver leaves. Yet Via San Lorenzo is also an occasional route for protesters, who saturate it with their chants, their whistles, and their banners as they march from one end to the other to ensure an adequate outreach to their grievances. Overall, many of Genoa's renovated and largely pedestrianized downtown areas do not cater exclusively to middle- to upper-class individuals keen on consuming the city (Zukin 1996). Instead, they provide a vibrant arena that condenses the three historically predominant forms of the Italian piazza—the religious plaza, the political space, and the market place (Isenghi 2004, in Dines 2012: 108)—to accommodate a plethora of urban publics (Gazzola 2013).

GeNova—The New Genoa

In the years that immediately preceded the Group of Eight summit of 2001, Genoa's downtown underwent large-scale renovations meant to valorize its historical heritage and increase its visitability; for many Genoese, this meant an opportunity to start small businesses that would earn them a living in the face of consistently high unemployment rates. Their hopes, however, were to be met only partially. The G8 summit, to which I devote a chapter in this book, turned its promise of showcasing the new Genoa to international audiences into a globally visible display of state repression. Shocked by what had happened under their eyes, many a Genoese resented how their city had been hijacked from them by a political performance, reduced to a battlefield, and then memorialized as nothing else but a dramatic event. Yet even in the aftermath of this disaster, many Genoese still had something to be hopeful for: namely the promise that, upon becoming Capital of European Culture for all of 2004, Genoa would conquer its own place in the sun as part of Italy's profitable tourist circuit. Even the 7.5 percent demographic increment reported between 2001 and 2005 pointed to an increased confidence among this city's residents, many of whom, instead of migrating, stayed on and started families (Arvati n.d.: 29).

The year 2004 was a special time for many Genoese, whose legendary propensity toward pessimism and despondency was, yet again, replaced by hopefulness. As indicated by its GeNova (New Genoa) logo, the city that welcomed visitors that year had changed remarkably. A considerable injection of national and EU funds helped establish a beautified cityscape that hosted a wide assortment of festivals, symposia, events, and exhibitions on topics ranging from ancient history to modernity, from art to folklore, from science and technology to industry, and from migrations to sports. By the summer of 2004, tourist flows had grown considerably; the number of museum visitors had increased from 163,000 in 1999 to 410,000 (Hillman 2008: 312), and at all times of the day groups of visitors could be spotted striding through Genoa's downtown, its centro storico, and the Porto Antico. Revenues for local businesses went up, and the excitement among the residents was palpable. More than once, while wandering about in areas of the centro storico that had previously been off the beaten track, I was stopped by elderly residents who, taking me for a tourist, proudly volunteered directions to freshly renovated historical landmarks. Some of these were in the very same area where, in the late 1970s, locals had pelted my schoolmates with stones during an art history field trip.

While the success of Genoa's tenure as Capital of European Culture had many hope for the best, the hardship was not over. The following year, Genoa experienced a sharp decline in tourist presences and revenues; with no great event in sight, hope dwindled. Many started wondering if anything would ever change after all. In 2002 the introduction of the Euro, the uni-fied European currency, had brought about a 100 percent price hike that took place almost overnight: due to speculations that went unchecked, all of a sudden what had previously cost 1,000 lire was worth one euro—that is, about 2,000 lire. Unfortunately, salaries, pensions, and savings remained unchanged. If the maneuver reduced Italy's public debt by half, it also deliv-ered a formidable blow to the financial stability and the well-being of Italy's middle and working classes. To make things worse, the financial crisis that had begun in the United States in 2008 soon spread to Italy; this country's large public debt, its lack of growth, and the limited credibility of its gov-ernment turned the crisis into a full-fledged recession that affected already vulnerable Genoa even more than other Northern cities. For years, ever since the onset of the recession, hardly a week went by without a protest taking place in downtown Genoa. In 2011, massive layoffs were announced by Fincantieri, Genoa's foremost shipyard. Months of convulsive street pro-tests ensued, during which workers placed a large excavator in front of the prefecture with the implicit threat they would launch it against the sixteenth-century building if their grievances were not to be heard. In 2013, employees of the local public transportation company went on a five-day strike against the privatization of their firm, thus bringing the whole city to a standstill. In the meantime, the escalation of property taxes (IMU) meant to help stem the public debt brought about a steep increase in rents for already struggling small business owners, estimated in the range of 70.1 percent for centro storico properties and 48.1 percent for the rest of the city.[13] Combined with the difficulty in obtaining credit and the collapse of consumer spending at the hands of a citizenry bogged down by high unemployment rates, low salaries, and record high taxation (Guano 2010a), these rent hikes caused many a small business to close, thus contributing to the impoverishment of a large section of the local middle class that had been a protagonist of Genoa's hopefulness.

The Uneven Distribution of Hope

Keen on escaping their predicament through strategies that ranged from installing a tiny dehors in front of one's hole-in-the-wall coffee shop to taking advantage of a municipality's subsidized loans by opening a small business for selling one's own handmade crafts, local small business owners had contributed with their poiesis to making the city from the bottom up (Calhoun, Sennett, and Shapira 2013: 197). Indeed, the promise of progress and the capitalist mobilization of hope brought about by affective urbanism (Anderson and Fenton 2008; Lashaw 2008) may, under certain circumstances, foster the rise of creative classes (Florida 2012 [2002]) endowed at the very least with cultural and social capital; however, processes of urban revitalization also bring about a deepening of existing inequalities. This happened in Genoa, too.

If, for segments of the educated middle classes, Genoa's revitalization seemed to prospect opportunities for employment and above all small-scale entrepreneurship, the hope fostered by affective capitalist urbanism was not evenly distributed—nor were its dividends (Anderson and Holden 2008; Appadurai 2013; Miyazaki 2013). Among those who did not expect to garner benefits were the residents of much of the industrial peripheries to the west of the city: those neighborhoods that had been disproportionately affected by industrial degradation, and that did not directly benefit from an increase in tourist flows (Hillman 2008) even as the local factories kept hemorraging jobs. Take, for example, Sampierdarena.

A former seaside village situated to the west of Genoa's dowtown and a favorite resort with local and international bourgeoisies, Sampierdarena was stripped of its beaches, its pleasantness, and its prestige in the early twentieth century due to the expansion of Genoa's port. After turning into a working- to lower-middle-class neighborhood, in the mid-1990s Sampierdarena went on to become the destination of a massive immigration from Ecuador. As the Ecuadorian community became the largest immigrant group in Genoa, tensions began between the newcomers and the Genoese residents. Nowadays, some of the most frequently voiced complaints about Sampierdarena are the neighborhood's rise in crime rates and the difficulties in syncronizing the schedules and habits of the (mostly aging) Italian residents with those of the considerably younger Latin American community. Within apartment complexes, for example, squabbles among neighbors frequently arise around the issue of noise levels that the Genoese are not willing to tolerate. Public space is just as contested: on one hand, Genoese residents complain about the street parties and the brawls that erupt at night, often leaving behind carpets of broken beer bottles (Gazzola, Prampolini, and Rimondo 2014: 120); on the other hand, Ecuadorian youth deprecate the scarcity of public spaces where to get together, play soccer, listen to music, and party without incurring the grievances of Italians

(Flores and Valencia León 2007). However, what singlehandedly triggers the most anxieties among the Genoese is the presence of *pandillas*: gangs of Latino youth such as the Latin Kings or the Netas who, unlike less sensational facets of Ecuadorian immigrants' life, receive considerable attention at the hands of the local media (Queirolo Palmas 2005).[14]

And yet, while ample coverage in local newspapers is devoted to crimes committed by Ecuadorian youths,[15] what is often disregarded is the impact on the neighborhood of a nearby mall and several big-box stores. In 2002, what had been an Ansaldo factory in Sampierdarena became Fiumara: a shopping mall (Genoa's first) hosting about 100 franchises, a multiplex movie theater, and a large grocery store. In the same years, an Ikea store opened in the nearby deindustrialized Campi area, soon to be surrounded by other big-box stores such as Castorama (now Leroy Merlin) and Decathlon. In 2000, one of Europe's largest designer outlets opened in Serravalle, an inland village about thirty minutes away from downtown Genoa and twenty minutes away from Sampierdarena. The proximity of malls and large franchises immediately led to the demise of much of what had been Sampierdarena's once thriving *tessuto commerciale* (commercial fabric) of small businesses. Described by Genoese writer Maurizio Fantoni Minnella (2014: 52) as a "parasite smeared with heavy makeup that uses its seductions to suck the lymph that used to flow in the urban core, thus impoverishing it mercilessly," the Fiumara mall gave a hefty contribution to the desertification of previously lively Sampierdarena streets. The ensuing takeover at the hands of drug dealers, pimps, and prostitutes did the rest, thus bringing about this neighborhood's current lack of security and its ill reputation.

During the second half of the twentieth century, Italy's department stores had already begun positing a strong competition for small, family-owned businesses (Scarpellini 2007) that supported a large segment of the Italian middle class (Ginsborg 2003). In recent years, U.S.-style shopping malls further intensified this trend. The creation of Fiumara, the Serravalle Designer Outlet, and assorted big-box stores affected family-owned shops not just in Sampierdarena but all over Genoa, too, including those situated in the centro storico that had been invested with the responsibility of generating foot traffic in degraded areas, thus supporting the revitalization of this neighborhood. Unfortunately, the competition of shopping malls has a crushing effect on small businesses. Not only can mall franchises afford higher rents and longer business hours, but, due to their business volume, they can also guarantee lower retail prices compared to smaller stores. Furthermore, the availability of large—and most importantly free—parking decks has been pivotal to reorienting the shopping habits of many Genoese shoppers. As one Genoese woman put it, "At Fiumara you can do all of your shopping plus the grocery in one go, and then you can load it all into your car without even having to get wet if it rains. Parking is never a problem, and you don't have to take the bus. Things are cheaper, and you have more choices all in one place."

Ironically, one of the charms of much of Genoa's revitalized downtown and its centro storico is its pedestrianization and the absence of traffic. However, the deep cuts in the public transportation system ensuing the recent recession have made transit increasingly complicated. Several bus lines serving densely populated uphill neighborhoods were cut, and service to the whole city was greatly reduced, even as fares increased considerably. Nowadays traveling by bus requires long waits at bus stops only to ride in vehicles that are so crowded that, as one woman put it, "you barely have room to breathe. Count yourself lucky if, by the time you get out, you still have your wallet and cell phone." Private cars are hardly a viable transit option for downtown shoppers, however. In recent years, the privatization of Genoa's already scanty street parking recast what had been a longstanding lack of service as a service to be purchased in return for steep fees. If going downtown has become increasingly complicated, a trip to the Fiumara mall or the Serravalle Designer Outlet is considerably easier: you may still have to brave the traffic, but parking is guaranteed—and, most importantly, it is free. And, if you do not have a car, you can still take one of the convenient shuttles arranged by the Outlet itself. While many a Genoese deprecate the disappearance of neighborhood stores with its corollary of desertification and impoverishment, they still cannot resist the lure of malls: the "degenerate utopias" that use shopping pleasures to dampen awareness of the social and economic ramifications of consumers' choices (Harvey 2000: 168).

Epilogue: No Alternative, No Hope

At the time of writing in December 2013, Italy is experiencing record unemployment, the fiscal pressure has reached its highest levels since the end of World War II, and most families struggle to make ends meet. In the meantime, more and more Italian companies are being bought by foreign corporations, small businesses are filing for bankruptcy, and the suicides of unemployed individuals and small business owners succumbing to hopelessness make the headlines on an almost daily basis. Writing about the Italian diaspora of the late twentieth century, Donna Gabaccia (2000) argued that the latter largely comprised educated young adults looking for professional and business opportunities that were denied to them in their home country. In recent years, this pattern has dramatically intensified. Young college graduates are leaving in droves, hoping to make a living in Germany, the United Kingdom, and the United States. What is new is that now even mid-lifers are doing so, too: "I am sick of this shitty city, it is impossible to get anything done here. Just look around, [the city] is full of old people, if you have any initiative they will kill it. The Genoese are all shitheads, I want to go away. I want to move to Spain and start a new life there. You are lucky to live in the US, if I could I would move there, too!" This tirade was delivered to me in 2012 by Giovanni, a man in his late thirties who ten years earlier had bought a small coffee shop in Genoa's centro storico because he believed in the transformation the city was seemingly undergoing. Like many of his fellow small business owners, Giovanni was exasperated by the difficulty of making a living. While his wish to move to Spain is somewhat unusual (Germany, the United Kingdom, and the United States are more common destinations), his upset is reminiscent of a series of complaints that were common in the 1970s and 1980s: "Genoa is a city that stifles initiative," "its residents are too old," "the Genoese keep their money in the bank instead of investing it in productive endeavors." Invectives and accusations such as these index the frustration and above all the hopelessness of many a Genoese who end up blaming the city as a whole for its structural inequities and conjunctures. The only difference, in this case, was that this frustration was set against the background of renovated Genoa. A few days after recording Giovanni's outburst, I met with Carla, a mid-level manager in a firm that was threatening yet another round of layoffs. Like Giovanni, Carla was thinking of moving: "You cannot make a living in this city, that's what it boils down to. They may have beautified and pedestrianized it and all that, but you cannot eat the landscape. As soon as [my husband and I] find a job elsewhere, we are out of here." By then Simona, one of Carla's former schoolmates, was already gone. She had left in 2011, at age forty-six and not without trepidation, to start a new life in the United States. "You cannot work in Genoa, you cannot get anything done here," she had told me before leaving, hinting at a hypothetical continuity between the stagnation brought about by the crisis, the stifling bureaucracy, and the nepotistic and clientelistic ethos of the local elites. Giovanni, Carla, and Simona's eagerness to leave was triggered by yet another wave of hopelessness that hit Genoa during the recession that began in 2008, after the austerity measures imposed in 2011 by the European Union and the Italian government led by Mario Monti led to a general impoverishment. While a decade earlier the neoliberal rhetoric of meritocracy had promoted hope, now the steep rise in taxation, the welfare cuts, and the downsizing of public services were being justified through the flip side of the same rhetoric—that is, the dystopic claim that there was "no alternative" to an uneven distribution of hopelessness that disproportionately affected Italy's middle and lower classes.

Hope is rooted in a linear, teleological, and eschatological temporality of meaning (Crapanzano 2003: 6). Tracing its origin back to both Christianity and the Enlightenment (Mayr 1992), hope for a better life is at the core of the myth of progress; it is an expectation of modernity that twentieth-century industrialization was supposed to fulfill (Ferguson 1999). Yet hope is by definition subjected to disappointment—first and foremost due to its orientation toward the future: a direction that implies, among others, the linearity of time and the commitment to change rather than repetition (Bloch 1998: 341). What unfolded in Genoa over the second half of the twentieth century was the renewed loss of a future-oriented linearity in the face of cyclical disappointment. The interruption of the progress spearheaded by urban revitalization and the failure of the salvific promise of a trickle-down effect (Comaroff and Comaroff 2000) came with a high cost. As the recession worsened, the return of hopelessness translated once again as an exacerbation of the exodus that has characterized Genoa's decline since the late twentieth century. For the first time since the early twentieth century, in 2012 Genoa's population dropped to a headcount of 580,000.[16] Out of those who stayed behind, one fourth were over sixty-five (Arvati n.d.).[17] Hope, for those who left, was elsewhere.

Chapter 2

Genoa's Magic Circle

> The arena, the card-table, the magic circle, the temple, the stage, the
> screen, the tennis court, the court of justice, etc., are all . . . forbidden
> spots, isolated, hedged round, hallowed, within which special rules
> obtain. All are temporary worlds within the ordinary world, dedicated
> to the performance of an act apart.
> —Johan Huizinga (1955)

> Genoa has not forgotten, because it is difficult to forget
> . . . .
> What remains is, bitter and indelible, the open spur of a wound.
> —Francesco Guccini (2004)

If the tale of Genoa's revitalization is often told as a linear sequence that is
neatly organized around great events (Mastropiero 2007), one of the latter
actually opened up a chasm in the city's attempt to recover hope. Hence,
while the previous chapter provided a diachronic narration of how this
sentiment has waxed and waned in Genoa over the last fifty years, this
chapter stops the clock at the Group of Eight summit of 2001. By delving
into the terrifying dynamics that ruptured this city's everyday to turn hope
into trauma, here I seek to provide my readers with a glimpse of what
happened when a Genoa that had been hijacked from its residents became
the theater of a violence with few antecedents in recent Italian history. The
purpose of this chapter is to highlight how the underlying agendas of the
great events that are often held to promote cities may overwhelm the promise of improving residents' lives; through my writing, I also hope to convey
the lingering anxiety caused by a social drama that never found closure.

Over the last several decades, great events have become a popular means to brand cities and contribute to their prestige and visibility (Richards and Palmer 2010; Smith 2012). Indeed, as they support the inflow of capitals and the beautification of the built environment, such events also promote hope: residents of host cities often expect a general improvement of their lives through the creation of employment, the alleviation of poverty, and the establishment of new infrastructures (Anderson and Holden 2008: 152). Yet, since their primary goals are to boost national and political prestige even as they generate large-scale profits, great events may in fact end up taking a toll on local populations. In developing countries, the renovation processes that precede great events often include large-scale slum clearings (Greene n.d.); in wealthier nations, urban beautification efforts may also cause the displacement of urban populations (Rutheiser 1996). Following a somewhat similar template, Genoa's 2001 G8 summit, too, entailed a considerable injection of funds, the transformation of the built environment, and above all the promise that the city as a whole would benefit from the event. Yet not only did this summit take place against the backdrop of a city that had been largely vacated of its residents, but, most importantly, it also came at a high cost.

Held shortly after the election of Silvio Berlusconi's second conservative government, the 2001 Group of Eight summit went down in history as the battle of Genoa due to the violent clashes and the extreme brutality of state repression. From July 20 through July 22, the leaders of the eight wealthiest countries in the world conducted their debates inside a militarized citadel—a magic circle—at the heart of downtown Genoa. In the meantime, the rest of the city became the theater of guerrilla warfare and police and army violence that had few precedents in recent Italian history. While most protesters sought to hold their demonstrations peacefully, Black Bloc anarchists carried out hit-and-run attacks on the police as well as on civilian targets, ravaging and burning down parked cars, banks, and small businesses. Instead of seeking to contain the Black Bloc's offensive, police and army corps responded by indiscriminately beating all of the protesters who happened to be in their way. Over three hundred of them were illegally detained; more than four hundred had to be hospitalized, and one young man, Carlo Giuliani, was shot in the head. The end of the violence coincided with the conclusion of the summit on July 21. By July 22, most protesters had left town; over the next several weeks, the devastated city slowly returned to a disconcerted normalcy. As cleaning crews moved in to pick up the burnt rubble and business owners began replacing their shattered shop windows, astonished local and global publics who had followed the events from afar wondered what on earth had happened in Genoa. Instigated by the media apparatus owned by Prime Minister Berlusconi, Italian conservatives blamed the social movements; progressives, instead, pointed the finger at the Fascist undercurrents in Italy's newly elected government.

Even as Italian political factions kept accusing each other, myriad reports on the events materialized not just in newspapers and television broadcasts all over the world, but also on the Internet. In a matter of weeks, countless sites documenting the battle of Genoa made their appearance on the web, while books and videos on the same topic piled up on the shelves of Italian bookstores. Drawing on such testimonials as well as on ethnographic interviews, this chapter is yet another attempt to make sense of the battle of Genoa.[1] Rather than compiling an investigative report, however, in what follows I use the tools of anthropological, sociological, and geographic theory to examine the narrative and spatial dynamics that contributed to the collective enactment of a starkly polarized political imaginary: one that, populated by discordant representations of righteous selves and evil foes, played an important role in triggering state violence.

More specifically, this chapter engages recent sociological analyses of social dramas as collective enactments of crisis and resolution as well as geographic debates on the resistive spatialities created by protest movements —an approach it complements by drawing on anthropological and sociological enquiries into the organizational and performative practices of global social movements (Eyerman 2008; Graeber 2007; Iveson 2007; Mitchell 2003; Juris 2006, 2008; Routledge 1996; Wagner-Pacifici 1986, 2000). However, while much of the anthropological and geographic literature on social movements focuses exclusively on the strategies enacted respectively by the protesters and by those seeking to police them, here I highlight the existence of yet another public, though one that was largely excluded from the event: that of Genoa's own residents whose urban everyday was forcefully interrupted through the creation of a highly contested, though ephemeral, spatiality invested with antagonistic political worldviews.

Political imaginaries are culturally negotiated landscapes of power in which a "people"—that is, a collectivity sharing an enemy—entitles a sovereign agency to wage war in its name (Buck-Morss 2002:12). As they legitimize sovereign power, such Manichaean narrative schemata (Gullí 2003;

Wertsch 2008) feed social dramas as public enactments of conflict and resolution (Eyerman 2008; Turner 1974; Wagner-Pacifici 1986). I argue that the
drama that took place in Genoa was precipitated by the inscription of a
political imaginary into a peculiar spatiality: a magic circle where the elimination of normal social life and the spectacularization and militarization of
political action enabled the performance of an "act apart" (Huizinga 1955:
10) of epic proportions. While, on one hand, the Italian police and the
army took it upon themselves to protect the free world from its communist,
anarchist, and Al-Qaeda-inspired enemies, on the other hand the social
movements lashed out at the symbols of global oppression and exploitation.
The epochal clash that ensued took place in the name of the "people" whose
rights and freedom had to be protected.

A Spectacle for What Publics?

In the story I am about to tell, the "people" were in the first place the highly
abstract signifier that emerged from the interpellations issued by Italy's
media, the majority of which were controlled by conservative leader and
President of the Council of Ministers Silvio Berlusconi. An important condition for the hailing of such a "people," I suggest, was the almost complete
erasure of those other populations who did not fit this abstract, hypothetical mold—Genoa's own residents in the first place.

The summit had been designed as a global spectacle to be watched on
television rather than seen in person; its imperial placelessness was to be
enforced through the threat of violence as well as through aesthetic intensification (Hardt and Negri 2000; Boal et al. 2005). Being particularly concerned with the performative aspects of the first world summit he would
ever host, the newly elected Berlusconi took charge of even the most minute
visual details of downtown Genoa. After all, this is where he would get his
first chance ever to be immortalized next to the likes of George W. Bush
and Vladimir Putin.

As a seasoned media tycoon, Berlusconi could not help fretting over a
beautiful city that was seemingly not beautiful enough. He had flowerpots
rearranged, ordered that lemons be hung from non-citrus trees, and had
unsightly buildings covered with *trompe l'oeil* sheets featuring baroque
façades (Ferraris 2001). His beautification measures included, among others, an embargo on drying laundry on window lines. Even as it drew much

ridicule, this bizarre imposition became indicative of the intent to exclude Genoa's residents from the event: implicitly redefined as "matter out of place" (Douglas 1966: 33) that should not be seen, citizens' everyday life was not an acceptable background to the summit.[2] Genoa's residents were not an intended public of observers, either.

The G8 summit had been planned as one in a series of great events meant to contribute to this city's revitalization; Genoa had been selected by the former President of the Council of Ministers and progressive leader Massimo D'Alema—allegedly for having been the city of his childhood, but also, and most likely, due to this city's loyalty to the Italian Left. Come 2001, however, little did it matter that the renovation of Genoa's downtown had been presented as a gift to the city and its residents: the Genoese were told they would have to wait to enjoy the restored buildings and the freshly paved pedestrian areas.[3] Their exclusion was operated in the first place through fear. "Genoese, in the weekend from July 20th through the 22nd, if you are not on vacation yet and if you have a chance to, go to the beach or the countryside"—this was the message issued by Achille Vinci Giacchi, the ad hoc minister for the G8 summit, in order to encourage Genoa's residents to vacate the city (Genoa Social Forum 2001: 16).[4] In the meantime, the militarized citadel that was being built right at the heart of the city made it obvious that the latter was to become unlivable for whomever resided or worked in that area. As the barriers were being erected, police officers went from door to door, issuing passes and informing residents that they were expecting riots and, potentially, even terrorist attacks. Leaving the city, thus went the message, would be the most reasonable choice in view of the summit.

Many Genoese heeded the recommendation. By the time the event began, at least one-third of approximately 600,000 inhabitants had left.[5] Others sought to use their sense of humor to lighten up what was becoming an unbearably tense atmosphere in a city that was no longer their own. In this vein, a group of unionists residing in the centro storico tried to drag a mock Trojan horse through a gate, reciting poems to stone-faced police officers who, as one activist told me later, "didn't find it funny." The presage of state violence inscribed onto the militarized cityscape—the metal fences, the massive presence of the army and the police, the sight of snipers on rooftops—was compounded by the worrisome news seeping in about the alleged plans of antagonistic social movements that were expected to ravage the city. This is how the owner of a small business in Genoa's centro storico described his feelings at that time: "On one hand, we saw the rising threat of state violence; on the other, we were being told that the city would be invaded by deviant youth (*spostati*) keen on destroying everything." Dismayed at the realization that the very same event that was supposed to promote the city on a global scale had turned ominous, he decided to close and barricade his shop for the duration of the summit. Many of his fellow business owners did the same. As an increasingly deserted Genoa took on the feel of a ghost city, some of those residents who had not left made a point of participating in the protests—at least until they figured out that it was not safe to be in the street. As one man told me, "I went with my wife to the migrants' march (*corteo dei migrant*); initially the atmosphere was festive, and there were a lot of people with their children. . . . However . . . the police in anti-riot gear looked scary. I saw them, and then I saw some of those [anarchist] kids dressed in black with their somber faces. . . . I figured that, if anything had happened, we could have been easily trapped between the two groups. Then I told my wife: let's go home, I don't like it here. And I was right." Like many others, he eventually opted for following the summit from his own home, monitoring the events from his windows whenever he could, but mostly through television.[6] Many fellow Genoese did the same. As they lost the right to their own city—to inhabit, use, and experience it as they pleased (Lefebvre 1996)—the Genoese who withdrew to their homes had to join the summit's global audiences of television viewers. They, too, became yet another atomized public in a public sphere that had been engineered as a consensus-making machine.[7] If the suspension of normal social life contributed to the onset of liminality in downtown Genoa, the narratives of danger that had engulfed the Italian public sphere provided the justification for a state of exception whereby fear legitimized sovereign violence (Agamben 2005; Hardt and Negri 2000).

Conjuring the Terrorist Enemy

Even as many of Genoa's residents had been persuaded to vacate their city, a multitude of social movements grouped under the umbrella of the Genoa Social Forum flocked to it for the sake of holding a counter-summit. Their goal was to publicly question and challenge the purposes and modalities of the summit while proposing an alternative model of globalization: "Another world is possible" was their slogan. The Genoa Social Forum (GSF) comprised a variety of movements ranging from environmentalists to feminists, from Catholics and unionists to indigenous groups, and from Roma, Sinti, and migrants to anti-IMF activists (Della Porta and Reiter 2006; Juris 2006). Regardless of their heterogeneity, though, what the GSF-affiliated movements had in common was their critique of forms of oppression and exploitation imposed by dominating powers (Della Porta et al. 2006; Juris 2006; Routledge 1996). The multifarious ideals and purposes of the over 200,000 GSF affiliates who convened for the counter-summit were thus summarized in an open letter to Genoa's citizens: "actions of international cooperation, environmental protection, valorization of citizenship and labor rights, the promotion of ethical and responsible economic models, development of forms of multiethnic coexistence and of intercultural exchange, affirmation of the principles of peace and struggle against injustice" (GSF 2001:41). The overwhelming majority of social movements also shared peaceful intentions and non-violent strategies. A few of those who planned to participate in the counter-summit, however, had pledged to carry out violent attacks in order to express their rejection of global capitalism. Prior to the summit, these groups obtained a disproportionate attention in the Italian public sphere.

In the weeks preceding the event, the Italian media had launched a fear campaign (Cristante 2003) that sought to inscribe and congeal a specific narrative of the GSF as the enemy of Western civilization (Della Porta 2006: 6; Eyerman 2008: 17). Conservative newspapers owned by, or aligned with, Berlusconi and his allies published daily reports on how the GSF movements were going to ravage the city and carry out indiscriminate attacks on civilians and police officers alike. The protesters would allegedly be armed with balloons filled with HIV-positive blood. They would also fling marbles full of a disfiguring acid; the most benign among them would use catapults to throw dung (Colombo 2002; Cristante 2003), and marginal youth groups such as the *punkabbestia* would unleash their pit bulls against the police (Sema 2001). As if this were not enough, rumors circulated about a possible Al-Qaeda attack. Osama Bin Laden himself was supposedly planning on instigating riots among the protesters in order to distract the police and the army while his drones and scuba divers would annihilate the leaders of the free world (Sema 2001: 22).

Concerned by the potential of extremist violence, even much of the moderate Italian Left led by the Democratici di Sinistra party distanced itself from the GSF (Della Porta et al. 2006: 148). This failure to provide a public counter-narrative in the mainstream media allowed conservative television channels and newspapers to shape and control the climate of growing anxiety. Little did it matter that the crowd of protesters spanned a highly heterogeneous multitude. Pacifists, human rights activists, migrants, environmentalists, feminists, and many other declaredly peaceful groups were all subsumed under the generic, and generically threatening, label of "*no-global*": a somewhat English-sounding sobriquet that not only simplistically homogenized them as antagonists to globalization, but also marked them as alien to local culture and society.[8] As such, a stark dichotomy of righteous selves and evil others became inscribed onto Genoa's physical territory, the tension was bound to escalate.

The Map Is the Territory

The officialdom's preemptive defense against the threat allegedly posited by the protesters had been the rearrangement of the area of the summit into a highly defendable citadel. In the days that preceded the summit, Genoa's airport, its railway system, and the port were sealed off, and 2,000 people were turned down at the Italian border (Della Porta et al. 2006: 3). Following a strategy that had been implemented in Quebec City during the Free Trade Area of the Americas summit of April 2001(Juris 2003: 55), much of the city center was turned into a red zone (*zona rossa*) meant to protect the sacred ground of legitimate power. This area was surrounded by a metal fence (and, in some cases, heaps of containers) that isolated the area of the summit and prevented any face-to-face engagement between the G8 leaders and the movements. Around the militarized red zone was yet another ring—a yellow zone (*zona gialla*) that included the remainder of the city center as well as adjacent residential neighborhoods.[9] Inside the yellow zone, social movements had been assigned thematic plazas (*piazze tematiche*): spaces for representation (Mitchell 2003) where they could not only hold their meetings but also performatively manifest their goals and express their critiques of dominant powers by directly addressing global publics instead of political referents (Chesters and Welsh 2004, 2006; Della Porta and Reiter 2003; Graeber 2007; Juris 2006 and 2008). As performative counterpoints to the theatricality of the summit, their banners, symbols, chants, music, and costumes sought to convey complex messages to their global publics (Chesters and Welsh 2004, 2006; Graeber 2007). Their carni-valesque antics criticized and mocked an ostensibly self-absorbed and self-referential establishment intent on discussing world poverty even as it played a major role in its perpetuation (Graeber 2007; Juris 2006). Commenting on the resistive quality of GSF practices in the yellow zone, one activist remarked: "There were two different cities. In [the yellow zone] there was an outdoor university with economists, pacifist, people like Rigoberta Menchù talking with the youth from other countries. On the other hand there was the police that kept pouring in, and the huge fences that created the ghetto of the powerful." For the protesters, the hierarchical separation between the red and the yellow zone constituted a ready-made physical and metaphoric terrain of resistance that lent itself to the spatialization of dissent (Routledge 1996). Yet the protesters were also painfully aware of how they were being kept in their place, both spatially and metaphorically (Cresswell 1996; Jansen 2001). In the words of a Ya Basta affiliate, the fence separating the red from the yellow zone was a material reminder of the "enormous wall" symbolizing the global conflict between the North and the South of the world: "Just as the symbol of the third world war was the Berlin wall, the symbol of [this war] is the enormous wall that starts at the Rio Grande and runs through to Turkey, passing Gibraltar and then north, leaving out Eastern Europe; it divides Australia and Japan from the rest of East Asia. This wall is an insult to humanity."[10] The fence, in this perspective, provided the ultimate evidence of how global political and financial elites sought to avoid a dialogue with the people they claimed to represent. Confined to the exterior of the citadel, the "people," in this view, were excluded from the process of making decisions that would affect them all. What many protesters had contemptuously dubbed "the cage" (la gabbia) symbolically reproduced the separation between the rich and the poor, the powerful and the dispossessed—or, as one activist put it, "the New World Order, the Global Empire, protected by 20,000 police and military, besieged by the new Global protest movement."[11] Signs displayed by the movements read, "8 stronzi in gabbia" ("eight shits in a cage"); "zona rossa di vergogna" ("the zone is red with shame"); "strada chiusa: muro della vergogna" ("dead-end road: wall of shame"; GSF 2001: 61, 37, 17). The fence effectively collapsed the global scale of inequality into a very tangible, very local, and very sizable symbol: one that posited an irresistible instigation to be torn down.

In her analysis of the spatial politics of standoffs, sociologist Robin Wagner-Pacifici (2000) observed how, as state representatives and anti-establishment groups confront each other, their moral and ideological polarization is reinscribed—and exacerbated—through the physical boundaries that surround the central point of containment. Almost inevitably, such a binary organization of space increases tension and leads to violence. On a similar note, I suggest that, by designing and building the fence, the Italian government did not just prospect and seek to stave off a violation attempt; it *invited* it. Prying open the red zone, even though only symbolically, became a categorical imperative (Wagner-Pacifici 2000: 8) for the protesters: one that was matched only by the army and the police officers' determination to prevent any trespassing. To them, too, the fence was the boundary where the enemy began to manifest.

Some movements sought to trespass the fence only symbolically, for example by throwing flowers and balloons over it. Others braved the mace cannons to pin messages to its meshes, thus seeking to draw attention to that very same reciprocal acknowledgment and dialogic communication with political leaders that had been denied to them. Occupying the ambiguous space between the declaredly nonviolent movements and the extremist fringes, the White Overalls (*Tute Bianche*) affiliated with Ya Basta (Caracciolo 2001; Vanderford 2003), instead, decided to try and physically violate the fence. A few weeks before the summit, their leader Luca Casarini added fuel to the fire by publicly declaring to the Italian media, "We shall block the G8 summit."[12] The White Overalls' agenda was ambiguous with regard to violence. Their strategy was characterized by a Gandhi-inspired passive resistance (Vitali 2001)—with the caveat that, even as they professed restraint from proactively violent attacks, the White Overalls intended to use the weight of their mass to tear down the red zone barrier (Callinicos 2003; Juris 2006: 44). In the words of one member, "The aim was to shut down the G8. The strategy was to attempt to breach the fortifications from a variety of positions. The tactics were direct action. The first task was to break through the myriad fortified police lines."[13]

Like Gandhi's freedom fighters, however, the White Overalls also explicitly sought to trigger police brutality in order to show the world the true colors of an essentially repressive state (Caracciolo 2001: 12). On July 20, movement members who were being hosted in the Carlini stadium prepared for their march by taping Styrofoam sheets and empty plastic bottles to their bodies: while symbolizing the waste produced by consumer capitalism (Vanderford 2003), these items were also meant to protect them from police attacks. Hiding behind Plexiglas shields, the White Overalls set out for the fence. They never made it. Riot police and carabineri corps attacked them when they were still in the yellow zone, about a mile away from the red zone fence:[14] "First a frantic barrage of tear-gas, lobbing over the front lines, deep into the heart of the demonstration. Nobody here had gas masks. The poisonous gas first blinds you, then hurts, and then disorientates you. It is immediate and devastating. The people, packed in tightly, panicked and surged backwards. The chaos was manic."[15] Armed with the toxic CS tear gas that had been banned by the 1997 Chemical Weapons Convention as well as with the T-shaped *tonfa* batons known to produce deep wounds (GSF 2001: 24, 108), the police pushed the protesters against a wall. The protesters fought back, and mayhem ensued. By that evening, hundreds of civilians lay injured in local hospitals, or detained in police stations and army barracks. One of them, Carlo Giuliani, was dead, shot in the head by a young carabiniere conscript under circumstances that were never fully clarified.[16]

The Black Bloc: Liminal and Elusive

The police attack had taken place in a yellow zone area for which the White Overalls' march had been authorized (Della Porta and Reiter 2003: 161); the alleged trigger had been an incursion by Black Bloc anarchists. Long before the summit, the Black Bloc had been singled out as a major security concern. Their participation at the 1999 World Trade Organization summit in Seattle, the 2000 International Monetary Fund and World Bank meeting in Prague, and the 2001 summit of the Americas in Quebec had been characterized by a high level of devastation (GSF 2001: 164). Due to their declaredly violent intent, the Black Bloc were feared not just by the Italian defense apparatus, but also by the majority of GSF movements who were concerned about the effects that their violence could have on their own efforts to promote their cause. As expected, the Black Bloc wreaked havoc in Genoa, too—and other protesters ended up paying the price for it (Juris 2006).[17]

In what follows, I suggest that the Black Bloc played the role of mythological tricksters who, positioned betwixt and between, simultaneously violate and establish boundaries (Babcock-Abrahams 1975). Frequently described as cunning deceivers and liars, tricksters are ambiguous and polyvalent (Makarius 1974; Hynes 1997a). Most importantly, they are shapeshifters, situation invertors, and metaplayers who break the rules only to reaffirm them (Hynes 1997b). Just like the tricksters of world mythology, the Black Bloc who took part in the 2001 G8 counter-summit used shape shifting, chaos, and ambiguity to help crystallize representations of the terrorist enemy, thus escalating a repression they invariably eluded.

Surprisingly enough, the Black Bloc' participation in Genoa's counter-summit was characterized by their lack of interest in the very same fence that had monopolized everybody else's attention (Juris 2006: 8).[18] Instead of targeting the red zone, the Black Bloc made quick, unexpected appearances in the yellow zone, where they carried out violent attacks against what they described as the symbols of global capitalism. Their objectives supposedly included the destruction of luxury vehicles, banks, chain stores, car dealerships, and the city jail; however, apartment complexes, small shops, and cheap cars were also hit in the process (Della Porta and Reiter 2003: 137). Black bloc targets included journalists, photographers, and— although from a safe distance—army and police officers.[19] In the words of one of them, "Firstly the Black Bloc did a lot of property damage, some of it sensible: banks, porn shops, petrol stations, expensive cars, supermarkets; some of it stupid: traffic lights, bus shelters, cheaper cars; and some of it lunatic: starting a fire in an office above which was an apartment bloc."[20]

Whenever they launched an attack, the Black Bloc donned their peculiar attire: black clothes, hoods, and surgical or gas masks. On occasion, they also enacted a ceremony of their own, waving black flags and marching in circles to the sound of their drums before lashing out at their targets. This visibility, however, was carefully restricted in time and space. The Black Bloc always materialized out of nowhere and they disappeared immediately after each attack, either by dispersing through Genoa's maze of shortcuts or by changing clothes and blending in with the crowds. Even their weapons were improvised out of materials that were quickly harnessed and just as swiftly discarded. The stones they hurled at the police were ripped from flowerbeds, and their Molotov cocktails were concocted out of bottles picked from recycling bins and filled with gas removed from parked vehicles. Masters of elusiveness, the Black Bloc met attempts to photograph or film their raids with violent attacks, during which cameras and camcorders were routinely destroyed.

Best described as a tactic of urban guerrilla warfare rather than a movement (Gustinchic 2001), the Black Bloc groups roaming Genoa's yellow zone were open to anyone willing to wear black clothes and join them in their attacks. Through their masks, the Black Bloc sought to deny the existence of subjectivities for the sake of becoming, as Edward Avery-Natale

(2010) put it, an undetermined "anything." Yet donning a black mask allowed *anyone* to become a Black Bloc. Interviewed by a journalist, for example, a man acting as part of a Black Bloc group self-identified as a British Nazi and declared: "I don't give a dime about the G8. . . . I am here to wreak havoc and I am having a hell of a good time" (GSF 2001: 68). The uncertainties about the Black Bloc's political affiliation also contributed to raising questions about the real purposes of their attacks. This was all the more the case since the latter took on the same modality again and again: after positioning themselves in front of a group of nonviolent protesters, the Black Bloc would lash out at the police, pelting them with stones and Molotov cocktails. Then, the police would attack—but never before the Black Bloc had vanished into thin air (Chesters and Welsh 2006: 84). Each time, peaceful protesters were left to bear the brunt of the repression: the blows, the tear gas, and the arbitrary arrests that the Black Bloc invariably escaped.

Along with their elusiveness, the organizational fluidity of the Black Bloc (Gustinchic 2001: 452) and their lack of a consistent, and consistently identifiable, public persona gave way to competing readings of their strategies and real identities. For the police and the military who had been bombarded with warnings about the terrorist threat, the Black Bloc were the proof that all GSF movements were essentially violent, and that, as such, all of them had to be repressed by using all means available (Sema 2001). Many GSF members, instead, were irked by the police officers' lack of responsiveness to the Black Bloc. Eyewitness reports but also films and photographs proved how the police consistently failed to contain the Black Bloc, targeting peaceful protesters in their stead. Black Bloc were also spotted and even photographed as they socialized on the roof of a carabinieri barrack (GSF 2001: 118–119). Others were seen as they filmed journalists and reporters at a check point; interacted collegially with carabinieri and police officers, and walked freely in and out of police precincts and army barracks, carrying guns under their black clothes (GSF 2001: 119–121). The suspicion thus arose that Black Bloc had been infiltrated by police officers keen on delegitimizing dissent and providing an alibi for state repression (Caracciolo 2001: 9).

While answering the question of the Black Bloc's real identity is beyond the scope of this chapter, here I wish to highlight their pivotal contribution to precipitating the drama of righteous selves and terrorist others inscribed onto the G8 summit. By holding a revolving mirror to the political fantasies of all parties involved, and, most importantly, by exacerbating the fear of an elusive, if dangerous, enemy, the Black Bloc enabled the sovereign violence that was exercised through police retaliations (Agamben 1988; Juris 2006). Tricksters, as has been observed, are made sacred by their violations; in turn, this sacredness separates them from society and puts them in the condition of those who can be killed with impunity (Babcock-Abrahams 1975: 164; Makarius 1974: 37).[21] Just like mythological tricksters, however, the Black Bloc also held the ability to divert the consequences of their actions onto others (Babcock-Abrahams 1975); hence, their sacredness was transferred to the other protesters, who consistently paid the price for the Black Bloc's raids.

Spaces of Death

The disruptive ambiguity that the Black Bloc injected into the battle of Genoa contributed to the creation of sinister liminalities: "spaces of death in the land of the living" (Taussig 1987: 4) where illegally detained GSF affiliates were stripped of their rights and subjected to a brutal repression, even as fellow activists, lawyers, and families were prevented from intervening.[22] In a plot that kept repeating itself throughout the duration of the summit, the alleged presence of the Black Bloc provided the pretext for the violent police incursion in the Diaz school that hosted the Indymedia center as well as several GSF members and journalists. On July 21, at about 11 PM, a police commando irrupted into the school. Unidentifiable because of their anti-riot gear,[23] the police officers who broke into the Diaz school that night beat up and severely injured sixty-two of the ninety-three journalists and GSF members who were staying there. The police reportedly walked around the rooms screaming, "Where is Carlo? [Giuliani, who had been killed earlier that day]" and savagely attacking people still in their sleeping bags. By the time they were done, the rooms of the Diaz school were splattered with blood, and sixty-two people had deep wounds and fractured bones (GSF 2001: 281).

During the incursion, a crowd amassed in front of the school: concerned GSF members, physicians and nurses, journalists, and even politicians, none of whom was allowed to enter the premises as the massacre went on (GSF 2001: 129–131). All they got to see was the bleeding bodies of the wounded who were carried away, to be taken into custody. As legality was restored few days later, Italian magistrates cleared all of the apprehended: none of them, they found, was a Black Bloc. The two Molotov cocktails that were exhibited as evidence turned out to have been planted by an officer during the raid.

The plight of many of the Diaz school victims did not end with their arrest, however. Seventy-five of them were taken to the Bolzaneto barracks. Along with the other detainees, they were to be subjected to physical and psychological abuses in an environment where legality had been suspended. Jailers would confiscate or even rip prisoners' identity documents as they told them, "See? Here you are nobody, you have no rights" (GSF 2001: 146). One detainee reported: "I requested a lawyer, and all I got was more blows" (GSF 2001: 143). Reduced to bare life that can be disposed of with impunity (Agamben 1988), the detainees were deprived of sleep, water, and food, and were not permitted to use the restrooms. Many prisoners, regardless of their injuries, were forced to lean against walls as they stood on their toes, their arms eagle-spread, for hours on end: "Those who showed signs of weakness and let their arms down were invariably slapped on their neck, kicked on their feet or shins, punched on their belly or hips. . . . As to myself, I was in that position . . . for about 15 hours" (GSF 2001: 142).

Signs of perceived deviance were forcefully removed from bodies: piercings were ripped away, and long hair was summarily shaven. Earlier on, the protesters' colorful clothes, costumes, and hippie garbs had mocked the dark uniforms of the police as well as the black suits of politicians (Graeber 2007: 329);[24] their upbeat music and improvised dances had challenged army discipline and the stiff formality of the officialdom. In the Bolzaneto barracks, however, the same unruly bodies that had made fun of the establishment were punished through degradation and violence. Women were molested and threatened with rape; prisoners were made to walk through two rows of soldiers who spat and urinated on them (GSF 2001: 142). Often, the blows were administered on existing wounds, so that the victims' bodies would bear no additional evidence (GSF 2001: 143). Even such distortion of the concern with legality was not consistent, though. At times, the viciousness of the abuses betrayed a bold confidence in the victimizers' impunity: as one prisoner reported, "All of a sudden, a policeman . . . took my hand, spread my fingers apart and pulled them violently, thus tearing my flesh and splitting my hand" (GSF 2001: 144).

The space of exception that had emerged inside the barracks—one whereby state powers dealt with the threat of terrorism by suspending legality in the name of the law (Agamben 1988: 2005)—dissolved with the end of the summit, when prisoners were eventually released. The injuries, however, persisted. Their signs scarred the violated bodies of the victims; they also lingered in the collective psyche of those publics who still grappled to come to terms with the events.[25] In the aftermath of the battle of Genoa, much was said and written about the seemingly inexplicable brutality of police and army corps. As part of a rising tide of conspiracy theories about the conservative government's explicit intent to repress the protesters, persistent rumors surmised that Gianfranco Fini, Vice president of the Council of Ministers and leader of the post-Fascist Alleanza Nazionale party, had taken a trip to Genoa during the summit. A Genoese woman who watched the events from the safety of her home told me: "I see a motorcade enter the barracks, and shortly after that I hear this loud chanting and applauses, so many applauses. Then, the following day I hear that Fini was in town. It must have been him, he came here to incite the violence (*metterli su*). Who knows what he promised them." On the other hand, apologetic explanations for police brutality singled out the conspicuous presence of inexperienced young conscripts along with that of corps that had never been trained in peaceful crowd control and de-escalation techniques (Della Porta and Reiter 2003) and only worked with dangerous detainees; such tenuous circumstances were further compounded by the lack of non-lethal weapons in police and army equipment.[26]

On a deeper level, however, the repression of dissent at the 2001 G8 summit shed light on the extent to which the military machinery activated by the government was, in fact, a self-standing political player capable of embodying and performing its own version of the state (Agamben 2007; Aretxaga 2003): one that owed less to utilitarian rationalism than to a highly abstract Manichaean worldview (Taussig 1987).[27] As this political imaginary was being called forth, it became appropriate for soldiers and police officers to chant hymns to Mussolini and Pinochet as they abused their victims, often even forcing them to sing along (GSF 2001: 142–143). A fantasy was at work that not only exceeded functional rationality, but also activated a sedimented Fascist repertoire: a root paradigm of "symbols, archetypal characters, and rhetorical appeals" that is still known to haunt the conservative Italian imaginary (Wagner-Pacifici 1986: 7). As soldiers and police officers inscribed their discursive, yet absolute Other (communist, anarchist, terrorist, queer, hippie, etc.) onto the humiliated and brutalized bodies of their detainees (Della Porta and Reiter 2003: 172), their

personal enactment of the dominant narrative became thicker, more inti-
mate, and more extreme. It became a rapt, and deadly serious, deep play
where everything was at stake (Geertz 1973), and whose bloodbath was
simultaneously highly symbolic and very real.

By then, captive GSF members had become anonymous blank screens
onto which a dangerous alterity could not only be projected, but also punished by means of the same brutality that had been imputed to it (Taussig
1987). Given the enormity of these Others' imaginary crimes, their retribu-
tion could reach above and beyond legality. Thus, in the magic circles
drawn around the Bolzaneto barracks and the Diaz school, the summit that
had begun as a ceremony meant to illustrate and celebrate the global world
order turned into a ritual of elimination of the chaotic Other.[28] Blending
the mode of the "world *as if*" (Turner 1980: 163) with that of real actions
with tangible consequences, the sovereign violence applied to the defeated
bodies of the protesters enacted the pretense of an epochal victory over its
absolute, if multifarious, enemy. The fiction of this victory, however, did
not outlast the end of the heterotopic spatiality (Foucault 1986) that had
been created for the summit.[29] As soon as the summit reached its conclusion on July 22, the magic circle of the Bolzaneto barracks was lifted, too.
This is when the spell broke, and news about the abuses committed during
the summit erupted in the global media.

The End of the Drama

While Italy's conservative television channels and newspapers had had a
considerable impact in framing the anti-G8 protests for the public opinion
before and during the event (Perlmutter and Wagner 2004; Snow 2003),
theirs was not the only gaze on the G8 events. The summit was characterized by an intense participation not only of international journalists, but
also of independent and amateur reporters and photographers who generated an alternative flow of information. Following Indymedia's advice
"Don't hate the media, become the media," hundreds of protesters armed
with camcorders and cameras produced a mass of evidence of police and
army brutality, thus assembling a counter-narrative that challenged the
official version of the events (Della Porta and Reiter 2003: 113).[30]

Once they flooded the media, the images of bruised, lacerated bodies,
and the myriad reports of police repression, torture, and violence generated

Figure 4. Anti-police march in 2002. Photo by author.

a global spectacle of horror that cast a deep shade on the G8 summit as well as Italy's conservative government. In the aftermath of the summit, the public confidence in the police and carabinieri corps reached its lowest levels ever. As one Genoese woman told me, "The presence of the police used to make me feel safe. Now when I walk by them I get nervous." Formal investigations began of the abuses of the Diaz school and the Bolzaneto barracks, followed by first- and second-degree trials that often failed to give the victims the closure they expected.

The loss of trust in the Italian state was just as stark on a global level. If the official narrative of the government had posited the need to defend Western civilization, globally circulating tales of a repression that was unheard of for a European Union country opened up a crevice in Italy's claims to the status of Western democracy. After the events of the Diaz school, even conservative media around the world began condemning the brutality of the repression (Juris 2005); furthermore, that such violence had taken place in twenty-first-century Europe made things even worse. Leading European and U.S. newspapers called Italy a "Chilean," "Argentine,"

"East European," or "Cuban" dictatorship (Fubini 2001; Colombi 2001), thus activating a transnational imaginary whereby the Italian state's attempt to confirm its membership in an ideal Western civilization had produced the opposite result. As it became clear that the violence that had been initially imputed to the social movements had, in fact, been committed by representatives of the Italian state, what had been regarded as the solution to the terrorist problem was singled out as the problem itself. In the weeks that followed the end of the summit, Silvio Berlusconi's legitimacy as a G8 leader and as Italy's prime minister became the object of intense, and intensely critical, debates, both at home and abroad. For much of the summer, Berlusconi's government seemed to be heading for a quick demise. All of a sudden, however, a highly dramatic event took place that provided a formidable validation for Italy's conservative government, its fear campaigns, and its violent repression of protesters.

On September 11, 2001, two hijacked airplanes rammed into New York's World Trade Center, destroying two towers and killing thousands; a third plane hit the Pentagon in Arlington, Virginia, and a fourth one crashed in Pennsylvania while presumably en route to the White House. Western civilization was, indeed, under attack. Now that the terrorist enemy had turned out to be every bit as dangerous as expected, the state of exception became a welcome—and permanent—necessity (Agamben 2005). As concerned citizens around the Western world stockpiled canned food and duct tape, the global indignation over the abuses committed in Genoa faded in a splashing of orange alerts. Berlusconi's government lasted until the end of its five-year mandate.

A Drama Without Closure

Rather than being a merely physical gesture, the act of drawing a magic circle and assigning meaning to it makes it possible to create a "sphere of activity with a disposition of its own" (Huizinga 1955: 8). By virtue of being "apart together" (Huizinga 1955: 12), participants in this circle enter a shared imaginary world where normality is interrupted. The tragic events that transpired from the G8 summit—the guerilla warfare as well as the violent repression—were at least in part a product of the creation of a sui generis magic circle: one that inscribed an ideological map onto a cityscape that had been transformed for the occasion. The suspension of normal social life, the crystallization of official narratives, and above all the creation of a militarized citadel inside the city were all pivotal to turning a highly abstract and starkly dichotomic political imaginary into lived experience.

Rather than improving residents' own lives, the restoration of Genoa's built environment prior to the summit turned out to be only the first stage of a deadly serious deep play: one whereby the creation of a peculiar place-lessness went hand in hand with the need to claim and defend territories at all costs. What had begun as a constellation of camera-ready vignettes (of world leaders celebrating themselves, and of GSF movements debating, marching, and performing in their thematic plazas) thus unfolded into a full-fledged social drama. The stakes were high for all those involved. What, for the officialdom, was the epochal clash between the free world and its terrorist enemies, for the protesters epitomized the chasm between human-kind and the agents of global oppression. While these imaginaries differed radically from each other, they both shared the same Manichaean organiza-tion of righteous selves and evil enemies. Hence, both the protesters and the state representatives respectively sought to enact their own narrative even as they recruited each other in the role of the "familiar stranger": the blank screen for projections of "predictable but unreasonable, unaccount-able, deeply flawed, possibly immoral" alterity (Mattingly 2008).

By skillfully blending violence and shape shifting, the Black Bloc intensi-fied the polarization, thus contributing to precipitating the events. Not only did their transgressions enable the Italian state to reclaim its monopoly over violence (Weber 1965), but they also made it easier for it to suspend the law in the name of legality (Agamben 1988, 2005). Death spaces thus emerged where the terrorist enemy could be punished or even exorcised, in an exercise in magical thinking whereby attacking the part became equiva-lent to vanquishing the whole.

After the end of the summit, as normality was reinstated, the realization of the brutality of the repression sent shock waves through the very same Western world whose defense had supposedly been at stake. This emotion was particularly strong in Genoa. In the days that followed the summit, the city began a slow recovery: the gates and the fences were dismantled; the burnt rubble, the destroyed cars, and the shattered windows were removed, and the graffiti were painted over. Little by little, even the acrid smell of the tear gas that had soaked the upholsteries of many a downtown home gave in. Clearing the material debris, however, did little to soothe the anxiety and the anger at the violence that had swept through the city. An intricate

Figure 5. Piazza Carlo Giuliani. Photo by author.

game of forgetting and remembering began. An anonymous hand had spray-painted "Carlo Giuliani, *ragazzo* (boy)" over "Gaetano Alimonda" on the plaque naming the piazza where the young Genoese protester had been killed, thus memorializing an event that the institutions seemed eager to cast into oblivion. Each time Carlo Giuliani's name was removed from the Piazza Alimonda plaque, the graffiti would reappear in a matter of days. In the meantime, Genoa became a disaster tourism destination: in a city that had pursued a painstaking transformation and sought to present itself as a hub for cultural tourism, all that visitors wanted to see was the place where Carlo Giuliani had been killed.[31]

Adding insult to injury, the placelessness imposed upon Genoa by Berlusconi's government and the G8 summit was mirrored by the degree of abstraction that this city took on in the collective imaginary of global social movements. In globally circulating post-2001 narratives, "Genoa" became a placeless time/space coordinate fully defined by state repression (see, e.g., Juris 2006: 194, 169). As the excluded public that had been denied the right to its own city both materially and symbolically (Lefebvre 1996), many

Genoese took exception at this categorization. Not only did they resist the reduction of the places of their everyday life to a theater of brutality, but they also found that such a designation complied with the conservative government's intent to mar Genoa's image as a traditionally leftist city. As one centro storico resident put it:

> When I say I am from Genoa people look at me and say "oh, that's awful!" I had friends [from another city] visit a couple of months ago, and all they wanted to see was Piazza Alimonda [where Carlo Giuliani was killed] and the Diaz school. This makes me very angry. . . . At the end of World War II, Genoa was the only Italian city that did not need to be liberated from the Fascists, because it set itself free, and this is why it earned a Gold Medal for Anti-Fascist Resistance (*medaglia d'oro alla resistenza*). The 1960 riots caused the [conservative] Tambroni government to fall after it had permitted a neo-Fascist rally here. Tambroni wanted to stick it up to the Genoese, but we didn't allow him to. What happened with the 2001 G8 [repression] has been a revenge of the Italian Right against a city that has always been loyal to the Left (*di sinistra*).

With the help of Genoa's glamorous performance as a 2004 Capital of European Culture, some of this ominous global aura dissipated. Yet the memory of the events still lingers. Ten years after the 2001 G8 summit, a somber march of 15,000 marked the anniversary of Carlo Giuliani's death. The police and the army were there, too; realizing that their presence could be interpreted as a provocation, however, this time around they chose to keep a low profile. Conducted among a crescendo of rumors that the Black Bloc would be back and would yet again wreak havoc on the city, the march culminated in the inauguration of a small memorial in Piazza Alimonda. In the meantime, PrimoCanale, the local television station that had provided 24/7 coverage of the G8 summit in 2001, commemorated the events by broadcasting the old footage the entire day. Early in the afternoon I got an anxious phone call from a relative: "The Black Bloc are back, they are ravaging Corso Gastaldi. You need to go home immediately!" she informed me in one breath. Being on edge about a possible outburst of violence, my relative had mistaken PrimoCanale's old footage for a live broadcast. As it turned out, thousands of concerned Genoese had committed the same mistake, and a subtle panic was spreading through the city. By the time I reached the Galleria Mazzini antique fair at 4 PM, I was surprised to see that many of the vendors were eagerly packing their wares, ready to go home well ahead of time. The rumor had reached them that the Black Bloc were back and that, once again, the city had become a battlefield for the war between Berlusconi's conservative state and the social movements.[32]

Social dramas, suggested Victor Turner (1980), heal through a process of redress culminating in the reintegration of the social groups that caused the crisis in the first place. This never happened in Genoa. The ten years that had followed the 2001 G8 summit were characterized by the GSF's often-thwarted attempts to secure at least some of the massacre culprits to a reluctant justice. Mario Placanica, the carabiniere who had killed Carlo Giuliani, was acquitted after claiming self-defense. In 2010, a conservative government led, once again, by Silvio Berlusconi and Gianfranco Fini, refused to ratify the suspension of the high-ranking police officers who had been found guilty at the trial for the raid on the Diaz school. In 2012, however, twenty-five police officers were found guilty by the Court of Cassation, and the victims were entitled to damages. Yet the latter were to be paid not by the perpetrators, but rather by the state on the basis of a recently approved ad hoc law meant to shield the defendants from a predictable verdict. As to the tortures in the Bolzaneto barracks, forty-four defendants were found guilty during the second-degree trial. However, in most cases their crimes became statute-barred before the final, third-degree trial was held years later, and only a handful of them were convicted. Of the only thirteen police officers who had been found guilty of the Diaz massacre, none served time.[33] To make things worse, in 2013 Giovanni de Gennaro, the prefect who had been indicted for the Diaz attack, was appointed president of Finmeccanica, Italy's foremost industrial conglomerate controlled by the Ministry of Economy and Finance. In 2014, de Gennaro became president of the Ansaldo Foundation, one of Genoa's most popular cultural institutions. Angry protests erupted on the occasion of his first (and to date last) visit back to Genoa. Much to the disappointment of social movements, of victims and their families, and of many a Genoese, justice was never served. Genoa's drama did not find closure, and in this city the memory of the G8 summit remains, indeed, an open spur of a wound.

Chapter 3

Gentrification Without Teleologies

> Since I landed [in Genoa's centro storico] in 1984, I have witnessed
> an ongoing skin change: the smell of exotic spices has replaced the
> stench of fried fish, and Latin American music has replaced
> Neapolitan songs. Yet, the background has remained the same: a nasty
> world of pushers and pimps, but also a normal world of families that
> try to get by the best they can, a world of children and elderly people.
> This is a small world in which, when you go home, you have to watch
> your step for rats and the syringes of tossici. Yet, this is also the small
> world where the tobacconist knows you and gives you your favorite
> brand of cigarettes as soon as you walk into his store without you
> having to ask, and where the neighbor keeps you in the hallway for
> half an hour to tell you about her struggle with triglycerides.
> —Paola Pettinotti (2007)

Surrounded by tall metal fences and with its rooftops guarded by snipers, during the G8 summit Genoa's centro storico had become an empty, if heavily militarized, shell. Some of the residents had barricaded themselves in their homes. Others, instead, had left, fearing both terrorist attacks and army raids. When the summit was over, life as usual resumed, and so did the challenges that centro storico residents face on a daily basis. Take, for example, Francesca.

Like many in her generation (Molé 2011), Francesca, a psychologist in her thirties, lives hand-to-mouth collecting precarious contracts with a variety of agencies and with little hope for professional stability, let alone a career. Francesca moved to the Maddalena area of the centro storico in

1999, to which she was attracted not just by its bohemian and multicultural environment, but also by the low property prices. Ever since, she has been living in a diminutive apartment on the sixth floor of a building with no elevator. Like most dwellings in the centro storico, her apartment does not get much sunshine; her back windows, in particular, face a roof that some residents use as a dump: "bags, shoes, empty crates, wallets, sanitary pads. And then there are the rats and the pigeons. We called the Public Sanitation office, but nobody ever showed up. I am not particularly sensitive, but at times [the sight of what's on this roof] really makes me feel like throwing up."

At the time of relocating to the centro storico from her mother's home, this apartment had not been Francesca's first choice: she had seen a better place in a nearby vicolo with a small balcony and a lot more sunshine; however, that apartment needed considerably more work and the cost would have been prohibitive for her parents, who were subsidizing the purchase. All things considered, however, Francesca is not planning to move out any time soon. Her centro storico apartment is conveniently located, and she does not need a car or even a bus to go anywhere. Cinemas, theaters, grocery stores, and Genoa's two main railway stations are just a short walking distance away, and she is fond of shopping in ethnic stores run by African and Indian immigrants. The centro storico has become her home to a fault: "At times I feel so contained [by the neighborhood] that I need to go somewhere else to have an aperitivo, otherwise I might as well spend my entire life inside here."

Francesca's neighbors include a dentist, a butcher with his wife, a clerk, a lawyer, the tiny office of a public health care provider, and the manager of a small family-owned chocolate firm with his family. The surroundings of her apartment complex are sketchier, though. For one, the street is a hangout for transient Latin American and African prostitutes who seem to rotate every few months. Francesca does not mind their presence, but her male friends hesitate to walk by because of the harassment to which they are subjected as potential customers. Then there is the call center: possibly a front for some kind of criminal organization that, for years, attracted an incessant flow of shady characters. "Luckily it's gone," Francesca told me. "One day a team of plain clothes police officers came in, slammed everybody against the wall, and shut down the call center for good." Another occasional presence on her side of the street is a young Moroccan pusher who hangs out there for months in a row, and then vanishes, only to appear again a few months later. "He is probably in and out of jail," she says, though she does not really feel threatened by him. For a while, a homeless man slept in her building's lobby; he was drunk most of the time and smelled of urine. Eventually, he left, too, and now he can be seen hanging out in the flowerbeds of the posh Piazza Corvetto, less than a mile away from Francesca's home.

Francesca is well aware that these nuisances mean little in the face of the actual risks posited by high crime rates in the area. For example, once one of her friends was robbed at knifepoint by a gang of young boys. Overall, this is not the kind of environment that Francesca would consider safe for a single woman. Yet she is not afraid. As she told me, "I don't look like I have money. If you see me, it's obvious that I have nothing worth stealing." Like many other centro storico residents, she firmly believes that "if they know you, and know that you live here, they leave you alone."

In much of the North Atlantic literature on gentrification, Francesca would exemplify the "marginal gentrifier": the single woman who, rich in cultural capital but little else, moves into a deteriorated inner city neighborhood where she can afford to live within her means even as she enjoys the proximity to her workplace as well as a vibrant and diverse environment (Beauregard 1986; Rose 1984). Marginal gentrifiers look considerably different from the upwardly mobile yuppies, the affluent professional-managerial class that is sometimes celebrated for its "creativity" (Florida 2012) but is most often reviled for its "revanchism" (Smith 1996). They are a far cry from the transnational elites that a North Atlantic Marxist scholarship casting cities exclusively as playing fields of planetary capitalism (Farías 2010, 2011; Ong 2011; Roy 2011) identifies as the trend-setters of an allegedly globally homogenous gentrification process (Hackworth and Smith 2001; Rofe 2003; N. Smith 2002). By crafting a global "concept city" deprived of its social and cultural peculiarities (De Certeau 1984: 159), such scholarship enacts a "sameing" strategy that disallows difference through the universalization of North Atlantic modernity (Blaser 2013: 558). While rich in cultural capital (Bourdieu 1984), marginal gentrifiers lack the financial capital that would either align them with the upwardly mobile yuppies, or that they would need in order to resist what some regard as the highly predictable—and almost teleological—displacement at the hands of the bourgeoisie (Clay 1979; Gale 1980; N. Smith 2002).

As anthropologists have long argued, ethnographic attention to details considerably complicates claims about the universal purchase of social and political processes hinging on the triumphant and seemingly unstoppable global advancement of capitalism. George Marcus (1995), for example, encouraged anthropologists to replace the totalizing narrative of Euroamerican capitalism and its ineluctable conquest of the world with a focus on the emergent nature of a fluid and ever-changing global; Sylvia Yanagisako (2002) advocated the shift from the notion of a universal capitalism to that of a plurality of capitalist practices, and Anna Tsing (2004) argued that the connection between globally traveling dynamics and local circumstances pivots on unpredictable forms of friction. Partly echoing these concerns, some geographers and sociologists have responded critically to totalizing "supply side" approaches according to which devalued downtown neighborhoods invariably attract gentrifiers (Smith 1979). By suggesting a closer attention to the local cultures and especially the tastes and political inclinations of educated and mostly liberal middle classes, this perspective posits the latter not only as a major determinant in gentrification processes (Ley 1994), but also as a complicating factor that may modify their outcomes (Brown-Saracino 2004, 2009).

Along these lines, in this chapter I argue that, even though gentrification in Genoa's centro storico has indeed been triggered by neoliberal rationality (Collier and Ong 2005), it still diverges from the global waves, stages, and other allegedly uniform patterns detected in North American cities that invariably end up with the displacement of vulnerable social sectors at the hands of wealthy newcomers. In fact, the ongoing repopulation of a formerly sparsely inhabited centro storico is driven not only by a declining middle class that, rich in cultural capital and low in financial resources, pursues and promotes affordable forms of cultural consumption (Jager 1986; Ley 1994, 1996), but also by a steady inflow of immigrants from African, Asian, and Latin American countries. I suggest that, while diverging from dominant teleologies of gentrification, the dynamic unfolding in Genoa's centro storico is largely promoted by the lures and the limitations of the centro storico's built environment. I thus conclude that gentrification in Genoa is best approached as an assemblage (Farías 2010; Collier and Ong 2005): an emergent set of "heterogeneous connections" between spaces, things, logics, and subjectivities (Farías 2010: 14) whereby not just neoliberal rationality, but also the built environment with its materialities and the people who both inhabit and shape it contribute to making a world whose dynamics are occasionally foreseeable, and at times much less so. While it is indisputable that trends toward gentrification have taken place worldwide, a closer look at cities that do not strictly conform to the Anglo-American template contributes to generating a more nuanced picture. Drawing on Aiwa Ong's (2011: 4) exhortation to approach the city as an emergent "nexus of situated and transnational ideas, institution, actors and practices," in this chapter I seek to escape the totalizing guidelines of the political economy model to capture instead glimpses of urban processes that can be reduced neither to the cataclysmic concern with a "diffuse and abstract capitalism as the master driver of globalization" (Ong 2011: 4) nor to the focus on resistance and class struggle as the only significant modality of urban exploration (Dines 2012: 17–18; Ong 2011: 8).

The issue at hand is not just a matter of paradigm, but also one of geographic focus. In examining Montreal and Brussels, geographers Mathieu Van Criekingen and Jean-Michel Decroly (2001: 2461) observed that gentrification dynamics in cities that occupy a more modest position in global hierarchies have generated mixed socioscapes that little resemble the homogeneous yuppie or bourgeois enclaves depicted by much gentrification literature. This blend, they suggested, is not a stage on the path toward a complete bourgeoisification of the neighborhood (Clay 1979; Gale 1980); instead, it is a form of gentrification in its own right: one that has often been discounted due to the almost exclusive focus placed on a limited number of "exemplary" global cities by North Atlantic urban studies (Krause 2013: 242). As Nick Dines surmised in his study of urban regeneration in Naples, the "heavy Anglo-American bias" that characterizes much of the empirical work on global urban processes runs counter to its claims to a universal understanding of spatial relations, thus limiting the latter's applicability to a restricted network of global cities (Dines 2012: 16). Writing against the grain of the North Atlantic literature on "fantasy cities" (Hannigan 1998) and the corporate reenchantment of cityscapes (Ritzer 2010), Italian urban sociologists Laura Bovone, Antonietta Mazzette, and Giancarlo Rovati (2005: 9–10) juxtapose the "city-with-long-history" to the "artificial-city-with-no-history." While the notion of "artificial city" is debatable, this distinction has the merit of highlighting a degree of dissatisfaction vis-à-vis a hegemonic approach to issues of urban revitalization and gentrification that uses broad strokes to paint a globally uniform picture. As Bovone, Mazzette, and Rovati suggest, much of the Anglo-American literature that sets the tone in the study of urban renewal applies to recent cities where entire neighborhoods can be razed to the ground and rebuilt to suit the globalized whims of the developers. Yet this literature ignores some of the processes that are taking place in older cities, whose sedimented spatialities and deeply ingrained lifeways cannot be just as easily overwritten by comparatively recent—and spuriously homogeneous—global dynamics. In a similar vein, geographer Lila Leontidou (1990: 3–5) argued against a type of scholarship that dismisses Mediterranean cityscapes as "exceptions" to the "regularities" prescribed in Anglo-American Marxist geography and glosses urban phenomena occurring in Mediterranean cities as residual (1990: 3–5). According to Leontidou (1990: 30), such an approach derives from the inability or unwillingness to take into account cities in peripheral capitalist countries whose urbanization predated the modern era and was not necessarily driven by industrialization, and whose downtowns always retained their vibrancy as the uninterruptedly mixed-use social, cultural, political, and economic core of the city (Leontidou 1990: 31). Even though they lack the global visibility of cities like New York, London, or Paris, Mediterranean cities are often characterized, as Gary McDonogh (2007: 150) put it, by "compelling experiments, mixtures and relations of city and society, region, state, and world."[1]

As one of the Mediterranean's foremost ports, Genoa provides a peculiar contrast to North Atlantic templates for urban renewal. Supported by an increasing interest in real estate development, a modernization process that began in the nineteenth century led to the partial abandonment of this city's historic center, which became surrounded by a new ring of modern buildings and streets meant to be the new downtown (Doria 1969). At that time, the bourgeoisie and much of the professional and administrative classes moved to the new city center (Doria 1969), and the centro storico underwent a rapid decline. The population left behind (mostly working-class families and elderly residents, with the much later addition of the southern Italian immigrants who had moved in during the 1960s) struggled with problems such as poor infrastructures as well as high crime rates. Even as a degraded and sparsely populated neighborhood, however, the centro storico retained its strategic location between Genoa's modern downtown and the port.

Writing about the "waves" of gentrification, Jason Hackworth and Neil Smith (2001) argued that this process unfolds globally through specific historical stages. The first wave, they suggest, took place between the 1960s and the 1970s when gentrification was still only a sporadic state-led phenomenon. When depressed markets recovered in the late 1970s, gentrification experienced an upsurge that lasted until 1989. In the 1990s, a third wave of gentrification unfolded that was characterized by the continuing support of the state and above all the massive intervention of corporations rather than small-scale capitals. When examined in a comparative perspective, several factors set Genoa aside from the allegedly global dynamics identified by wave theorizations. For one, in Genoa gentrification begins much later than in the global cities described by Hackworth and Smith: while the onset of Genoa's industrial decline began in the early 1970s, its revitalization starts only in the late 1980s and the early 1990s. If it is true that the public administration played a role in the gentrification of Genoa's centro storico—among others by selling public housing units, by promoting the proliferation of small businesses, and by supporting the renovation of historic buildings—by the same token it also contributed to stemming it through heritage protection and rent control laws.[2] Furthermore, unlike what Smith and Hackworth propose for what they regard as a global third wave, the gentrification of Genoa's centro storico drew mostly on smaller— rather than corporate—capitals. In turn, the latter were driven by state- and municipality-funded interventions on the built environment that promoted the restoration of existing buildings rather than their demolition. This kind of intervention usually focuses on one building at a time, allowing for restored buildings and dilapidated ones to continue to exist side by side. What Genoa has in common with gentrification dynamics observed elsewhere in the world, however, is the specter of displacement that has periodically haunted its centro storico. In fact, Genoa's blueprint for displacement has deep historical roots dating back at least to the sixteenth century: the time when the local aristocracy decided to move back to the city. Now known as Via Garibaldi, the much-celebrated Strada Nuova with its UNESCO-hallowed mansions emerged on the fresh ruins of what had been a populous plebeian neighborhood. Such a predatory approach to the housing of the poor was implemented yet again in the 1930s, when parts of the centro storico were demolished for the sake of urban modernization, as well as in the late 1960s, when the Madre di Dio area was razed to the ground and then rebuilt, a few years later, into the Centro dei Liguri administrative complex. In the 1980s, the administration's plans for a revitalized centro storico in the face of a rapidly declining industrial economy caused many public housing residents—mostly elderly women—to be displaced to Begato's "dykes" (dighe): a recently built and just as rapidly degraded housing project. Devoid of infrastructures and far removed from a downtown to which displaced centro storico residents still had deep social connections, Begato's modernist dykes became immediately notorious for their squalor.[3]

Yet in Genoa's centro storico the trend toward displacement has not continued unabated. In fact, in recent years it has been somewhat curbed by factors including the relative abundance of vacant apartments, the protection afforded at least in principle by the Italian legal system to tenants belonging to vulnerable categories such as young families and the elderly, and the high incidence of property ownership that is characteristic of much Italian society.[4] What is peculiar about the gentrification of Genoa's centro storico, in fact, is the repopulation of formerly deserted spaces: as census reports show, even though no new buildings were erected, in 2008 this neighborhood experienced a population increase of 28.99 percent vis-à-vis the 0.15 percent growth reported in the rest of the city (Salerno 2010: 129). Just as importantly, this repopulation was simultaneously carried out by immigrants and by middle-class gentrifiers.[5] Indeed, the Maghrebis who were among the first to migrate to Genoa had been settling in the centro storico since the 1970s (Notarangelo 2011), thus preceding the onset of the gentrification process. However, the Nigerians and the Senegalese who first arrived in the 1990s moved in at a time when the revitalization process was well under way, often making a home for themselves in areas that, like the notorious Via Prè, are extraordinarily resilient to regeneration. Students and young professionals, instead, started settling in other parts of the centro storico such as the Castello hill, Piazza delle Erbe, and the area surrounding Piazza Campetto. This gave way to a mottled socio-spatial patterning locally known as *a macchia di leopardo* (leopard-spot style; see Gastaldi 2003) that keeps reproducing itself with each immigration wave in the face of the allegedly homogeneizing and segregating forces of capitalism. Yet, while for many immigrants the crowded storage rooms for which they pay exorbitant rents are still their first landing pads in Genoa, others move out as soon as their livelihood becomes more stable. Among them are Latin Americans, who prefer housing in Sampierdarena: a semi-peripheral neighborhood where they have access to affordable, sanitary, and more spacious apartments with better amenities. Furthermore, since the early 1990s, the pockets of degradation and crime that have historically existed in the centro storico have been shuffled about—not blotted out—by interventions on the built environment that target a few buildings at a time, displacing prostitutes and pushers by a few blocks, often on the same street. Finally, yet importantly, the architectural peculiarities of Genoa's centro storico have played an important role in limiting the mass displacement of vulnerable social categories such as immigrants and the elderly, allowing instead for the vertical stratification that is typical of some Mediterranean cities (Leontidou 1990: 12).

Stacked just a few feet away from each other, the buildings of Genoa's centro storico may provide their residents with shelter from traffic and a short walking commute to the Porto Antico and Genoa's modern downtown; however, they often also lack the sunshine and the large windows that choosy buyers would expect of pricey homes. As the bane of developers, the density and verticality of the centro storico's architecture has triggered controversial (and to date ineffective) calls for a "*sfoltimento*": a "thinning out" to be achieved through the selective destruction of the least appealing buildings for the sake of valorizing the historical ones. The latter have the peculiar configuration required by aristocratic living from centuries bygone: the first floor has no access to sunshine, but it has high ceilings and sometimes a beautiful internal courtyard; the second floor, traditionally occupied by servants, has low ceilings, small windows, and no sunshine at all. The bathrooms are often little more than latrines, or what people call in local dialect "*loeghi*": tiny closets with a diminutive sink, a small toilet, uneven whitewashed walls lined with webs of external pipes, and a window that measures at most a few inches in width and height. The third floor of some of the buildings hosts the so-called "*piano nobile*" (noble floor) where the aristocratic families that originally built the house used to live. The piano nobile usually has large windows, high (and often frescoed) ceilings, and spacious rooms; finally, the floor under the roof is again likely to have low ceilings, though in many cases it receives more sunshine and may have a better view than the rest of the building. Between 1999 and 2008, property values for top floors increased by 60 percent, and in several cases rents all but doubled (Hillman 2008: 313); the considerably less prestigious lower floors, however, are still frequently inhabited by the elderly and low income families, often of immigrant origin. This is how Michela, a tourist guide who is renting an office space in the centro storico, describes the occupancy in her building: "The frescoed floor belongs to a lawyer who lives there and owns the building; then there are a bunch of artists, and on the lower floor there are Sri Lankan immigrants who make a living as domestic workers. On the ground floor there is a small coffee shop run by a young man who was accused of hitting a cop during the G8 summit and is currently under trial."

While the lawyer enjoys a fair amount of sunshine, the Sri Lankan immigrants have to keep the lights on all day—that is the origin of the

Genoese saying "Don't go house hunting in summer, when sunshine falls even into storm drains." Be they rich or poor, none of the building residents has access to an elevator, because the municipality will not allow the installation of an elevator in an historical building. This is one of the reasons why even the most luxurious apartments in the centro storico are usually regarded as appropriate for young singles or professional couples with no children and no health complaints. Furthermore, the kitchens and bathrooms in the apartment on the noble floor are likely to have been renovated, though not so in the servants' quarters. Not to mention that, in some areas of the centro storico, first- and second-floor apartments swarm with cockroaches crawling out of the decrepit sewage system as soon as the sun sets, with no regard for differences between popular and aristocratic architecture. Just as importantly, both the lawyer living in the frescoed apartment and the immigrants on the second floor have to deal with the many problems affecting the centro storico. These include the spotty security, the poor overall sanitation and the frequent rat infestations, the questionable quality of tap water, the lack of accessible parking, and the dearth of green spaces that often exasperate young families—just to name a few.

In the late 1980s and 1990s, the historic centers of cities and towns all over Italy began a transformation that turned them from merely historical and symbolic resources into material ones (Cavanaugh 2009: 126; Dines 2012; see also Aiello 2011). Mutating, in the words of a local municipal councilor, from a "liability" to an "opportunity" (Gabrielli 1999), Genoa's centro storico was no exception. In the early 1990s, this neighborhood's combination of excellent location and low property prices posited a fertile ground for gentrification processes (Smith 1979) that attracted young and educated, though not necessarily wealthy, members of the middle class. As in Francesca's case, for many of the new residents the lure of the centro storico consists of a variety of factors that entail, of course, affordable property prices as well as the possibility to walk to work, but also the proximity to restaurants, theaters, shops, bars, and museums. Some are drawn to the centro storico by the nostalgic feeling of living in a small community where nobody is anonymous (Salerno 2010: 148): a sensation that compensates for the alienation of modern city life (Caulfield 1989; Simmel 2002 [1903]). The perceived premodernity of the centro storico also transpires through an architectural and historical uniqueness that appeals to educated aesthetic sensibilities (Berry 1985; Jager 1986): a process that has been enabled by the twentieth-century chasm in occupation and by a degradation that also

Figure 6. A centro storico alley. Photo by author.

allowed the centro storico to be cast as both "authentic" and "antique," and hence desirable (Lowenthal 1985: 59). Furthermore, the appeal of the centro storico to many young and educated new residents includes exposure to diversity in the form of proximity to immigrant communities—especially their commercial venues such as restaurants and shops—that can

Figure 7. Genoa's centro storico. Map by Jessica M. Moss, based on source material from OpenStreetMap contributors.

be thus perused and consumed. While at times the engagement with diversity is only a form of skin-deep neo-bohemianism that is more aesthetic than socially committed (Brown-Saracino 2004: 140; Salerno 2010: 148; Van der Berg 2012: 164), it may also manifest as an activist commitment. This the case with Cristina, the anthropology graduate who, after earning her doctorate, devoted herself to teaching young Maghrebi students, or of

Marco, the young bartender-cum-filmmaker who, in his work, documents the degradation but also the social vibrancy of some of the most hidden areas of the centro storico. This constellation of ideas about what constitutes a desirable quality of life in this neighborhood—and the practices enacted to pursue it—highlights the role of the centro storico as a site for an intensified collective imaginary that feeds on a broad range of experiences and caters not just to a variety of social groups, but also and just as importantly to a plethora of perspectives.

Romancing the Centro Storico: The Mediterranean Noir

The coexistence of poverty, degradation, and crime with a bohemian middle class fascinated by diversity has contributed to the emergence of a cultural production in which the centro storico has become the favorite setting for a new fiction genre: the Mediterranean noir. Revolving around the standard typology of jaded private detectives of working-class origin, this genre casts Genoa's centro storico as a sui generis Gotham City populated by a variegated socioscape of prostitutes, bohemian intellectuals, immigrants of various provenances, petty criminals, and elderly residents. It is in this vein that in 2007 Genoese walking tour and tourist guide Paola Pettinotti published a thriller entitled *Ghetto. Un'indagine nei caruggi dei travestiti* (Ghetto: An Investigation in the Alleys of Transgender Prostitutes). Fabio Bozzo, the protagonist, is a cynical detective who lives in Vico della Croce Bianca, an alley in a particularly rundown area of Genoa's centro storico known as the medieval Jewish ghetto. Now populated by transgender prostitutes and Maghrebi immigrants along with a small cohort of marginal gentrifiers, the ghetto is not only considerably degraded, but it is also devoid of the web of small businesses that attracts foot traffic to other areas of the centro storico (Bertora and Grippa 2011). As such, it is an ideal setting for a thriller where detective Fabio gets unwittingly involved in an intricate story. Sudden murders of local transgender prostitutes, unexpected street brawls conducted by Latino gangs, and attacks on Muslim immigrants at the hands of neo-Nazi thugs are propelling the ratings of an up-and-coming local television station whose anchor is always again on site minutes before the crime takes place. In the meantime, young real estate employees are combing through the neighborhood to convince concerned elderly residents to sell their apartments. With the aid of his girlfriend

Donatella (a transgender prostitute), as well as his bohemian elderly neighbor Eulalia, his home ghost Clelia, and a range of other characters from the local Moroccan, Tunisian, and Ecuadorian immigrant communities, Fabio manages to tease out an intricate web of collusions between the real estate agency SuperCasa, the Axum bank, the Apulean mafia known as Sacra Corona Unita, and the television station, stopping short of uncovering even more disquieting connections to the upper echelons of Italy's state administration and its financial world. The purpose of this scheme is to generate a climate of anxiety among the residents of the ghetto to persuade them to sell their homes for a pittance just before a large injection of restoration funds is due to be delivered by the national government. Thanks to Fabio's intervention, the plot fails. Yet not all of the villains are stuck with the bill; in the end, the mysterious instigator (possibly a politician or a millionaire—or most likely someone who is both) manages to buy Fabio's silence in return for a conspicuous amount of money to be shared with the residents of the ghetto.

A seasoned ghetto resident and a marginal gentrifier herself, Paola Pettinotti describes her thriller as a *mappa antropologica* (anthropological map) of the centro storico that pays a particular attention not just to its ever-changing socioscapes, but also to the gentrification that has been taking place since the early 1990s.[6] Indeed, the neighborhood Pettinotti so perceptively describes is a variegated potpourri of ethnic and social groups coexisting peacefully, if not without tensions. When push comes to shove, however, residents will find ways of getting along, pooling resources in the face of a common threat from outside. In Pettinotti's fiction, this dynamic is exemplified by the Tunisian maid who does not think much of Fabio but ends up regarding him as a brother when he risks his life to protect her son. Such is also the case with the Italian woman who does not want her daughter to date an Albanian teenager and yet is indignant at the thought that real estate speculators are trying to drive out immigrants, as well as with the elderly lady who ends up striking a friendship with the transgender prostitute she initially mistrusted.

Aside from showing—and romancing—a centro storico that is rife with the potential for both conflict and solidarity, Pettinotti's thriller astutely depicts some of the salient qualities of gentrification in Genoa: qualities that set it apart from the dynamics often described in the North Atlantic literature. One of these is the high rates of home ownership in Genoa's centro storico; just as in much of Italy, in Genoa, too, it is impossible to evict most residents simply by raising rents or denying lease renewals. Recent forms of displacement of centro storico residents affect predominantly individuals and families who sell their apartment either because they find it profitable, or because they cannot afford the restoration costs agreed upon by their better-off neighbors (Gastaldi 2003; Salerno 2010). This is why, in Pettinotti's thriller, local residents cannot be forcefully evicted, but they can be driven out through the fear of the violence that may erode their living spaces (Zukin 1996: 38).

Indeed, as Pettinotti surmises, such a diverse neighborhood is a potential hotbed of tensions among the various social groups that inhabit and use it. Elderly historical residents are often unhappy about the presence of immigrants in their neighborhood, and a few real estate speculators are rumored to have given free leases to Gypsy families for the sake of driving out of the building all other tenants and home owners. Whether this ever happened or not, the rumor indexes the discomfort some centro storico owners feel at the thought of sharing quarters with a highly stigmatized ethnic group. As to young and highly educated marginal gentrifiers, they are more likely to have, at least in theory, an open-minded approach to diversity. In fact, for many of them diversity was a core factor in their choice of relocating to this neighborhood; on the other hand, this openness does not necessarily translate as direct interactions across ethnic boundaries (see also Gastaldi 2003; Salerno 2010). Genoese residents, too, may clash with each other over a variety of issues. At times, for example, residents and shopkeepers are at odds over competing definitions of *vivibilità* (quality of life). This includes in the first place the pedestrianization of the centro storico, which, though supported by many residents as a desirable form of sustainability (see also Bromley, Tallon, and Thomas 2003), is regarded as a blow to local commerce by some of the older shopkeepers. On the other hand, while old and new residents alike appreciate the spread of small businesses that feed a constant foot traffic—and, with it, an "eyes-on-the-street" kind of self-policing community (Jacobs 1961; Zukin 1996)—they are also often averse to an intensification of the nightlife (*movida*) that does little to improve their quality of life, even as it compounds sanitation, safety, and public order issues. Just as importantly, both business owners and residents have had to strike a compromise with mafias, prostitution, and drug trafficking. The relationship between residents and the local crime scene is particularly ambiguous: on one hand, safety is a core concern for many who work and live in this neighborhood, and who periodically attempt to elicit disciplinary interventions at the hands of a reluctant municipality (Jacquot 2011). On the other hand, the realistic appraisal of the neighbor-hood's variegated socioscape and the bohemian romanticization of the local underworld support the common belief that centro storico residents enjoy, after all, a degree of immunity. This assumption is also an extension of the perception of the centro storico as being, as many residents are fond of saying, "Like a village, everybody here knows everybody else" (see also Salerno 2010): a comforting premodern *Gemeinschaft* that offers respite from the anonymity of city life (Gazzola 2003). In Genoa's centro storico, this face-to-face community also includes prostitutes, pimps, and pushers. A friendship with *prostitute storiche*—elderly prostitutes who have worked their entire life in the centro storico—is a badge of honor for some middle-class residents, who thus demonstrate their belonging in the neighborhood. And, even though the relationship with local mafias has to be negotiated more carefully, it may still have its benefits, too. As one small business owner told me, "A week after I opened my store I received the visit of a man with two women who looked like prostitutes. He told his girls to look around and buy whatever they wanted. I sold them a couple of purses, and I treated them just like any other customer. I think they were checking me out to see how I would respond, whether I could fit in in the neighborhood. After that, I never had any problem; at times the prostitutes still come and shop here, and that's fine. In fact, they are great customers because they don't ever request a fiscal receipt, and I save on taxes."[7]

Yet even the relative familiarity with the Genoese underworld is no guar-antee of safety for centro storico residents. At times, in fact, they are still vulnerable to crime: Antonio, a shopkeeper, was attacked in broad daylight by a group of men who sought to take his camera just a few yards away from his store. While he managed to protect his gear, he also received a severe beating. Giovanni, instead, was robbed at knifepoint close to his home by a group of young men, whom he identified as "Moroccans": a broad vernacular category that includes all Maghrebis. Both Antonio and Giovanni imputed the attacks to "somebody from outside" or to young thugs who are not aware of the centro storico's informal truce between residents and criminals. In spite of a high incidence of crime, many new residents feel that they have learned how to navigate the complex socioscape of the vicoli. Marina is one of them. A college-educated woman in her late twenties, Marina makes a living by alternating gigs as a professional photographer, a model, a bar-tender, and a salesperson in local shops. Nothing ever happened to her in the centro storico, except for that one time when a man attacked her: "I was walking through this vicolo and it was late at night, there was nobody in the street. A man came behind me and pushed me against a wall. I got really scared and cut him in the belly with the small Swiss army knife I always keep in my pocket. It's a small blade, but if it cuts you it sure hurts. He let go of me, and I ran away."

From then on, she began paying closer attention to her surroundings, and she figured she could benefit from entering an implicit agreement with the local underworld: "I make a point of walking through the vicoli where all the drug dealers and the pimps are. For one, if pimps and pushers get used to you, they will do nothing to you. Besides, neither pimps nor pushers want any trouble in their vicoli, and they will protect you, too. The last thing they want is for the police to come and mess with them if something happens in their vicolo."

However, while crime generates obvious concerns among marginal gentrifiers, what many of them regard as a real threat for the centro storico is its crass commoditization.

Studentification and the Movida

A conspicuous group among marginal gentrifiers comprises university students, especially those of the School of Architecture that, in 1990, moved to the Castello area in the heart of the old city, thus igniting the gentrification process. This decision brought about the relocation of a large population of students and faculty members, and triggered the revitalization of a sizable portion of the centro storico. In order to encourage its student and faculty body to make full use of the neighborhood, the School of Architecture intentionally scrapped its plans to build an internal cafeteria.[8] All of a sudden, eateries, restaurants, and coffee shops mushroomed at every corner of its centro storico surroundings, bringing with them an unprecedented foot traffic—at day as well as at night. Not only did this relocation encourage students and faculty members to move to the centro storico, but more and more residents from other neighborhoods also began venturing into the old city, thus ending the longstanding centro storico curfew that, until the early 1990s, would begin every day at sunset. Few Genoese would dare go to the vicoli at that time—unless, of course, they were looking for drugs or sex, and at dusk many centro storico residents would barricade themselves in their homes till the next day.[9] Until the early 1990s, the centro storico section to the west of Via San Lorenzo had somewhat better luck at attracting, during the day, a reasonable amount of pedestrians through its businesses. The eastern portion of the old city, instead, had gone almost completely deserted. The arrival of the students, however, changed all this.

Defined by geographers as "studentification" (Smith and Holt 2005), the kind of gentrification that is brought about by college students has characterized predominantly cities that have fewer financial and cultural resources compared to global metropolises. As "anchors and landlords in urban regeneration" (McDonogh and Peterson 2012: 13), universities may encourage students (who as a social group are endowed with cultural capital and presumably a professional future, but have limited financial resources) to find accommodation in dorms and private housing in low-income neighborhoods surrounding the universities. Some of them choose to stay on after graduating even as they pursue employment.

Since Genoa's university does not have a self-contained U.S.-style campus, its centro storico location boosted the gentrification process by attracting highly educated residents whose ranks include not only students and faculty, but also young graduates looking for an affordable yet historically meaningful accommodation even as they seek to establish themselves professionally. Just as importantly, the presence of students in Genoa's centro storico brought about a peculiar nightlife known as *movida*: the intense nightlife and groove scene that begins after sunset and ends in the wee hours, and whose epicenter is Piazza delle Erbe.

During the day, this piazza has a pleasantly quiet feel to it. The bars open at 11 AM to cater to the lunch needs of employees, professionals, and business owners working in the area. In the afternoon, small groups of passersby may sit on their outside tables to sip a cappuccino or to sample snacks with their evening *aperitivo*. It is at night, however, that things change. After sunset, the piazza becomes increasingly more crowded; the crowd usually peaks after 11 PM—the time when the price of a beer jumps from three to eight euros. This happens especially on Friday and Saturday nights, when throngs of youths descend upon Piazza delle Erbe, impossibly crowding its tiny pubs and occupying the piazza not just with their bodies but also with their laughter, their music, and their revelries till the wee hours.

Initially hailed as a sign of the centro storico's revitalization (a vibrant nightlife is, after all, still better than no life at all), the movida phenomenon drove up the prices of property in the area. Yet, as it often happens, the intense nightlife brought about its own challenges (Thomas and Bromley 2000). Exasperated by the noise that lasts well into the night, old and new Piazza delle Erbe residents alike immediately started expressing perplexities. Soon enough, this resentment took on forms of more or less violent aggressions. Such was the case of the elderly woman who threw a glass bottle from a window, severely injuring a young woman and ending up in serious legal trouble. Better-advised residents douse revelers with buckets of cold water, or—as one woman told me with a smirk—they use slings to hit them with ice cubes, which "hurt like hell, but leave no evidence." These, however, are poor deterrents for the thousands of youth who pour into Piazza delle Erbe, determined to make the most of their time there.

As they face the challenge of sharing their living spaces with the movida, Piazza delle Erbe residents do not feel protected by the municipality. Even when noise levels become intolerable, the consensus is that calling the police is useless: the police will not venture into Piazza delle Erbe at night because it is too crowded anyway—or, as some surmise, because they do not want to get involved in dangerous situations. The scarcity of police surveillance does not get past petty criminals, either. The movida is known to attract pushers, pickpockets, and youth gangs that, emerging from the vicoli around Piazza delle Erbe, prey on revelers and residents alike, occasionally making headlines in the local newspaper. Be they the aristocrats and professionals of the noble floors or the schoolteachers, immigrants, and retirees of the lower quarters, in the morning Piazza delle Erbe residents tiptoe around the glass shards and the occasional urine puddle to discuss their sleepless nights. Their opinions are epitomized by the words of a local resident and shopkeeper: "This is not the way to revitalize the neighborhood. They cannot turn Piazza delle Erbe into a theme park for bratty students lest all the residents move out and all the regular businesses close."

The Waterfront

Another fundamental trigger in the partial gentrification of Genoa's centro storico was the inauguration, in 1992, of a globalized waterfront known as Porto Antico. Designed by architect Renzo Piano, Genoa's Porto Antico rose on what had been for over 2,500 years the city's port. In the sixteenth century, walls were built around the port, and access was restricted through checkpoints (Gazzola 2013: 123). For centuries to follow, the centro storico was denied a physical connection to the very same sea from which it drew its livelihood. By replacing the inaccessible old port with a wide-open esplanade, Porto Antico reunited the city center with the sea; it also provided an outlet to centro storico residents who had been historically starved for fresh air and sunshine.

The waterfronts that have proliferated in renovated cities all over the world are often described as playgrounds for tourists and wealthy residents (Guano 2002; Kane 2012). In this vein, Genoa's Porto Antico features restaurants, stores, museums, one of Europe's largest aquariums, a panoramic lift, an outdoor theater, a swimming pool, a public children's library, a clinic, two lines of ferries to the Riviera, and upscale apartment complexes. There is no doubt that the motive that led to the creation of Porto Antico was the valorization of centro storico properties, thus contributing to the escalation in property prices and tax revenues. Yet, Porto Antico's relationship with the centro storico has been hardly unproblematic, in that, in spite of its much-vaunted role as a *volano* (flywheel) for tourism, it immediately showed a propensity toward co-opting and containing the visitor flows that were meant to become a resource for the whole city. Furthermore, as the local intelligentsia often laments, the postmodern and high-tech architectural style of Porto Antico cannibalized the history (Jameson 1991) of what had been the most ancient nucleus of Genoa's port, allowing only fragments of the fifteenth-century docks to emerge from the cement of its streamlined environment. Environmentalists and traditionalists alike, instead, criticized the choice of planting Egyptian palm trees in the Porto Antico instead of more sustainable local plants. Yet to many Genoese the creation of this marina was tantamount to gaining access to an area that had been walled off from the rest of the city for centuries. Porto Antico was rapidly incorporated into the urban everyday, becoming a favorite site of socialization and leisure regardless of age, social provenance, and ethnic affiliation (Gazzola 2013): a participatory public space (Mordue 2010: 179) that caters to both locals and visitors.

On any given day and until late in the night, Porto Antico hosts a variety of people from all social classes and ethnic groups. Retirees, employees from nearby stores and offices, Latin American and Eastern European *badanti* (caregivers) with their elderly clients, old and new centro storico residents, Indian, Sri Lankan, and Pakistani families, North and West African peddlers, Genoese mothers with young children, and teenagers and young

Figure 8. Passeggiata in Porto Antico. Photo by author.

adults of assorted ethnicities walk about or sit on the circular benches around the trees. They look at the sea, the ships, and the cityscape, they take their children out for a romp, chat with each other, read the newspaper or a book, walk the dog, smoke cigarettes, eat ice cream and focaccia, listen to music, skateboard, play soccer, sell their merchandise, and engage in people-watching. Occasional events such as markets and fairs, concerts, festivals, and air acrobatics shows may increase an already robust visitor flow to the point where walking becomes difficult. In the Porto Antico area that surrounds the aquarium, Senegalese vendors have established an informal outdoor market where they sell African carvings and knockoff Louis Vuitton purses they purchase from Chinese wholesalers. The Porto Antico market is illegal, and it periodically attracts the complaints of shopkeepers who fear the competition. Every now and then, police officers seek to shoo the peddlers away, occasionally detaining those whose papers are not in order and handing them a *foglio di via* (expulsion order). After realizing the futility of trying to control Senegalese peddlers, however, in recent years the municipality started enacting a new strategy—punishing customers. Every now and then, the police will levy fines of 2,000 euros from customers caught in the act of purchasing a counterfeit designer purse from Porto Antico peddlers. By making sure that the event is widely reported in the local media, the police will not only make an example of it, but they will also temporarily pacify concerned business owners. As the water settles on the issue, however, business as usual will resume between the Porto Antico Senegalese peddlers and their customers.

Culture Change: The New Business Owners

Be it of the legal or the illegal variety, commerce has always been intrinsic to the life of Genoa's centro storico; hence, the latter still enjoys a remarkable reputation for its artisan workshops, its specialty food stores, as well as for the overall good quality and low prices of the wares sold in its shops. Even more than other Italian cities, Genoa is known as a *città di bottegai*, a city of shopkeepers. A traditional bulwark of the Italian economy, small businesses support a large portion of its middle class, soaking up this country's labor in family-owned shops and artisan firms that usually employ fewer than three family members (Ginsborg 2003: 50; see also Blim 1990; Ginsborg 2003: 12; Scarpellini 2007: 18; Yanagisako 2002). Until the recent recession decimated shops all over the country, many Italians still regarded opening a small store as a last resort against unemployment. Small businesses have always existed in the centro storico, and it would be a mistake to interpret their presence in this neighborhood as exclusively an outcome of gentrification and urban revitalization. On the other hand, however, it is also true that their numbers have grown since the early 1990s, and that their role in the eyes of centro storico residents and visitors alike is not limited to the kind of services they offer to their customers; instead, it extends to the foot traffic they generate in formerly deserted vicoli, thus contributing to a general perception of safety (Jacobs 1969; Zukin 1996). This is why, since the 1990s, the municipality has sought to boost small commerce in the centro storico by handing out subsidized loans that enabled the creation of a variety of new shops. Located not just in streets that had a well-established tradition of commerce, but also in alleys that, for much of the twentieth century, had been regarded as off-limits to most, many of these stores feature goods that are likely to appeal to middle-class customers such as crafts, interior decor, jewelry, apparel and accessories, books, herbal remedies, and traditional and specialty foods, often at competitive prices. The new entrepreneurs who sell them are an integral part of the revitalization process.

Ever since the early 1990s, global gentrification dynamics have often entailed the integration of housing with shopping and dining facilities with a cultural flavor meant to increase their allure in the eyes of educated consumers from the managerial-professional classes (N. Smith 2002; Zukin 1996). Yet the role of small-business owners in urban regeneration and gentrification has received comparatively little ethnographic attention, remaining in the background of the activities of new and old residents. A notable exception is Michael Chernoff's (1980) description of social displacement in Atlanta's Little Five Points: a neighborhood whose gentrification process entailed, among other things, an influx of younger small-business owners whose style and mindset triggered a clash with older shopkeepers. In Genoa's centro storico, however, the conversion from old to new businesses has been considerably smoother. As possibly the centro storico's most celebrated shopping street, Via Luccoli is a good example of this seamless (if incomplete) transition. Even those Genoese who have always been wary of setting foot in the centro storico are familiar with Via Luccoli and some of its most famous stores, such as Moisman, Ghiglione, and the historical Erboristeria San Giorgio. Via Luccoli connects the aristocratic Piazza Fontane Marose to Piazza Campetto, which in turn is located just a few yards away from Piazzetta San Matteo: a well-known gem of gothic architecture that used to belong to the local aristocratic Doria family and now hosts famous architect Renzo Piano's office. Even when the decline of the centro storico was at its worst, Via Luccoli always retained some of its flair and its popularity. In the late 1990s and early 2000s, however, this street experienced a renaissance through the arrival of new—and younger—business owners: mostly college-educated young men and women, consumers and producers of culture who created work opportunities for themselves in the face of unrelenting unemployment rates. While older small-business owners are a traditionally conservative category (Ginsborg 2003; Scarpellini 2001, 2007), some of their younger colleagues are more progressive; among them, many of those who set up shop in the centro storico did so because of their interest in participating in this neighborhood's diverse environment. Often combining small bank loans with moneys garnered from their parents' savings, several of these individuals replaced older owners who were ready to retire, and in several cases they purchased or rented venues that had already been closed for a while. Unlike what happened in Chernoff's Little Five Points (1980), most of the new shopkeepers found a modus vivendi with the old ones, creating an atmosphere of mutual support and, in some cases, friendship. On most days, many of Via Luccoli's business owners socialize at the local coffee shop over lunch or the mid-afternoon espresso; they chat standing on the stoops of their shops, they lend each other a hand when need arises, and, once a year, the men engage in a soccer match with a team of Via Luccoli white collar employees. Most importantly, the new shopkeepers have introduced new ways of doing business—and, with them, new ways of shaping the urban experience.

A New People Climate

Writing about the role of revitalization in promoting urban economies, Richard Florida (2012) extolled the importance of what he calls "people climate"—a neighborhood's friendliness to the needs of its residents and users. In the case of Genoa's centro storico, this includes, among others, safety and aesthetics. Genoa's shopkeepers have been pivotal to increasing what the local administration and residents alike define as the livability (*vivibilità*) of the centro storico: a category that appeals to new residents and visitors alike. In the attempt to support the revitalization process, since the early 1990s the municipality sought to encourage small entrepreneurship in the centro storico—especially by women—with subsidized loans. In the 1990s through the early 2000s, several small businesses appeared in the old city; many of them featured crafts and artisanry inspired by nostalgia for local and national traditions, thus contributing to turning Genoa's centro storico into a "site of delectation" (Zukin 1996: 9) for consumers of Genoa's new identity as part of a global economy of value that reifies local cultures to consume them (Herzfeld 2004: 19).

Blending personal and work life, talent and professionalism, the new wave of entrepreneurship that blossomed in the city was ridden mainly by educated individuals whose personal passions fueled their businesses. Some of these new entrepreneurs are artisans who produce their own goods. Unlike older artisans who began exercising their trade after a long apprenticeship in a *bottega* (workshop), usually under the guidance of a close relative (Herzfeld 2004: 116), and still offer their services in the centro

storico as restorers, shoe cobblers, silversmiths, clockmakers, and chocola-
tiers, many of the new artisans often transform a self-taught hobby into a
business. Their ceramics, leathers, papier-mâché products, accessories, and
custom jewelry reconcile the need to pay higher dividends in the face of
rising rent and property ownership costs by specializing in the production
of items that are less labor- and training-intensive (Herzfeld 2009: 47). Such
are, for example, the tiny business of the laid-off airline stewardess who
makes terracotta tiles reproducing quaint architectural features from the
centro storico, or the diminutive store of the former political science major
who, after raising her children, decided to find a venue to sell her own
handmade earrings, necklaces, and bracelets. Giovanna, a tile maker in her
fifties, somewhat complicates this trend by combining personal passion
with formal training in her business choices. While still in her twenties,
Giovanna began a career as an art history major at the local university;
however, those were years of political turmoil, and she soon became disillu-
sioned with college. She dropped out short of graduation, and, at age
twenty-three, she went on to take a ceramic class taught by a master cera-
mist from Albisola, a small town in the Riviera known for its pottery. For
Giovanna, this was a life-changing experience. This was when she decided
to undergo a rigorous training, and, from then on, ceramics became her
life's work. Giovanna's store is a feast for the eyes, with hand-painted
ceramic tiles in all shapes and colors affixed to the walls and displayed
on tables: Portuguese-inspired *azulejos*, white and blue Albisola motives,
reproductions of Escher's lithographs, and Persian miniatures. Her artistic
production is the result of training with some of Italy's most renowned
master ceramists; however, it also draws on her ongoing engagement with
visual arts and artisan traditions as well as her flair for experimentation. A
true pioneer, Giovanna moved her workshop and store to the centro storico
in the late 1980s. At first, her customers from the upscale Albaro neighborhood were wary of following her; eventually, though, they capitulated and
began visiting her in her centro storico store.

Unlike Giovanna, some of the other business owners purchase their
wares from artisans and wholesalers—though always with an eye to strictly
"made in Italy" quality and tradition, or, alternatively, to posh exotica from
Tibet, India, and Indonesia. In many of these stores, the quality of the
goods also draws on their cultural histories, which is part of their allure.
Terre del Gattopardo, for example, is a store featuring handmade ceramics
from Sicily installed on the ground floor of an ancient building. Like the

overwhelming majority of shops in the centro storico, Terre del Gattopardo is small; and yet, its visually intriguing architecture and the beauty of the items on display compensate for the lack of space. Erika, the owner, inscribed her motto on the medieval vaulted ceiling: "Do not believe anything that does not come from your heart." Like many of Erika's fellow centro storico business owners, her husband has a heightened aesthetic sensitivity, too, which he expresses in his work as a professional photographer for a glossy magazine. The store originated from their shared interest in interior decoration: "We thought that, given the Genoese's well-known passion for interior décor, there would be enough demand for high-quality ceramics. We did not want souvenirs or cheap mass-produced goods, we wanted refined wares. And the centro storico is the ideal place for this kind of store. No offense meant for Benetton, but in an ancient city, I expect to find handmade goods, not mass-produced stuff."

Once Erika showed me the best pieces in her collection: a large serving platter exquisitely decorated with an okra rim and deep green leaves spiraling from the center: "This is made by an artist in Caltagirone, and there is no other piece like this in the whole world," she said, beaming with pride. She then pointed to a pair of earrings featuring replicas of Greek coins that had been found at an archaeological excavation site in Syracuse; next to it was a beautiful set of necklace and earrings made of salt paste: a material that looks exactly like coral, and that, as Erika would explain to her customers, was traditionally worn by breastfeeding Sicilian women for protection. Made by Erika herself, the salt paste jewelry she displayed in her store was virtually indistinguishable from coral; in fact, knowing that it was artfully made out of a simple, and above all sustainable, material added to its appeal to environmentally conscious shoppers. This blend of unique beauty and popular tradition was exactly the kind of image Erika and her husband pursued for their business. As Erika told me, "*La cultura è alla base del nostro negozio*: Culture is at the basis of this store, and being able to convey this to our customers is part of our job." Hence, her choice of the centro storico as the location of her store had been almost inevitable: "As a shopper looking for quality goods," she added, "I expect to be able to walk about without worrying about traffic, enjoy the environment, and have a pleasant shopping experience. People in a centro storico are more relaxed than in a shopping mall." Erika's critical stance toward shopping malls, their mass-produced goods, and the homogenized experience they offer was—and still is—shared by many business owners in the centro storico, who regard

Genoa's shopping malls as their cultural and experiential antithesis and a threat to their livelihood.

An Uncertain Future

At the time of writing in 2014, Erika's store does not exist anymore; her shop has vanished along with scores of other small businesses, both in Via Luccoli and all over the centro storico. Some of these stores had been in existence for only a few years; others, instead, were well established with a solid reputation and a broad clientele. None of them could resist the world-wide crisis that, beginning in the United States in 2008, hit Italy consider-ably harder than other European countries. As Italy's GDP began to fall precipitously, the country's unemployment rates rose just as rapidly. Silvio Berlusconi's conservative government did little to stem the mounting crisis, preferring instead to deny it even as the president of the Council of Minis-ters became increasingly embroiled in a number of financial, sexual, and political scandals. As Berlusconi devoted most of his time and energies to defending himself against real and imaginary enemies, he severely under-estimated the crisis the country was facing.[10] In the meantime, he also lost what little credibility he still had in the eyes of foreign governments and international institutions. His government fell in November 2011, to be replaced by a cabinet led by technocrat Mario Monti. Pressured by the European Union, Monti's government enacted austerity policies that caused much grief to the Italian population. These included, most notably, the reintroduction of an unpopular property tax, deep cuts in public spend-ing, and a steep increase in fiscal pressure even in the face of the continuing failure to contain Italy's rising public debt and to secure fiscal probity from all sectors of the population. Like his predecessors, Monti's government kept enacting the usual strategy of harvesting the low-hanging fruits—that is, increasing taxation on the already-dwindling income of retirees and the salaried classes—in order to stem Italy's soaring public debt (Guano 2010a). While Monti's goal was to reassure EU leaders about Italy's sol-vency and to restore market confidence, such austerity measures took a deep toll on the general population. The combination of steep, and often regressive, taxation on one hand and high underemployment and unem-ployment rates on the other caused poverty and despair to spread rapidly; as consumer confidence plummeted, many small entrepreneurs had to deal with the growing fiscal pressure exercised by a seemingly insatiable state even as their business volume shrank rapidly. Many stores closed at that time, casualties of a recession that caused a spike in financially motivated suicides, especially among small-business owners (De Vogli, Marmot, and Stucker 2013). Yet such crisis did not seem to affect all businesses equally; instead, it singled out those retailers that catered to the middle classes even as it spared the upscale ones.

At the onset of the 2013 summer sales season, a long line of cars jammed all access routes to the Serravalle Designer Outlet. Inside the outlet, all stores were packed with customers: better-off Italians who had not been affected by the recession, shoppers on a budget who would rather spend their little money on a single but deeply discounted designer item during an all-day weekend outing, and foreign visitors looking for bargain prices on high-end Italian-made goods. For all the interest generated by promotions at the Designer Outlet, the majority of Genoa's stores, however, went empty. The main shopping streets were crowded; yet people would look at shop windows and walk away without buying anything. On that occasion, Giorgio, a seasoned Via Luccoli business owner, told me, "You know when they won't buy anything from you, because they will turn their back on you as they look at the shop window. They do so to avoid eye contact." I spent the next day with him in his apparel store. Plenty of people peeked at his window with their back on us, and, by closing time, not a single customer had stepped into his store. Giorgio made no mystery of his concern: the shop costs him an average of 200 euros a day, weekends included, and his revenues have been in the red for several years by now. "If the crisis does not end soon, I might as well have to sell [the store]," he told me, with a look that betrayed his pain.

Like many of the new business owners, Giorgio has strict standards: "I buy only Italian knitwear, and I get it personally from the factory, because I want to check the quality. People who buy my goods know the quality; before the recession, they would keep coming back, year after year." Giorgio loves his store, and he is proud of it the way a father is proud of his child: Whenever he pulls a sweater from the shelf to show it to a customer, he has an endearing way of stroking the fibers as he showcases the "Made in Italy" label on his knitwear. Although Giorgio is only in his early forties, this is not his first business. Together with his father, he has owned a similar, though considerably larger, knitwear store in the proximity of what was to become the Serravalle Designer Outlet. Soon after the store opened in the early 2000s, however, he had to close it due to the impossibility of withstanding the competition. At that time, Genoa's centro storico seemed poised to become a popular shopping venue—even more so in that Genoa was scheduled to host the 2001 Group of Eight summit, thus attracting international visibility and scores of visitors: "We decided to open our store in Via Luccoli because it's a traditional shopping venue. It's close to the Carlo Felice [opera] theater, and it's halfway between the Palazzo Ducale [and its exhibitions] and the Porto Antico [waterfront]. Tourists who come in with cruise ships, they take them from the port to Palazzo Ducale, and they have to walk through here." This is what Giorgio told me when I first met him in 2003. Back then, his very recent business had already taken a few hits. For one, the 2001 G8 summit had not turned out to be the kind of event many had hoped for. Furthermore, the introduction of the Euro in 2002 had brought about a steep rise in wholesale and retail prices, and a consequent decline in sales and revenues as consumers' purchasing power went down. While Genoa's visibility as a capital of European culture in 2004 did much to boost tourism, the success was not really sustained in subsequent years. Costa Crociere, Genoa's foremost cruise ship company, moved to the nearby Savona port, thus diverting much tourist traffic to other routes. Not to mention that the proximity and popularity of the Serravalle Designer Outlet and of Fiumara, Genoa's largest shopping malls, continued to erode the revenues of centro storico small businesses. As Giorgio frequently complains, "Many of the tourists that still come in are loaded on a bus and taken directly to the Serravalle Outlet—so much for supporting small businesses in the centro storico!" The crisis that began in 2008 and turned into a full-blown recession in 2011 did the rest, vanquishing many small businesses all over the country, and positing a formidable challenge for the small entrepreneurs who had invested in Genoa's centro storico. What attracted Giorgio and some of his fellow business owners to Genoa's centro storico was the promise of this city's great events: the G8 summit of 2001 as well as Genoa's 2004 role as the capital of European culture. What keeps him there, in spite of the crisis, is the hope provided by yet another great event, though one that involves another city: Milan's 2015 Expo, which was expected to spread its flow of visitors to nearby cities, Genoa included.

Yet, in spite of Via Luccoli's reputation as a hub of local commerce, by 2013 many of its stores—all of them small family-owned businesses—had vanished, including some of the historical ones. Giorgio's shop, instead, is

still open, though nobody knows for how long. Unlike many of his colleagues, Giorgio has been fortunate enough to find a job: a permanent
clerical position, which came around at the right time for him. However,
this also meant that he had to hire a saleswoman to sit in the store for most
of the day, five days a week—which is further eroding his scanty revenues.
Even though Giorgio cut all non-necessary expenses and reduced considerably the variety and quantity of his stock, his business volume became so
low that he had to use a sizable portion of his salary to subsidize the losses
from the store. As the crisis deepened, Giorgio became even more despon-
dent: "At this point things are so bad that I would even be willing to sell
my store to a Chinese [entrepreneur], if one ever asked me," he told me.
Yet the very thought sent shivers down his spine: "This would be a nasty
blow to my fellow shopkeepers," he said—one he could not deliver light-
heartedly: Genoese small-business owners blame Chinese entrepreneurs for
driving the competition into the ground through their pricing policies and
their exceptionally extended business hours.[11] At the time of writing in
2014, however, even this prospect was moot: the crisis was so deep that not
even the dreaded Chinese buyer had materialized yet.

Writing about gentrification, students of political economy keen on
identifying universal patterns have postulated that this phenomenon goes
through similar stages worldwide: initially a dismissed area attracts pioneer
gentrifiers, who, in turn, awaken the interest of developers and investors.
As the media begin to advertise the urban renaissance, the number of
middle-class residents grows, eventually replaced by members of the affluent business and managerial class (Clay 1979; Smith 1996). To date,
Genoa's centro storico shows no evidence of a progression toward a bourgeoisification of the neighborhood at the hands of a class of managers,
professionals, and entrepreneurs. This is not to claim that the centro storico
has remained entirely immune from an inflow of elite residents—take, for
example, the posh penthouses that are rented at exorbitant prices to traveling business people, or the local media tycoon who has taken up residence
in a frescoed apartment designated by UNESCO as a world heritage site.
However, impeded by the neighborhood's own architectural configuration,
this flow looks more like a trickle than a stream: wealthy new residents are
the exceptions rather than the rule in a place where the majority of gentrifiers resemble Francesca, the psychologist living hand-to-mouth, or Marina,
the college graduate who temps at multiple jobs rather than the revanchist
bourgeoisie of North Atlantic literature keen on blotting out the underclass

(Smith 1996). Moreover, if they are entrepreneurs, these gentrifiers are more likely to be small-business owners struggling to keep afloat like Giorgio and his colleagues rather than corporations raking in profits through their "cathedrals of consumption" (Ritzer 2010). Genoa's marginal gentrifiers may well be participants in transnational urban trends; however, as members of a declining middle class, they are also collateral damage to global dynamics that erode their livelihood both from above and from below: the crisis that affects them so deeply is instead sparing, or even emboldening, Genoa's luxury outlet and its shopping malls even as it beefs up the revenues of the lower-end businesses catering to an impoverished clientele.

Chapter 4

Cultural Bricoleuses

> Even the value of the merchandise that sellers display in their booths
> is not intrinsic to them; rather, it is a sign of other things.
> —Italo Calvino (1972)

Even though upon beginning the ethnography for this book I had been living in the United States for about ten years, my frequent visits home had enabled me to follow the profound transformations in Genoa's built environment: the extensive restorations of a number of historic buildings, the creation of a globalized waterfront, and the beautification of several downtown streets and plazas. What I did not expect, however, was the festive atmosphere, the thick crowds, and the proliferation of festivals, fairs, and artsy businesses in a city center that, until the early 1990s, had been remarkable only for its dullness and occasional blight. Even more striking was the extent to which groups of middle-class women contributed to this vibrancy.

As tourist and museum guides, middle-class women were competently lecturing on local art, history, and traditions. Women had opened quaint hole-in-the-wall stores in Genoa's centro storico, where they sold terracotta pottery and handmade accessories. Women organized multicultural festivals that framed symposia on the rights of immigrants with belly-dance performances and ethnic foods. Last but not least, middle-class women had invaded the traditionally working-class and predominantly masculine space of the street markets, not to sell produce and plastic kitchen tools, but to sell valuable antiques and crafts made with their own hands. In short, middle-class women had become the enthusiastic foot soldiers of a culture industry that flourished in the shade of revitalization.

Recent statistics have showed how, over the last several years and in spite of a deep recession, Italian women's entrepreneurship has grown faster than that of men, most likely as a result of a gender discrimination on the job market that hinders women's access to stable salaried employment (CENSIS 2013: 17–19).[1] While an analysis of national trends in women's entrepreneurship is beyond the purposes of this book, in this chapter I draw on an ethnography of the self-narratives and the experiences of women antique dealers active in Genoa's fairs to explore how, with their practice, middle-class women have increasingly complicated the boundaries between entrepreneurship and domesticity. By taking up Carla Freeman's (2000, 2014) exhortations to adopt a more nuanced approach to the analysis of women's roles in neoliberal economies, I explore how these women agentively engage, subvert, but also reproduce structures of domination. Drawing on Moore (1994), Freeman (2000, 2014), Yanagisako (2002), and Ortner (2003, 2006), I suggest that the key to this endeavor is a deeper understanding of the complex relationship between constructions of femininity and middle-classness in Italian society, as well as of the role of women's poiesis (Calhoun, Sennett, and Shapira 2013) in the making of the new Genoa.

Real Ladies Don't Need to Work

The birth of the Italian middle class dates back to the economic boom of the 1960s, when per-capita income and white-collar employment rose exponentially due to the quick industrialization of the north of the country (Ginsborg 1990: 237). The social and economic transformation of much of Italian society also determined a shift in women's roles: specifically, their increased domestication. As the new Italian industries meted out state-of-the-art washers, stoves, and kitchen appliances, the rising advertising industry disseminated mediatized images of smiling housewives who, with the help of their high-tech domestic accoutrements, ruled over their spotless homes. Encouraged to embrace the joys of modern domesticity by the media, the Church, and society, middle-class women all over the country withdrew into their homes. Throughout the 1960s, the percentage of women in the Italian workforce hit a historical low (Ginsborg 1990: 244).

Even though the feminist struggles of the late 1960s and the 1970s opened up new venues for women to return to the labor market, the inscription of the domesticity of middle-class women in Italian society continued to be reiterated and legitimized through a discourse that was—and still is—classed as much as it is gendered.

Coming of age in the postfeminist Italy of the 1980s,[2] I had to get used to the notion that "proper" middle-class ladies would not hold jobs (except, of course, as teachers). The shibboleth proudly put forth by my male relatives, my parents' friends, and my girlfriends' fathers alike was "My wife does not need to work."[3] In this rhetoric, the exclusion of middle-class women from the public sphere was constructed as their own class privilege: as a liberation from the "need to work" that instead afflicted working-class women. While drawing on notions of work as *travail*: a painful imposition on the individual (Gamst 1995; Accornero 1979), this rhetoric denied not only the inequality intrinsic to the modern doctrine of the separation between the domestic and the public sphere (Pateman 1987) and of "women's place in the home" (Massey 1994), but also the importance of employment in the construction of one's self-image and in the attainment of social power (Gamst 1995: 13).

Frequently accused of "stealing a man's job," well into the 1990s middle-class women who worked outside their homes often had to cope with a widespread resentment against what was perceived as their encroachment into men's sphere of competence as the providers (Valentini 1997; Reyneri 1997).[4] Little did it matter that the jobs to which women were gaining access were those for which men would not care to apply (Barbagli 1974; Massey 1994). In many cases, the threat that professionally active middle-class women seemingly posited to their own husbands' gendered and classed identity was, and often still is, exorcised through a reconceptualization of women's work as a "hobby" rather than a "necessity"—as in "My wife doesn't need to work, but she does it because she enjoys it / for fun / to keep herself busy."

The task of casting women's work as a "pastime" in Italian society was made easier by the salary range of the lower-end, part-time, and now often precarious clerical, secretarial, and teaching jobs to which educated women have often been confined (Molé 2011; Neve 2002; Valentini 1997). In addition, while men's *travail* supports their entitlement to finding dinner ready, the house tidy, and the children clean and disciplined when they return home, the superfluity of women's work in the public sphere prevents them from sharing their domestic responsibilities with their spouses.[5] In turn, this forcibly reiterated domesticity haunts women who seek to enter the job market by feeding the prejudice that they cannot be reliable and dedicated employees because of the assumption that their time and efforts would be devoted primarily to their families (Reyneri 1997; see also Di Leonardo 1985).[6] Quite often, women who are successful in securing employment are steered toward dead-end, lower-paid, and part-time jobs meant to "allow" them to take care of their domestic duties.

The continuing marginalization of middle-class women in Italy's labor market draws on shifting redefinitions of public/private boundaries whereby, as Coole (2000: 347) put it, women who enter the public sphere are "followed" by a residual "aura of domesticity." Yet it appears that, under certain circumstances, women's gendered skills, knowledge types, and experiences may be converted into valuable professional tools. In particular, I suggest that some of the middle-class women who work in Genoa's culture industry have turned the expertise in the forms of consumption that characterize "proper" middle- and upper-class femininity (Gibson-Graham 1996; Mullin 2001; Scanlon 2000) into an instrument to legitimize their newly found professional identities.[7]

Already back in the 1980s, middle-class Genoese women occasionally complemented the care of the home with the sale of sweaters, purses, and custom jewelry. Others would "keep themselves busy" by producing and informally marketing papier-mâché stationery, hand-painted T-shirts, and artsy crafts. Yet, until not too long ago, this type of activity was usually very loosely organized and confined to the domestic sphere, with the goods being casually sold to friends and neighbors during social visits. It is only in the 1990s that middle-class women started taking their business out of their homes. This happened, at least in part, because of the reformulation of the private/public boundary promoted by neoliberalism.

According to sociologist Bill Martin (n.d., 1998), neoliberal labor regimes in the Anglophone world brought about a redefinition of the professional personae of middle-class individuals who seek to enter the professional-managerial job market. More specifically, Martin coined the term *bricoleurs* for those new middle-class individuals who combine their formal training with personal talents and skills, thus blending public and private components of their selves to tailor their own usefulness to the ever-changing demands of neoliberal job markets. Martin's model only partially suits the experiences and efforts of many middle-class Italian men, who still pursue employment stability and often struggle to reconcile their role as providers with the demands and the whims of an increasingly flexible labor market.[8] Women, however, are often more open to experimenting with a flexibility and an *arte di arrangiarsi* (literally, the art of making do with whatever you have) that is already part of their variegated experiences as homemakers, caregivers, and occasional wage earners (Freeman 2000: 46). I argue that many of the middle-class women who are at work in Genoa's culture industry are, in fact, *bricoleuses* who utilize their gendered skills and knowledge types to establish their own public and professional identities. Specifically, the milieu in which Genoa's bricoleuses move is that of the aestheticized urban experience and the competent consumption of symbolic goods (Bourdieu 1984; Zukin 1989, 1996; Harvey 1990; Featherstone 2007; Lash and Urry 1987; Ley 1996) that are promoted by a culture industry keen on turning postindustrial Genoa into a city of consumable heritage. Since the early 1990s, much of this transformation has taken place through the intervention on the built environment. However, Genoa's transformation could only succeed if the renovation of the built environment was to be integrated with a change in the spatial practice and the urban imaginary of Genoa's publics.[9] What was needed was the help of cultural intermediaries (Bourdieu 1984: 270; Featherstone 2007: 19) capable of carrying out a capillary intervention on how culture is perceived, experienced, and consumed in the urban everyday. Educated and yet severely under- and unemployed middle-class women were ideal candidates for this role.

Culture as Privilege, Domestic Responsibility, and Resource

Ever since they gained access to higher education in the late 1960s and the 1970s (Barbagli 1974), women students in the Italian school system have tended to outperform their male peers academically. Yet there is an increasing disconnect between gender politics in the classroom and gender politics in the job market. Throughout their school years, women are encouraged to believe that, once they graduate, they will compete with men on the same footing. Unfortunately, this is not the case: the Italian labor market is structured to protect the employment of men—the breadwinners (Valentini 1997; Reyneri 1997)—at the expense of women.[10] The rates of precariousness, unemployment, and underemployment for Italian women are consistently among the highest in Europe.[11]

The "uselessness" of women's pursuit of higher education is only a recent chapter in an ongoing struggle over the definition of professional knowledge types in relation to gender and class identities. Well into the mid-twentieth century, high school and college education in humanistic disciplines and the classics was the domain of bourgeois males who were destined to become high-ranking civil servants, political leaders, scholars, and professors. The social upheavals of the late 1960s brought about a profound transformation in the gender and class politics of education—a transformation that was soon to be met with a decrease in the social value of recently democratized types of knowledge.

Thanks to the push for women's liberation, during the late 1960s and the 1970s more and more middle-class women pursued college degrees, thus making inroads into an all-male domain. Formerly prestigious humanistic disciplines became feminized, and middle- and upper-class male college students moved en masse to medical, law, and business schools, the sciences, and engineering. The few male students who still majored in disciplines like history, philosophy, and the classics were mostly destined to pursue a career in the upper ranks of the civil service, in politics, or academia: paths that were considerably more impervious to women. Educated women, instead, found an employment venue in the school system, both public and (though more reluctantly because of the lower salaries and exploitative work conditions) private. As it became feminized, however, the profession of middle and high school teachers lost much of its previous status. Its part-time structure was then reconceptualized as ideal for women, who could thus devote most of their time to their domestic responsibilities. To make things worse, in the 1980s the teaching job market that had boomed after the educational reforms of the 1960s began imploding. As fertility rates plummeted and conservative Italian governments showed less and less interest in safeguarding the public education system, thousands of educated middle-class women lost their main venue for employment. For many of them, the only choice left was between menial clerical jobs or the care of the home.

Once de-professionalized, the cultural capital women had acquired through their academic efforts was squeezed into a new mold for their old domestic role (Valentini 1997; Neve 2002). Ever since the 1970s, middle-class women have often been expected to act as the cultural managers of their families (Valentini 1997: 62; Yanagisako 2002: 106)—that is, the ones who are in charge of reproducing middle-class status by, among others, bringing books into the home, supervising their children's education, and organizing theater and museum outings for the whole family.[12]

Just as, in the Genoa of the late 1980s and early 1990s, "culture" suddenly became a "resource": the public rhetoric about the need to discover this city's hidden heritage that was accompanying the restoration of the built environment spurred many educated middle-class women to consider recasting their gendered and classed cultural capital into a tool to find, or most often invent, employment. In a society where women's entrepreneurship had consistently been very low (Blim 2001), the transformation was remarkable—all the more so since the traditional entrepreneurship venues for women had a strong working-class connotation, focusing on low-prestige services such as domestic work, beauty salons, or the care of children and the elderly. In revitalized Genoa, instead, many middle-class women grabbed the opportunity to create new "cultural" niches for themselves: they became vendors in antique and artisan fairs, and took up jobs as intercultural operators, tourist and museum guides, and cultural animators. In what follows, I explore the experiences and self-narratives of a group of women who—almost to their own surprise—entered the street antique trade between the mid-1990s and the early 2000s.

Genoa's Antique Fairs

A common opinion in the antique business is that the wealth of valuable items circulating in Genoa is due to the local aristocracy's habit of investing in precious furnishings and lavish decorations for the interiors of their homes rather than in outward displays such as extravagant clothes and imposing façades. Starting in the mid-1990s, the entrails of Genoa's homes started pouring into the city's public realm, and women were complicitous with this process.

On a weekly basis, several streets and plazas in downtown Genoa would host antique fairs where it was possible to peruse and purchase valuable silvers, paintings, porcelains, embroideries, and furnishings.[13] Traditionally, Genoa's street markets are places where produce and cheap goods are bought and sold through curt interactions (Black 2012), and the vendors who work there have always had, and still have, a low social status. The *new* markets of antique dealers and artisans, instead, offered a quite different scenario. They specialized in highly symbolic commodities that required at least a minimal degree of aesthetic, symbolic, and historical expertise to be fully appreciated.

The first antique market was organized in 1995 by the company that manages Palazzo Ducale (a restored thirteenth-century building that hosts, among others, a museum, a library, a historical archive, and a number of upscale businesses with a cultural aura). The immediate purpose was to showcase the Palazzo's antique stores and art galleries whose business volume had been sagging for some time. The Ducale market turned out to be a success both in terms of vendors participation and for the massive public it attracted. Rather than being contained in the courtyard, the fair immediately spilled into the plaza in front of the building. In its subsequent editions, the antique market invaded Via San Lorenzo and reached the edge of the waterfront. As it did so, it drew large middle-class crowds into an area that, during weekends, had been mostly deserted. Given the success of the Ducale fair, the city government encouraged the creation of other markets in a number of downtown locations.

Starting off their social life (Appadurai 1986) as commodities produced for the purposes of capitalist accumulation, the paintings, the vases, the crystals, the china, and the silvers on sale at street antique markets had been temporarily removed from the market to become props in a domestic display meant to valorize gendered and classed identities. Once put back on sale, however, these things would still carry their patina as a "means for status representation" (McCracken 1990: 32), which they would transfer to their urban surroundings the way they would pass it on to the domestic interiors they were meant to decorate. In the plans of the city administration, the antique markets were to help promote a relatively accessible form of aesthetic and cultural consumption in—and most importantly *of*—the city center. Their purpose was to keep Genoa's downtown lively and viable in the face of the increasing attraction exerted by the malls and big-box stores proliferating in the deindustrialized periphery.[14]

Upon being created, the Ducale fair immediately triggered the attention of many (and mostly male) owners of well-established antique shops, several of whom saw this market as an outlet for their less expensive items as well as a self-paying advertising venue for their businesses. It also attracted retirees, who envisioned the possibility of turning a hobby into a source of revenues. Most importantly, the fair also helped create a new category of vendors: lower- to upper-middle-class women ages thirty to fifty-five, many of whom had college degrees and little or no prior working experience, and who enthusiastically embraced their new role as street antique dealers. Elena is one of them.

Women Antique Dealers: Domesticity and Entrepreneurship

Trained as an opera singer, Elena gave up her career after getting married because, she explains, "the life of an opera singer is like that of a Gypsy, always on the move." Instead, she needed more stability. Her husband is a professor at the local university and currently holds a consulting position in Paris as well. Even though Elena does not care for nomadic lifestyles, she did not think twice about moving to Paris with him. However, rather than "sit at home knitting away (*a fare la calzetta*)," she decided to become an antique dealer. Once a month, Elena packs her car with the items she purchases at Parisian flea markets and travels to Genoa to sell them. Living in Paris, she explains, really helps, because with its museums, antique stores, and auction houses, this city gives her plenty of opportunities to hone her skills and expertise. Yet, she volunteers, "if you want to become an antique dealer you need to have a sensibility and a 'good eye' (*occhio*) for beauty and antiquity that is innate." Rather than being born with it, however, Elena acquired her good eye by growing up in a home that was decorated with beautiful antiques. Next came her musical training: an aesthetic education that taught her how to appreciate beauty and historical depth both intellectually and through her senses. Now all Elena needs is to keep studying and doing research to build on her knowledge and her good eye.

Like Elena, Tiziana and Daniela are married to successful professionals. Like her, they became antique dealers only later in life: being fully in charge of the care of the home and their children, they would not have had time for a job. One of them, Tiziana, had worked during her college years: she sold designer clothes out of her home as she majored in philosophy. After graduating and getting married, however, she devoted herself entirely to her husband and children. It is only in the late 1990s that the two friends started their joint business as street antique dealers. They did so almost by chance: challenged by a friend, one day they took their "old stuff" to the Ducale fair, set up a table in a corner, and, almost to their surprise, managed to sell all of their old wine glasses and crockery within a few hours. Once they had run out of their own things, they started selling their friends' crystal vases and porcelains; in a matter of months they built a solid customer base, and people would approach them whenever they had a house to empty.

Out of the several themes that emerge from the self-narratives of women who, like Elena, Tiziana, and Daniela, are in the antique business, the importance of education is a central one. In general, a solid background in the humanities and an intellectual interest for "culture" in its high, folk, or ethnic variants are prerequisites for many of the new professional niches created by middle-class women who work as tourist and museum guides, cultural animators, intercultural operators, and artisans. Antique dealers, in particular, are adamant about the need for a good grasp of European, Italian, and local history and art history along with a pronounced aesthetic sensibility and solid research skills. Women with this type of cultural capital find that the antique trade provides them with arenas to hone and establish their professional identities through a process that is both intellectually stimulating and socially rewarding.

Part of the excitement street antique dealers often draw from their trade derives from the research component of their business. Not only do antique dealers need to spend long hours studying books, journals, catalogues, and the web, but they also have to pore over museum exhibits and items on display in auction houses. The knowledge they acquire through their research is further polished through their interactions with colleagues and collectors. These exchanges create the arenas in which, after a period of informal apprenticeship, women antique dealers may eventually be hailed as "experts": a gratifying experience for many of them who are new to any form of professional recognition.

While a solid educational background is an asset for antique dealers, the women working in this field capitalize just as much on their gendered expertise in symbolic capital. The competent consumption of symbolic goods pertaining to the domestic sphere is a traditional expectation of middle-class women who are often in charge of managing the family's taste and its distinction for the sake of generating an adequate performance of class identity (Bourdieu 1984; Mullin 2001). In the self-narratives of bricoleuses like Elena, the gendering and the naturalization of a class-specific expertise predispose middle-class women to the profession of antique dealers, many of whom form the "good eye" by growing up in a family that can afford to socialize them to it. However, there are also other ways in which the bricoleuses' domesticity irrupts into the public realm of business.

In many cases, middle-class women like Tiziana and Daniela "discover" their potential as antique dealers when they take their own old furnishings

Figure 9. Antique dealer at her stall. Photo by author.

to a fair and sell them. This first experience is usually a turning point: this is when the *consumer* of symbolic goods figures out that she can be a *marketer* as well.[15] As the bricoleuse suddenly finds out, the skills she has been perfecting in her domestic sphere may have a professional value after all. Yet this transition is hardly risk-free.

For one, women have to be very careful with the style of their business interactions. In fact, they are often expected to be less profit-oriented than their male colleagues. While men antique dealers predictably seek to maximize their profits "because they have to support their families," as a collector put it, women should be gentler and more generous—after all, he suggested, they are in the business not for the money, but for the "fun of it." Hence, women antique dealers have to be more cautious when they bargain for a better price, lest they end up alienating customers, sellers, and colleagues alike.[16] However, this is hardly the only pitfall they may encounter.

When her aunt died in 1990, for example, Teresa found herself confronted with the ungrateful task of emptying her large apartment. Even

though Teresa worked full-time and had a family to take care of, her retired brother refused to help—emptying a house was a woman's job, he
said. Their aunt's heirlooms included several pieces of eighteenth- and
nineteenth-century furniture, and a variety of valuable silver, crystal, and
porcelain objects worth several millions of Italian lire. Faced with the choice
between throwing her aunt's treasures into a landfill (charities and churches
would not accept bulky items) or taking a shrewd dealer's offer to acquire
everything for pennies, Teresa decided to hold what was probably the first
estate sale in the history of Genoa—and, to date, still the only one. After
asking an antique expert to price every item, she opened her aunt's apartment to neighbors, friends, and acquaintances, who would rummage
around in search for a deal. The sale was very successful, and generated a
few million lire worth of revenues, which Teresa dutifully split with her
brother. Yet acquaintances and family members took exception to Teresa's
entrepreneurial decision, and even her brother criticized her heavily for
"making a market" of what had been her aunt's belongings. By selling her
domestic treasures, Teresa had fallen short of her role as the guardian of
her family's symbolic capital, and by giving in to the vulgarity of commerce
(Jackson 2002), she had cast a shadow on her family's respectability.[17]

Given the slippery ground on which they tread and the risk they faced
of tainting their own and their family's decorum, it is not surprising that
many of the women who work in Genoa's antique fairs were still carefully
sitting on the fence between the public and the domestic sphere. Even
though they added a somewhat subversive public layer to their roles as
managers of their families' cultural and symbolic capital, in the early 2000s
many women antique dealers still saw their domestic life and their duties
as the family caregivers as taking the precedence over their business com-
mitments. For many of them, the choice of working in street markets rather
than owning a store was dictated by the need to fulfill their domestic
responsibilities. As Alessandra put it, "The beauty of this profession is that
you are completely flexible. When my daughter got sick and had to stay
home from school, I did not go to the fair. . . . If you own a shop, you
cannot afford to stay home even one day." While some of them did not
exclude eventually investing in a store, they all agreed that this would only
have been possible after the children had grown up and become
independent.

In addition, regardless of the income they were generating, in the early
2000s few of the women antique dealers I met saw their trade as a "real"

profession.[18] Many described their business as a way of keeping themselves busy and as a rewarding pastime. The time-honored representation of women's work as "superfluous" resurfaced in the conceptualization and the use of women's earnings. Several of the women antique dealers with whom I spoke explicitly characterized their profits as a supplement to their husbands' income, and claimed to use them for sumptuary perks rather than regular household expenses. For example, when I met her in 2003, Marina told me how, after making a record 16,000 euros at a Christmas fair, she had utilized part of the money to take her daughter on a Nile cruise. As her sale volume kept being consistently large (on a good day, she could easily make up to 700 euros), the following spring she used her earnings to buy an air conditioner for her apartment: a luxury item that, back then, very few Italian homes had. At that time, she was planning to use the profits from the last few fairs to take her daughter to Paris.

During our conversations, Marina admitted to having started her trade because her husband's own business had been faltering for a while. At first, she said, he had been skeptical of her entrepreneurship; now that things were going so well, however, he had even started helping her a little: "He allows me to keep my things in his garage, and he sometimes helps me fix them," she told me, with a twinkle in her eye. Finally, her husband was willing to acknowledge her financial success. For all her confidence, though, during our conversations Marina consistently made a point of downplaying the importance of her earnings in the conduction of her household: her money, she kept insisting, was used exclusively for the "luxuries." The core expenses, instead, were all covered by her husband.

Why was Marina so adamant about the "superfluity" of an endeavor that she cherished, and that absorbed so much of her time and effort? Was she protecting her husband's masculinity, or was she perhaps trying to dispel the shadow of a "need to work" that could have tarnished her own middle-class identity? In many ways, Marina's conceptualization of the relationship between her entrepreneurship and her domestic role is indicative of the ambiguity that characterized the experiences and self-narratives of other bricoleuses. Thrilled though they might have been about their newly found professionalism, in the early 2000s several of the women who worked in Genoa's antique fairs still dealt—and often complied—with a definition of their work as a "hobby" that reinscribed the gender contract (Gottfried 2002) embedded in dominant representations of middle-classness.

Antonella's Trade

While in the early 2000s several women antique dealers still conceptualized their trade mainly as a gratifying way of keeping themselves busy, ten years later these dynamics had shifted. As the recession hit, several of the first generation women dealers quit their business: not only was their trade no longer enjoyable, but they also had to cut their losses. Those who stayed, instead, made no mystery of their need to earn a living. Their biographies demonstrate an intricate relationship of work and life (Freeman 2014: 207) unfolding as a plot where the challenges of maintaining a viable business at a time of crisis and the demands of an intensely physical labor still go hand in hand with different forms of gratification derived from their entrepreneurship. Embedded in a thick social network comprised of colleagues who are at times friends and at times competitors, customers to whom they sell and from whom they buy, friends and acquaintances who are at times customers and at times sellers, and an uninterrupted flow of strangers, Genoa's street antique dealers still live a life in which the personal and the professional are inextricably merged in ways that are both stimulating and challenging. Their stories illuminate the rewards of professionalization, the excitement of discovery, and the pleasures provided by a flâneur-like window on urban life; however, they also highlight the difficulties intrinsic to a physically demanding, and substantially nomadic, profession that has been deeply affected by the economic downturn of 2008.

During the course of my ethnographic research I became close friends with Antonella, a former technical designer who had turned to selling antiques after losing her job: "Since I was the only woman at the office, I was the first to be let go during the layoffs," she told me. Antonella is single. Unlike some of her better-off colleagues, Antonella comes from a working-class family. Her interest in antiques had started later in life. It was only in her late thirties that she realized the existence of a world of things whose patina carried interesting stories. At that time, Antonella had planned to move in with her fiancé, and had started looking at secondhand furniture to decorate her home. Her marriage plans fell through, but her interest in antiques continued. Later in life, this passion morphed into a full-blown business.

Her first fair happened almost by chance when a friend of hers loaned her a small section of her stall: "I brought a few things from my home inside a gym bag. A woman approaches me and she asks me the price of some little glasses. I was so excited that I couldn't even talk. My friend replied, '10,000 [lire]' and the woman said, 'I'll take them, please wrap them for me.' My hands were shaking with excitement. I kept telling myself, 'I can do it!'" First Antonella sold her own things, then her friends gave her items to sell; she also used word of mouth to buy from families. In a matter of years, her business was well established. She acquired a formal license, had business cards printed, and little by little people started calling her when they wanted to empty out a house—a task that requires not just expertise and solid negotiation skills, but also a degree of stamina. The profession is physically demanding. Many women antique dealers have a husband or a partner who helps them with carrying heavy items; Antonella, however, does not. On any given market day she has to wake up very early to load her station wagon with small items of furniture, china, canvasses, figurines, crystals, and whatever else she has acquired in previous weeks. This cannot be done the day before: once she left her car with all her wares inside; the car was stolen, and her insurance company reimbursed her only for the value of the vehicle.

Once she reaches her destination, Antonella has to find parking (not an easy feat in Genoa), set up a stall of three camping tables, line it with a black satin cloth and display cases, and neatly arrange her wares. Then she sits at her booth, waiting for customers to come by. This is the best part of her trade: "When I sit at my booth on a beautiful spring day surrounded by my things, I feel like a queen," she told me. Friends and acquaintances frequently come by to say hello and share a smoke, and she is rarely sitting alone. Then there are the return customers: those who have learned to trust her, purchase after purchase. "There are so many forgeries in this business that you need to be able to trust the person whom you are buying from," she told me. "There is a stall at this fair that is completely covered with forged goods; they are made by Tuscan artisans and they sure look nice, but they are worth nothing." Antonella, instead, selects her wares with great care and guarantees their quality. People come by, peruse the goods on display, ask questions, and, sometimes, make purchases. Like all small business owners, Antonella learned the basics of customer behavior while in the trenches: "Whenever there are a couple of people looking at my goods, more people are likely to stop by. Crowds attract crowds," and a crowd at your booth potentially means good business. She also learned how to bargain with customers who often request deep discounts. "They would never do this in a brick-and-mortar store," she told me. "Sometime I will give them a good discount if the day is slow or if I want to get rid of something; otherwise I'll take a couple of euros off just to make them happy." If the potential customers are obnoxious, however, she will quote an outrageous price just to get rid of them: "I may lose some business, but I will feel all the better for doing that."

Spending long hours at a stall—sometimes in cold, damp, and gusty weather—also means that one must find a way to pass the time, especially on slow days. This is why Antonella always welcomes the chance to catch up with other vendors and to visit with the friends who stop by. Her downtown market days are also made more interesting by a handful of picturesque individuals who hang out at fairs. One of them is a talented Genoese painter with a disturbed soul who is known for roaming around Genoa's streets talking out loud to himself, often arguing with imaginary enemies. The painter is friendly to Antonella, though, and he frequently stops by to ask her for a cigarette or for money to buy coffee. In return, he gives her drawings of abstract landscapes that Antonella keeps in a box: "You never know what they may be worth some day," she told me. And then there is Gavanello, a soft-spoken man in his fifties who, gifted with an extraordinary memory and a hefty inheritance, spends his life reading every single book, magazine, and newspaper he can get his hands on. Everybody at antique fairs knows Gavanello because, devoid of any interest in things mundane, he walks around in tattered clothes; Gavanello occasionally sells heirloom pieces to Antonella such as exquisitely framed nineteenth-century prints and watercolors; just as often, he buys boxes of old magazines and dusty books that will help fill his days. Antonella's fairs rarely go by without at least a quick visit with the elderly aristocrat who, sporting a blond wig and a nineteenth-century sense of gallantry, always makes a point to stop by Antonella's booth and engage in small talk with her. He is fond of old jewelry and trusts that Antonella always has the best selection.

Yet not all encounters are quite as pleasant. For one, selling in the street means having to keep a close eye on your wares at all times. Occasionally people pick something up from your booth pretending to look at it, but if you do not pay close attention, they may walk away with it. This is why a stall should never be left unattended. Whenever you need to take a coffee or restroom break, a colleague will have to fill in for you. At times, however, even the closest vigilance is not sufficient to prevent thefts: "Once a woman came by with two men. She grabbed a necklace, wore it, and then walked a few steps away and looked at me as if to say 'Do something if you dare!' I was furious, but I was by myself and she was there with two men, what could I do?" And then there is the drag of bad market days, when nobody shows any interest in your wares—or worse, when people stop by, try on your accessories, take selfies with them, and leave without buying anything.

Depending on the pace of business, between 6 PM and 7 PM Antonella slowly starts packing her wares. All vendors are tired after a long day of work, and this is potentially the most dangerous time for robberies. As Antonella learned the hard way, antique dealers who are setting up or dismantling their booths are easy targets for thieves who, taking advantage of the confusion, walk away with boxes of wares. This is why, if her sister is not available to help, sometimes Antonella hires Ali: a young Moroccan man who makes a living as a peddler, and who, for twenty euros, will help her carry the heavy boxes and load them in her car. As a petite woman in her early sixties, Antonella is aware of the strain her trade puts on her. "Being an antique dealer is hard work," she told me. "You have all the freedom in the world, but the physical labor is demanding, especially for a single woman." Yet Antonella is tenacious. I first met her in 2004; over ten years later, she is still active in Genoa's fairs.

Poiesis from the Margins

First created in 1995, Genoa's antique fairs experienced a boom in the early 2000s. As the recession hit in 2008, however, their success began declining. Vexed by rising taxation levels, a high cost of living, and declining wages, the Genoese started cutting down on all non-necessary expenses. Clothes, accessories, books, and home décor went first, igniting a downward spiral in the corresponding business sectors. Soon enough, the Italian media were debating the alarming decline in food sales during the third week of the month, when people were stretching their salaries thin. A few years later, the drop in food sales began to be recorded by the second week of the month. In the meantime, local newspapers started reporting heartbreaking cases of retirees who had taken to shoplifting at grocery stores and to scavenging in garbage bins in their quest for food. In this climate, the antique business experienced a sharp decline, too. Genoa's antique fairs continued to exist; however, the business was no longer profitable. Several of the vendors I had known had quit. Others stayed on—not because they were keen on cultivating a "hobby," but rather due to their continuing need to support themselves.

Since the onset of the crisis, many of Antonella's customers stopped buying antiques from her; instead, they were now proactively trying to sell their own heirloom pieces. One evening, a well-dressed elderly woman came by with a life-size ceramic beagle. Antonella greeted her effusively, but also politely informed her that she had no money to buy anything: that day she had only sold merchandise for twenty euros, even as the fair stall and parking had cost her eighty euros. "I wish I could buy it," she said. When the woman left, I realized that Antonella had tears in her eyes. "[The woman] used to be my customer," she told me. "Now she has cancer, and she needs money for her treatment." Over time, the flow of former customers and strangers trying to sell their heirloom items to Antonella increased: once it was the young couple with the crystal figurines; at another time it was the retired man with the gold watch and the elderly women with the silver vase and the porcelain teapot. All these people looked quite uncomfortable peddling their goods; however, Antonella was not surprised: "They are ashamed of selling their family things in a public setting, and they are probably also sad to let them go," she told me.

Every now and then, Antonella would buy the items that people sought to sell her—at times because they were good deals, and just as often out of compassion. In the meantime, however, her business kept dwindling. Attendance at the antique fairs had remained unchanged: as originally planned by the administration, these events continued to provide free entertainment for the citizenry. However, making a sale became increasingly difficult, and on most days Antonella would go home with a handful of euros after incurring considerable costs. Inevitably, Antonella had to adjust her marketing strategies. She began displaying cheaper mass-produced items next to her antiques. Custom jewelry, purses, and sunglasses from China made their appearance on her booth as she hoped to capture the impulse buy of even the most frugal shopper. Several of her colleagues followed suit. This adjustment, however, created tensions with some of the fair managers, who were concerned that the cheap items would erode the aesthetics and the prestige of the events. One of them, in particular, threatened to shut down his fair for good, complaining that the "garbage" on sale did not behoove the historical settings that hosted it. In December 2015, the manager followed through on his threat: through a stern selection process based on his personal taste, he informed about half of all antique dealers at his fair that they would not be allowed to participate in subsequent editions of the event. Antonella was excluded, too. When I saw her a few hours later, she was both anxious about her future and angry at the manager's decision: "I confronted him and all he could say was 'I am sorry about your predicament, but my decisions are based on aesthetics.'"

Writing about how the city is crafted from the bottom up, Craig Calhoun, Richard Sennett, and Harel Shapira (2013: 196) argued for the importance of exploring ways in which the city is "made by everyday people, contending with everyday problems and everyday restrictions": theirs is a poiesis that is considerably different from that of upwardly mobile and specialized creative classes engaged in rarefied artistic endeavors (Florida 2012). Genoa's antique fairs contribute to enhancing this city's aura as a cultural tourism destination by drawing to a considerable extent on the labor of social groups that are marginal to the job market. At a time of crisis, however, irreconcilable tensions may emerge between publics as collective actors pursuing different purposes and enacting various modalities of reciprocal address (Iveson 2007: 8). While the antique dealers' goal is to make a living, their role is perceived quite differently by the managers and administrators who seek to embellish the city. Furthermore, at a time of crisis even visitors are increasingly regarding antique fairs as an opportunity for sightseeing rather than as shopping venues. Most of them walk through the stalls, peruse the goods on sale, but rarely make a purchase. As one dealer put it, "Nowadays [visitors] stop by, ask me questions about that bracelet that looks just like their granny's, they touch everything, make faces at the prices, and leave without buying anything. They think we are here to entertain them and they come to fairs just to spend a couple of hours, but I am here to try and make a living."

Drawing fractal boundaries (Gal 2002: 810) between the domestic and the public urban sphere, Genoa's women antique dealers have allowed the privacy of the home to erupt into the publicness of the street, thus causing the classed patina of its décor to spread to its new urban surroundings. They have crossed over by carrying, literally, their middle-class domesticity with them and by putting it on the market, even as they gave their customers the opportunity to do the same.[19] If, on one hand, this afforded them the emancipation and the professionalization they had been previously denied, on the other hand it also perpetuated the domestic and decorative aura of their endeavor by framing it as a "hobby." When the recession began to decouple commerce from the experiential consumption of the city, antique dealers often found themselves facing the difficult choice between privileging the patina for the sake of visitability, on the one hand, and retaining economic viability on the other. Prodded by the city administration to favor the former at the expense of the latter, they now risk seeing their efforts relegated once again to the role of a decorative, status-making hobby that is detached from the needs of commerce.

Chapter 5

Touring the Hidden City

> It may also happen that, as you walk close to Marozia's tight walls, a crack opens before your eyes when you least expect it, and a different city appears: one that, a moment later, is already gone.
> —Italo Calvino (1972)

It is a Sunday afternoon, and a group of visitors is following a woman in her mid-forties who is leading a tour titled "Secret Cathedral" (*Cattedrale Segreta*). The general public is usually denied access to the sanctuary's innermost quarters, and the experience promises to be both unique and remarkable. Leaving from the familiar space of this magnificent medieval cathedral, the visitors—a group of twenty-one Genoese women and men—are led through stair flights that culminate in a sumptuous internal balcony overlooking the altar. This is where, in centuries bygone, Genoa's Dogi would listen to the Sunday Mass while keeping a safe distance from commoners. We take pictures, crack a few jokes about Genoa's aristocratic families, and move on. The next and last stop is the lodge on top of a tower where one of Genoa's most famous cardinals practiced his contemplations. The lodge offers a breathtaking view of the city framed by a blue stripe of sea on one side and by the hills on the other. The tightly knit mosaic of ancient slate roofs floating above Genoa's centro storico makes it difficult for visitors to locate even the most familiar markers. We all struggle to identify well-known places that, all of a sudden, are thrust into a new perspective. The guide smiles, and then

Figure 10. Centro storico rooftops. Photo by author.

patiently points to landmarks that help us clueless tourists-at-home orient ourselves.

On any given weekend and on most weekday evenings, Genoa's
walking-tour guides lead groups of visitors in the discovery of an intricately
layered city. Largely compelled by the scarcity of employment opportunities
but also by their own education and sensibilities, for over two decades
walking-tour guides have been at the forefront of the attempt to transform
formerly industrial Genoa into a "city of culture." Drawing on an analysis
of walking-tour guides' professional histories and experiences as well as of
their narratives of the city, I suggest that these protagonists of Genoa's
newly found tourist vocation are members of a sui generis creative class
(Florida 2012) that is both empowered and restrained by Genoa's own marginality. As they exploit the layered and barely legible quality of much of
Genoa's cityscape, these guides generate venues of self-employment by
spinning tales of concealment and discovery around the master narrative
of Genoa's hidden potential.

Narratives of the Hidden City

At any time during the year, visitors interested in exploring those parts of Genoa that are hidden in plain sight can choose from the following selection of tours offered by a well-known local guide association:

> *Unusual Genoa.* A different stroll for the sake of understanding the past of a true and intense Genoa: one that you never imagined before, and that tells you the most unexpected stories—stories of commoners, great doges, Risorgimento heroes; war stories etched into the stone by arrows; love stories. . . . *Hidden Genoa*: Genoa is a city that hides its secrets behind its façades, behind the apparent strangeness of curious street and square names. All of a sudden, you will find yourself in an unknown city that, from alley to alley, from palace to palace, will reveal its most intimate essence, whispering to you its hidden and fascinating secrets. . . . *Genoa's mysteries*: from one emotion to the next, you will be led into Genoa's most hidden heart; stories and legends will be revealed that are still veiled by time's arcane patina, but that are nonetheless still throbbing with life. . . . *Things never seen before*: even those who already know Genoa very well will notice how, little by little, the small secrets hidden in the grand monuments and absolutely unknown aspects of the old city reveal themselves. You will discover the many stories that hide side by side with the great official history of the Superb [city].[1] The concealed charm of small plazas and unexpected alleys, the most hidden treasures of churches, palaces that are not exactly such . . . , secret tombs, mysterious frescoes. Traces of a past that awaits eyes capable of seeing it, and of reading its fascinating stories through the filigree of time.[2]

"Unusual," "hidden," and "mysterious," the Genoa thus characterized holds enough "things never seen before" to exercise its appeal on a variety of visitors, especially those who already know the city. What these tours offer is a different experience of walking in the city: one that is considerably more focused than aimless flânerie (Richardson 2008: 148) as well as, in most cases, less performative than the Italian passeggiata (Del Negro 2004; Guano 2007). Local visitors go on such tours not to be seen—although, as I suggest later, some amateur historians may do just that—but rather to attain a deeper, if temporary, intimacy with their own city even as they escape the banality of the urban everyday (Reed 2002: 137; Richardson 2008: 167). The focus of this chapter, however, is not on the tourist experience per se, but rather on that of those who craft it by highlighting different aspects of this city's history, culture, and society. As they do so, walking-tour guides feed both the fluid urban imaginary (Iveson 2007: 41) and the variegated field of experience (Cinar and Bender 2007: x) that are grounded in the sensory quotidian of those who inhabit the city and engage its materialities on a daily basis (Malpas 1999). Their tales of the urban blend high and popular culture within the framework provided by residents' own narratives.

Narratives, Margaret R. Somers (1994) suggested, shape experiences even as they emerge from them, molding memories but also expectations and actions. Narratives connect places and selves, both at the individual and the collective level (Malpas 1999), but they also frame choices and prospect possibilities (Beauregard 1993: 197). Embedded in the collectively negotiated master narrative of Genoa's past mercantile splendors, its industrial heydays in the twentieth century, its subsequent decline, and its recent attempts to convert to a tourist economy, multiple perspectives articulate the theme of this city's "hiddenness" (Gazzola 2003) and its potential for "discovery." According to residents, twentieth-century industrialization was pivotal in occulting the city and creating a "hidden Genoa" (Gazzola 2003). As Italy's largest port and one of its foremost industrial cities, during the twentieth century Genoa surrendered part of its territory—and especially its formerly pleasant western seaside neighborhoods—to shipyards and factories. Genoa's modernist urbanism was characterized by a rationalization of urban space (Lefebvre 1978) that consistently prioritized industrial production as well as the interests of developers at the expenses of residents (Gazzola, Prampolini, and Rimondi 2014). As Genoa's industrial prowess declined rapidly in the 1970s, its modernist twentieth-century cityscapes came to be regarded as one more liability that occulted Genoa's natural and historical beauty.

Yet, following a trend common to several Italian cities undergoing revitalization (Cavanaugh 2009; Dines 2012), the master narrative of hidden Genoa entails not only the theme of loss, but also that of a potential that can be profitably tapped through revitalization. Some of these narratives focus specifically on Genoa's degraded centro storico as the shrine that holds much of its history and above all its promise as a tourist destination.

One of them is a tale of class and wealth accumulation in the Genoa of centuries bygone: according to it, this city's complex cityscape lacks the grand plazas of cities like Venice, Florence, or Rome due to the intentional concealment operated by a dominant class that eschewed ostentation, preferring instead to invest its wealth in lavish decorations for the interior of their homes. This narrative, which underscores the alleged sobriety and introversion of local elites, also intersects with a popular explanation of Genoa's exclusion from mainstream tourism. As the story goes, for the longest time the peculiarly occult quality of Genoa's cityscape has also determined this city's segregation from highly profitable national tourist circuits. Bereft of the legibility (Dicks 2004: 12) that characterizes popular tourist destinations, many of Genoa's splendors are hidden in the dark and convoluted entrails of its centro storico. As such, they have to be proactively sought out in a neighborhood that often eludes (or even intimidates) those tourists who are driven by flashy landmarks and postcard-like imageries. On the other hand, the tale of Genoa's subtlety also emphasizes the belief that only discriminating visitors are capable of appreciating the nuanced experiential cues offered by its intricate centro storico, with its dark alleys and its narrow spaces. However, this is a feat that not everyone can accomplish on her own; in fact, most will need an expert guide: a cultural intermediary (Bourdieu 1984; Featherstone 2007; Wynn 2005; Zukin 1991) who, by drawing on a flexible toolkit of talents, is capable of revealing this city's "hidden" cultural and aesthetic potential.

Seizing a Hidden Opportunity

"The job they offered me may have given me stability, but I would have had to sit behind a desk in a small room for eight hours a day. Being a guide is a beautiful profession, why should I give it up?" This is what Michela recently told me after declining a tenured clerical position, perhaps feeling that, in the Italy of precarious employment (Molé 2011), such a decision required some defending. Michela, whom I have known since 1987, is a representative of the cohort of Genoese walking-tour guides who got into this profession in the 1990s: mostly women, all of whom are flexible entrepreneurs who utilize traditionally feminine skills such as good social graces, empathy, patience, and a taste for the arts, but who are also not afraid to break out of established gender molds to establish their

Figure 11. Michela leading a tour. Photo by author.

authority (Freeman 2014). Michela is one of the founding mothers of this professional category, most of whom are now in their late forties and early fifties. Coming of age in the 1980s and early 1990s, this generation faced the unemployment wave that characterized the deindustrializing Italian society. In 1992, Michela had recently earned a master's degree in modern languages with a minor in art history: a degree that had instilled her not just with a passionate interest for visual and literary cultures, but also with the ability to see the city and its past through different eyes (Reed 2002). Faced with a dismal job market, one day Michela convinced a group of friends to post an announcement on the local newspaper advertising a tour of the centro storico: "The phone operator I talked to was hesitant, and she asked me whether I was really sure I wanted to do this. 'What if I post the announcement and then you won't do it?' she asked me. 'We'll do it,' I told her. Come Sunday, we approached the meeting point with some anxiety, expecting not to find anyone. Lo and behold, we turn the corner and eighty people were there waiting for us!"

This is when Michela and her friends realized that times were ripe for local tourism: in the late 1970s and throughout the 1980s, Italy's cities of arts (Florence, Venice, and Rome) had become a favorite destination for Italy's growing, and growingly educated, middle classes keen on honing their cultural tastes. What Michela and her friends were about to tap into was a rising public of cultural consumers (Munt 1994; Richards 1996) who, being interested in learning about places that may sustain identity through the discourse on its roots (Lowenthal 1985: 42), were keen on cultivating a more explicitly reflexive habitus (Bourdieu 1977) of integrating place into identity narratives grounded in a set of dispositions, tastes, and sensibilities (Giddens 1991: 54; Malpas 1999: 177). Only a few months later Michela and her friends founded Genoa's first walking-tour guide association, *Genova insieme* (Genoa Together), which now has a stable clientele and a regular schedule of tours. The story of Erminia, another walking-tour guide, is somewhat similar: after graduating in the early 1990s, she started posting notes on her gym's bulletin board. She would charge 3,000 lire per person (equivalent, at that time, to about three U.S. dollars) to lead walking tours of Genoa's centro storico churches. Not more than four people would show up each time, and Erminia would put in three hours of work for 12,000 lire. Not much, really. However, since she was then still living with her parents, she could afford to be persistent. Finally, she managed to develop a niche for herself, and above all a new public: local residents who already know the city, but who are also eager to look at it, for a few hours, through different eyes.

In targeting a public of locals, Michela, Erminia, and many other young women like them were breaking new ground.[3] Up to the day when Michela posted her newspaper announcement, Genoa's walking-tour guides had catered exclusively to tourists from other cities: mostly cruise passengers in transit, whom they would pick up at the airport or the port, load up on a bus, and take for a cursory tour of downtown Genoa. Those days, the guides would show them the Fascist architecture of Piazza della Vittoria, the view of Genoa's rooftops from Castelletto, and the San Lorenzo cathedral—though only from outside. Since Genoa was thought to be less attractive than Florence, Venice, or Rome, there was no need for tourists to step out of the bus. As sixty-year-old Ornella reminisces, "Back in the 1970s, there were only about six guides in Genoa. None of them had a college degree: a middle- or at most a high school diploma was sufficient to memorize those two or three pieces of information for those few tourists who would disembark in Genoa for a quick tour. Back then, the city had little to offer."

At the time of writing, however, Genoa has about one hundred official walking-tour guides. Most of them are university graduates who started almost by chance, grasping an opportunity to earn a living even as they waited for more stable employment, accidentally stepping into a profession that they had not seriously considered before at a time when the job market was particularly discouraging. Michela, Erminia, and many others who became guides in the early 1990s had to exercise their inventiveness to establish a new market, conjuring "hidden Genoa" out of its concealment for the enjoyment of foreign tourists, but also and above all for locals. In order to do so, they had to both challenge and exploit gendered discourses about safety.

Hidden Danger, Hiding Danger

Port cities are said to keep bad company, and Genoa is no exception. Until recently, the predominance of a transient masculine population of sailors, the port's unsettling openness to the world, the protection afforded to illegal traffics by the degradation, the darkness, and the convoluted map and layered architecture of Genoa's *vicoli* (alleys), as well as the poverty of a sizable segment of its population all fed into an anxious imaginary that excised the centro storico from the everyday life of many a Genoese (Leone 2010). In the 1950s and 1960s, a stroll through a centro storico that still bore the ravages of World War II used to be regarded as a "descent to the *inferi* (netherworld)" (Fusero et al. 1991: 86). As the port began to decline in the 1970s, the prostitutes and smugglers of the centro storico were joined by a sizable population of drug dealers and heroin addicts. The latter, in particular, frightened many Genoese by aggressively panhandling passersby, but also by occasionally robbing them. Starting in the early 1990s, a partial gentrification rearranged the crime map of this neighborhood, improving the livability of some areas, but also concentrating all prostitution, drug dealing, and smuggling in others. Nowadays, the area surrounding Piazza delle Erbe comes to life every night with revelers lured by the bars and the restaurants; drug dealers haunt the nearby vicoli, attracted by potential customers; prostitutes, instead, have moved, mainly to the Maddalena area, which used to host a thriving community of small businesses, and is now regarded as a mafia haven. In all this, the fear of crime is hardly gone.

The media frequently describe Genoa as *capitale italiana degli scippi* (Italian capital of purse-snatchings): a claim that concerns in particular the centro storico.[4] Gendered narratives of violence cast male *scippatori* who, whether on foot or riding a scooter, snatch their victims' belongings, and then take a quick plunge into an intricate maze of escape routes where nobody will ever catch them. The victimology is consistent, pointing to women with purses or gold jewelry—necklaces, bracelets, and watches, in particular, because of the ease with which they can be grabbed. Stories of egregious *scippi* where the victims are injured are broadcast through the media, but minor incidents often go unreported due to their frequency and the abysmal success rates of police investigations. Such stories, however, invariably travel from mouth to mouth, from woman to woman, often creating patterns of individual and collective avoidance in which certain locations are marked as dangerous.

This is why, until the early 1990s, many Genoese women from other Genoese neighborhoods would rarely venture into the centro storico. In the years prior to the centro storico's partial revitalization, women who lived in the nearby better-off neighborhood of Castelletto would take occasional trips to the small stores in a select number of vicoli to hunt for quality food at bargain prices. Those who lived in the more distant (and homogeneously wealthier) Albaro neighborhood, instead, were intimidated by its reputation, and were more likely to avoid it. In the early 2000s, some of these anxieties still lingered. In the words of Gabriella, a guide in her forties, "There are still women who are afraid of going to the centro storico. I went out for dinner with a group of friends a month ago, and there were women who said they would never go to the centro storico because it is dangerous. I looked at them and thought, 'Poor things' (*poverine*). It's all a question of culture. If you are not well educated, you have no idea of what is there in the centro storico. Obviously, if you have never taken an art history class in your entire life, you don't go to the centro storico." Gabriella is, indeed, well educated. In fact, she is one of those women who, in the late 1980s and early 1990s, earned college degrees in traditionally feminine disciplines such as the humanities, preparing for a gendered and classed future as teachers that never materialized. Gabriella then decided to become a walking-tour guide, embarking in the discovery and reenchantment of a heritage that had been "hidden" by a cloak of institutional neglect and social fear. For Gabriella and her colleagues, such decision obviously required an adjustment of gendered avoidance patterns, so that the guides' femininity and their middle class-ness would not become a liability as they take the plunge into particularly dangerous sections of the centro storico.

In Italian society, performances of middle-class femininity are regulated by dress codes and behavioral norms meant to produce a *bella figura* (positive impression: see Del Negro 2004; Guano 2007; Pipyrou 2014). Exploring Genoa's centro storico, however, requires keeping a low profile: one's clothes should be chosen carefully as not to attract attention, and all accessories are best left at home: "When I am designing a new tour, I put on flat shoes, take off all jewelry, leave my purse home, and go for a walk (*vado a farmi un giro*) in the centro storico to look at places and create an itinerary. Nothing has ever happened to me. It's all a matter of what you wear and how you carry yourself. Obviously if you look like you know where you are going and you know what you are doing nothing really happens to you." In their role as urban explorers, Genoa's walking-tour guides do acknowledge the existence of an embodied discourse of sex and danger (Mehta and Bondi 1999) whereby displaying proper middle-class femininity can expose them not just to unwanted sexual attention, but also to robberies. Their strategies, however, empower them to stroll through places where few outsiders would dare go, men included. As Giovanna puts it, "Prostitutes harass men, but if you are a woman they leave you alone. And drug dealers don't give a dime about a somewhat drab-looking woman staring at medieval friezes and taking notes," especially if she looks confident, "like someone who got her bearings"—a skill that guides have mastered to perfection.

In and of itself, the gesture of removing the highly visible accoutrements of middle-class femininity—elegant clothes, high heels, jewelry, a purse— displaces its vulnerability, removing it from one's body in the form of things that attract unwanted attention and impede mobility but can be easily discarded. The guides thus become free to behave like androgynous flâneurs: invisible viewpoints in flux (Keith and Pile 1993: 33) rather than highly visible bodies exposed to danger. A topographical knowledge that is embodied and displayed through one's confidence and poise allows guides to navigate what is otherwise cast as a space of danger. Such knowledge helps them build their authority as they guide their own tours, not only by protecting their clients from the antics of the occasional pickpocket, but also, and most importantly, by decrying clichés about the danger of the centro storico.

Few things annoy walking-tour guides more than exaggerated fears about crime in the centro storico, especially when they are leading a group of visitors. At times, undercover police officers may approach a tour group to inform the visitors of the criminal activities that take place in that area. This obviously creates a climate of anxiety, and guides have to make additional efforts to reassure their clients: "Just be aware of your surroundings (*state un po' attenti*). Nothing can happen to you as long as you are part of a group." The guide's words reassure the tourists—be they local or not—even as they reinforce her own authority and her protective role in the face of a reasonably moderate risk. In Michela's words: "Once I was walking a group and two young men approach us. They show us their police badges, and they say, 'Be careful, because they reported a lot of scippi and pickpockets in this area.' I got really upset. I mean, how dare you? Don't you see I am walking a group of visitors? We [guides] are going out of our way to convey a positive image of the city, and you come and tell us these things? Sure, every now and then some kids will pickpocket a Japanese tourist, but that's not an everyday occurrence." Representing the "Japanese tourist" as the alien whose lack of familiarity with the place casts him as a preferred victim, Michela reiterates her expert belonging in the centro storico: a belonging that combines topographical knowledge, cultural capital, and a performative confidence that allows her to navigate an unsafe terrain either alone or in the company of vulnerable visitors, whom she guides and protects with her expertise. Yet the very same social fear she removes from herself along with her jewelry whenever she takes a field trip is also what protects her findings (be they a medieval portal, a quaint artisan shop, or a picturesque corner) from a public gaze that may make them *too* well known and accessible. For excessive accessibility not just of local landmarks, but also of the tales that surround them, may posit a challenge for the guides, too.

Betwixt and Between

"How many of you are from Genoa?" asks Maria Teresa, a diminutive but energetic woman in her late twenties. Almost all of the approximately thirty people in the group raise their hands. A couple from Turin cracks a joke about being a minority, and everybody looks at them and chuckles. Maria

Teresa is leading us through the main sites in the history of a local aristocratic family, which has generously decided to sponsor a one-day event to claim back some of the prestige that has been obscured by centuries of strife. The first site of this tour is the church dedicated to a saint born to this family in the fifteenth century. Though located in downtown Genoa, this sixteenth-century church is barely visible from outside, and is off this city's main sightseeing paths. As Maria Teresa begins expounding on a painting, an elderly woman on her way out interrupts her: "You better do a good job here, because these are all Genoese with a very good handle on history!" Then off she walks. One of the visitors winks to his friend. Maria Teresa blushes for a moment, but she immediately regains her poise and continues with her explanations. Later on, she will concede that, for guides, dealing with a group of locals may be more challenging than entertaining tourists from other cities: "Generally speaking, most Genoese know more about their city than the average tourist from elsewhere. They ask a lot more questions, and you occasionally also find the smartass who seeks to contradict you to show off his knowledge. You have to prepare a lot more when you take locals on a walking tour, but you also need to be ready to gently contain [overbearing individuals] because you are still the one who is leading the tour after all."

If, to use Pierre Bourdieu's (1993) terminology, local history is a field, it certainly is a contested one where different actors compete to establish domination. While an assessment of the social importance of historical knowledge in Italy is beyond the scope of this book, it bears mentioning how this discipline is particularly popular in this country not just among academics but also—and possibly even more so—among amateur historians. Working solo or as part of cultural associations, the latter conduct their own archival research, organize small symposia, and self-publish their own books.[5] Overall, this field is a predominantly masculine one: a gendering that may put guides at a disadvantage in their necessary pursuit of legitimacy. As popularizers of high culture (Wynn 2005), however, women guides can draw on other essentialized talents: for one, their "natural" proclivity to interpersonal relations. As Doretta, a pleasant-looking woman in her sixties, put it, the guide is "the hostess who knows how to deal with guests; [she] needs to be flexible and to be able to relate to all sorts of people; you have to intuit what to say and what not to say. For example, for each Italian group [from each region of the country] there are things that are appropriate to say, and things that are not appropriate. . . . Men, instead, just stand there and pontificate, regardless of who stands in front of them. They may know everything about every single building, but they are unable to convey it." The value of the guides' emotional labor (Hochschild 1983) is compounded with additional, supposedly feminine qualities, such as the ease with which women are said to learn and speak foreign languages, and even the passion for art history is often interpreted as an extension of women's essential taste in fashion and decorating. On the other hand, guides also need to master masculine skills: not just a knack for fearless urban explorations but also assertiveness. Take, for example, Ginevra, a petite thirty-year-old who is capable of projecting a remarkably stentorian voice for hours in a row without ever tiring, and who during her tours likes to joke that "I can speak like this all day long for the whole week, and nobody can ever shut me up." Ginevra's swagger helps her build her authority even when dealing with the most difficult groups.

Genoa's guides are also trespassers vis-à-vis the academic dimensions of history, a discipline in which most of them have a solid educational background. Not only do the majority of guides have college degrees (and, in some cases, even aborted academic ambitions), but theirs is also a work of research that leads them to spend long hours in libraries as well as bookstores, attending conferences and public lectures, and keeping abreast of the most recent developments in local history and archaeology. Not to mention that some of them, like Marisa, even publish their own history books. As "thinkers, intelligent historians, and passionate storytellers of the urban landscape" who straddle the line between scholarship and entertainment (Wynn 2005: 400–402), guides can earn the attention of even the most authoritative publics. Sabrina, for example, regularly leads a group of local professors on walking tours of the city: "We have been doing these tours for years. [The professors] know me, and they appreciate my work. This recognition is very gratifying for me," she said, reporting with pride how she has earned the academics' respect as a skilled researcher. On the other hand, however, the guides' status is hardly homogeneously established vis-à-vis the local cultural establishment. Marisa's repeat brushes with a local edutainment conglomerate are indicative of the guides' tenuous legitimacy:

On occasion of Rubens's exhibition, I had an idea: I organized a dinner with baroque recipes at [a local restaurant]. I pored through ancient cookbooks in the library and then modified the recipes to fit our tastes. I then proposed this to [a famous local edutainment conglomerate]. . . . I would not make any money on the dinner, because I did not feel comfortable asking for a kickback; however, my profit would come from the guided tour. I wrote a nice presentation, which [the edutainment conglomerate] published in the local newspaper; however, even though the text was mine, my name did not show anywhere and they claimed this initiative as their own. At the end of the day, they made a handsome profit, but I did not get a penny. I called [the edutainment conglomerate] and they blamed the newspaper. Then [a well-known television show] shoots an episode in Genoa, and they are interested in baroque dinners. An acquaintance of mine who works at [the edutainment conglomerate] gives my contact info to the crew. They ask me to attend the dinner to explain the dishes. I was happy because being on national TV during prime time is good publicity, but when I get to the restaurant I bump into professor Bidalco, who had been my thesis advisor and is a culinary history expert. I smile at him and ask him, "What are you doing here?" He had been called by the [edutainment conglomerate restaurant] to present my recipes in my place. The TV crew had called a different office, which informed them that I was not qualified and nobody knew me, and they needed a famous historian instead. However, nobody ever bothered to inform me.

"This is what we are to them: just *bassa manovalanza* (unskilled labor)," was Marisa's bitter conclusion in the face of how nonchalantly her intellectual property had been handled.

The tension between high and popular culture also haunts Alberto, a poet and semiotician with a day job at the local Soprintendenza ai Beni Culturali (Heritage Management Office) and a passion for designing and leading walking tours of the city. Alberto is a former student of Umberto Eco, and after earning a graduate degree with a thesis on semiotics, he wanted to continue doing research. However, his family was not wealthy; unlike many aspiring Italian academics who can afford to keep volunteering their time as research and teaching assistants well after graduation, he had to support himself. Not to mention that, as a man, he had to find a job before he could even consider getting married. Hence, he eventually accepted a position as a railway employee, which he later managed to convert to his current job as a computer technician at the Heritage Management Office. He moved back to Genoa and went through a full-fledged culture shock. While Umberto Eco's Bologna was a vibrant and stimulating city, the Genoa of the 1980s came across to him as a cultural wasteland. Trying to connect with the little intellectual life the city had to offer, in 1995 he made a substantial contribution to designing and launching the first edition of Genoa's Poetry Festival; on that occasion he wrote and led the first two *Percorsi poetici* (Poetic Tours). Almost twenty years later, Alberto has designed, led, and, in some cases, published a repertoire of nine *Percorsi*: tours of the centro storico, the uptown neighborhoods, the monumental Staglieno cemetery, the seaside Nervi promenade and park, the fortresses that surround the city—to name a few—during which Alberto and his partners (whom he recruits among actors, professional walking-tour guides, academics, and assorted literary buffs) read poems and novels to help visitors gain a new appreciation of the ties between literature and Genoa's cityscape. Given the extent of his commitment to helping others see Genoa through the lens of literary culture, he also wrote a book where he thus conceptualizes his tours:

> In the Poetic Tours, poetry and fiction authoritatively complement traditional descriptions of art and history, and, not rarely, they include information on the surroundings, both natural and urban. This is not simply a game of citations; instead, it is one of the thousand ways in which one can broach the inexhaustible theme of the relationship between *literature* and *reality*. . . . Our tours are a quest for *scrittura toposensibile, toposensitive writing* of any kind, level and form, a quest for the writing of / in / on the "territory" in its broader sense of "inscription," from oral *traces* to elevated poems through the mediation of historical, journalistic writing as well as freer connections. (Nocerino 2013: 13; emphasis in the original)

During his tours, Alberto leads visitors in the exploration of unusual sites, and he has them pause to peruse urban objects that often go unnoticed (Reed 2002: 138): a tombstone, a marble bust, a ruin. Through the rediscovery of these materialities and the evocative power of his words, Alberto generates an aesthetic experience that involves both the senses and the intellect (Richardson 2008: 141). In his attempt to use urban locales as props to interrupt the quotidian and inject unusual depths into everyday life, Alberto seeks to induce

> residents (*cittadini*) and strangers alike [to be] "tourists" in a more conscious and productive sense than usual. For one tries to go beyond the surface of things, beyond the *monuments* as illustrious islands of historical memories and beautiful vestiges, for the sake of 'seeing' places rather than 'sightseeing' in them, to experience them again through the images, the emotions and the ideas that they have variously inspired at different times, and that have become *literature, writing* in the broader sense of the word. (Nocerino 2013: 13; emphasis in the original)

As the superficial "sightseeing" becomes a "seeing" charged with aesthetic potential, everyday life is bracketed out to allow for a focus on alternate experiential dimensions—a shift in consciousness that, unlike traditional tourism, interrupts ordinariness without the need for a geographic elsewhere (Lengkeek 2001: 178).

Such feat is made possible by Alberto's background as a semiotician and a poet, which provides him with an in-depth knowledge of literature and a flair for the power of language. Yet his Poetic Tours are also partly enabled by his position at the Heritage Management Office, which gives him access to the first-hand historical, architectural, and artistic information about the territory that he needs for his inspiration. "I had to learn to be pragmatic and make do with what I had," he says. Embodying a kind of neoliberal flexibility that merges one's education and talents with the opportunities and the limitations provided by life circumstances (Freeman 2007; Guano 2007; Richards 2011), Alberto is aware that designing the tours was a way to reconcile himself with Genoa after giving up his academic ambitions once he had returned from Eco's Bologna: "On one hand, the tours originate from the fact that I did not know Genoa all that well. I did not know the centro storico, and I did not know the local poets, either, but I had a historical frame for the literature. The tours were a way for me to get to know the city as well as local literary history. But I also felt I had something to express, and the tours are a way to communicate it to people in the hybrid form of a mix between theater and walking tour."

Just like professional walking-tour guides, Alberto invested much of his own background, talents, and above all passion as both a consumer and a producer of culture into the creation of his Poetic Tours. And, just like professional walking-tour guides, Alberto, too, straddles the line between scholarship and popular culture in his attempt to popularize and disseminate poetry and semiotics by inscribing them onto Genoa's cityscape. In spite of his desire to ennoble walking tours, however, Alberto received a sharp criticism from fellow intellectuals who did not appreciate the association between literary culture and tourism. Undeterred, he dismissed it with a shrug of shoulders: "After all, this is what Umberto Eco does by writing fiction," he told me. "If an intellectual of his caliber can write for broader audiences, why shouldn't I?" What distinguishes Alberto from professional walking-tour guides, however, is his status as a part-timer. Both Alberto and the professional guides share similar backgrounds and experiences in their role as cultural bricoleurs and bricoleuses (Martin 1998) who combine their formal training with personal talents and curiosities to establish and tailor their competence as walking-tour guides. However, Alberto would not consider quitting a job he dislikes in order to fully embrace his passion for designing and leading walking tours. "I would do this only if I knew it would make me a living," he told me on several occasions.

In the Italy of precarious labor (Mólé 2011), where flexibility in pursuing often underpaid short-term contract work has become the lay of the land, stable employment is still regarded as desirable. This is especially the case for men, who, even in the face of considerable changes in gender dynamics, are still under pressure to fulfill their traditional role as providers. Genoa's professional walking-tour guides—the vast majority of whom are women—are aware of the gendering of their profession: "This is not the kind of job on which you could raise a family," Giovanna, who has two children, told me. Luckily for her, she concluded, she is married and her husband has stable employment. Unlike what happens with the upwardly mobile yuppies of the creative class described by Richard Florida (2012), the creative content produced and disseminated by Genoa's guides is not bound to engender large capitals; instead, it only generates a modest livelihood. "Ever wonder why most tourist guides in cities like Rome and Florence are men, while here in Genoa we are all women?" Antonietta, a woman in her early forties, quipped during the brief pause she had between tours. "It's because in this city there is little money to be made in this profession." Not all guides have a gainfully employed spouse or partner, though. Hence, they alternate tours with gigs, for example as substitute teachers or as contractors in clerical positions. Those who are single, in particular, have to intensify their efforts and creativity to generate a steady income. Among them is Michela, who, aside from designing and leading city and museum tours for her Genoese publics, accompanies foreign tourists through the city and the Riviera, takes groups of Italians to Scandinavian countries, serves as an interpreter, and temps as a study-abroad program administrator at the local university. In the off-season, Marisa writes books, produces artsy lamp shades to be sold in local stores, and paints trompe l'oeil murals. Indeed, Genoa's walking-tour guides are cultural bricoleurs and bricoleuses (Martin 1998) who creatively combine their formal training with personal talents to establish and hone their competence (see also Freeman 2014). Yet they do so as freelancers who constantly have to negotiate their legitimacy betwixt and between a variety of fields, and as members of a gendered niche with considerable limitations. In an economy of labor where women even more than men are steered toward flexible forms of work (Molé 2011), walking-tour guides' professional trajectories differ considerably from those of Richard Florida's (2012) upwardly mobile yuppies: their efforts are not bound to create prosperity, but rather only a modest livelihood. Hence, Genoa's walking-tour guides have to utilize all their creativity and their cultural capital to generate a steady output of original stories and tours.

The City as a Creative Canvas

Aesthetically inflected labor dwells in an ambiguous space between high culture and commerce: one where creative inspiration goes hand in hand with the necessity to make ends meet (Win 2014: 6). Since he earns a living elsewhere, Alberto can afford to have only a few select Poetic Tours in his repertoire and offer them mostly for free. For professional walking-tour guides, however, the need to enrich their repertoire through original offerings may take on a more urgent quality. A well-known city of art such as Florence, Venice, or Rome does not need much effort to attract visitors and to entertain them.[6] No matter what, tourists will make a beeline for its museums and churches, and what guides have to do, day in and day out, is mostly dish out the same information to visitors who have never heard it before. In cities that converted to cultural tourism only recently, instead, the use of original narratives to generate experiences partly compensates for the scarcity of officially recognized and widely known material heritage

(Richards and Wilson 2006: 2118). Compared to Rome, Florence, or Venice, Genoa occupies a different space: one where the material evidence of historical depth is hardly absent, but until recently has received comparatively little tourist and commercial attention. A city that is devoid of many of the permanent enshrinements that characterize stable tourist landmarks (MacCannell 1976: 45) thus becomes a malleable "creative environment" (Richards and Wilson 2006: 1218) replete with sites on which guides can spin different stories, depending on the theme of their tour. The places that are under everybody's eyes and whose familiarity has determined a degree of indifference to them (Taussig 1991) can still become viable cultural products in an economy of novelty, The guides, however, will need to isolate and bring to life a specific theme or a historical era, often with the help of a visual cue: a plaque, a frieze, a pillar to anchor their specific historic narrations to trigger the kind of experience that is usually bracketed out of everyday consciousness (Lengkeek 2001). Hence, the same street can be described—and thus experienced—in light of its Roman vestiges, its medieval layout, its seventeenth-century architectural splendor, the devastations of nineteenth- and twentieth-century wars, or the lives and works of the poets, philosophers, and writers who resided there. Each aspect of a composite, multilayered architecture will become part of a different narration and a different tour offering access to a range of emotions: the horror at the ravages of war, the melancholia of love lost, the nostalgia for a simpler life, or the amusement at past debaucheries. Heritage tourism hinges predominantly on visuality (Copeland 2010; Poria 2010; Urry 2002; Watson 2010; Watson and Waterton 2010); when the latter cannot be sustained, markers often compensate for the thinness of visual experience (MacCannell 1976: 113). The guides' evocative storytelling is just as important in offsetting the opaque materiality of tenuous or illegible visual cues. As Viviana explained: "If you walk through Via Canneto, you can walk through it ten times and still see different things: for example the Roman walls, or the medieval things, or niches, portals, decorations and nymphaeums. There is a Roman settlement and then there are strata all the way through to the twentieth century. The cleverness of the guide consists in not saying 'Here you can see a medieval thing, and over there is a renaissance or baroque thing,' but rather in covering one style and century at a time. This way, visitors come back to listen to other descriptions." The visitor's experience, in such cases, is shaped predominantly through narrations (Malpas 1999;

Somers 1994) that, while compensating for the limited legibility of an intricately layered urbanscape, become all the more persuasive if set against the
backdrop of the diffuse aura of antiquity (Lowenthal 1985: 244) permeating
Genoa's centro storico. The streets, buildings, and plazas of ancient Genoa
thus become canvases where the guides' scholarship, expertise, and creativity inscribe different perspectives, evoking a temporal depth that suspends
familiarity to allow for the eruption of the unexpected. In Giovanna's
words,

> At times, I organize tours where you don't see anything at all,
> because people really like thematic itineraries. For example, last year
> I designed all itineraries entirely based on anecdotes and curious
> stories: stories of the kind "this is where, in 1502, King Louis XII of
> France met [local aristocrat] Tommasina Spinola, who fell in love
> with him after sharing a dance, though she never saw him again."
> Then, walking to Piazza dell'Amor Perfetto, I explain that "this is
> where Tommasina Spinola, upon hearing that Louis XII had passed,
> locked herself up in a dark room and let herself die. King Louis XII
> wasn't dead, but she did not know." Then I explain that Amor Per-
> fetto does not mean "perfect love," but rather "the love that is no
> more"—which usually nobody knows, and people are awed.

Depending on the tour theme, Giovanna can also choose to showcase
Piazza dell'Amor Perfetto, a minuscule square in the centro storico, as one
of the very few plazas ever built in medieval Genoa: a bit of trivia that she
uses to discuss how the local merchant aristocracy had no interest in publicly flaunting their wealth, preferring instead to impress their guests with
their extravagantly decorated homes. If the theme of the tour verges on the
arts and the crafts of the centro storico, Piazza dell'Amor Perfetto exempli-
fies the positive change brought about by the industriousness of an immigrant who, by opening a small kebab eatery, managed to dislodge the local
drug traffic. By using the cityscape as a canvas for their creative storytelling
practices, walking-tour guides valorize different elements of Genoa's composite history and lore. As they do so, they sustain their business by proposing ever-new perspectives on sites that are often taken for granted, thus
conjuring a range of emotions, ideas, and experiences that cast a different
light on the urban everyday.

Hidden and Liminal

Rather than being a product of corporate city branding choices (Dicks 2004; Hannigan 1998; Harvey 1988, 1990; Ritzer 2010; Zukin 1991, 1996), Genoa's reputation as a "hidden" city is created and managed at a grass-roots level by self-employed walking-tour guides. A cautious comparison with Florida's (2012) notion of the creative class helps illuminate how, rather than being just passive consumers of culture, Genoa's walking-tour guides utilize their cultural capital and skills to transform this city's public image, "worlding" it (Ong 2011) from the bottom up through their creative storytelling practices. Unlike Florida's "talents," however, guides are not upwardly mobile yuppies. Rather, they are a residual group that emerges out of this city's intellectual underemployed and unemployed workforce (Arvati 1988). Owing their sustenance to a hiddenness that is both a limita-tion and a source of opportunities, Genoa's walking-tour guides are mostly women who creatively draw on scholarship, popular culture, and personal talents to operate in liminal ways. As they create a professional niche in the shade of urban revitalization, the guides provide emotionally inflected labor; however, they also challenge gendered representations of urban dan-ger; they claim a place for themselves in the traditionally masculine field of urban history; and they tread the tenuous line that separates academic knowledge from cultural consumption. Drawing on their inventiveness as well as their understanding of local history and lore, walking-tour guides strategically inscribe ever-new stories onto Genoa's densely layered city-scape and its "hidden" landmarks. Yet, even as it is often cast as a source of opportunities waiting to be seized, Genoa's hiddenness is also a limit to the guides' trade. If, over the last twenty years, Genoa's walking-tour guides have managed to establish a cottage industry where there used to be none, this city's concealed treasures can still only support a limited volume of business. This is why Alberto never managed to leave his job as a computer technician to single-mindedly invest in his Poetic Tours, and this is why most women tour guides supplement their income with an assortment of gigs and short-term contracts. Prodded by the need to make a living as well as by the desire to find an outlet for their talents, Genoa's walking-tour guides aptly exploit this city's "hidden" potential despite the limitations they encounter.

Chapter 6

Utopia with No Guarantees

> Beware of telling them that, at times, different cities succeed each
> other on the same ground and under the same name, for they are
> born and die without knowing and communicating with each other.
> —Italo Calvino (1972)

Imagine a Festive Space

It is a steamy June afternoon; the sky is crispy blue with no clouds in sight.
The sun is heating up the fabric of the yurta installed on Genoa's Porto
Antico waterfront. Sitting on rugs scattered on the floor, several of the
occupants wear ethnic jewelry and colorful scarves that make a stark contrast to the earthy tones of the tent. The heat is sweltering, and we all
frequently wipe the sweat beading our foreheads. The setting is Genoa's
Suq (Souk) multicultural festival, and the occasion is the 2012 publication
of the Italian translation of James Kilgo's *Deep Enough for Ivorybills* (1988).
The debate is hosted by Massimo Morasso. A poet and a writer, since the
early 2000s Massimo has also earned a reputation as an organizer of Genoa's prestigious Festival of Science. It is in this capacity that he explains to
the Suq's audience how in the contemporary world the loss of vocabulary
pertaining to natural diversity underlies a detachment from it. A poetics of
the elsewhere, Massimo suggests, can only emerge from the effort to establish an imaginary landscape through which it becomes possible to relate to
that which is other to us. *What a fitting metaphor for the festival's project,* I
jot down in my notes. *If imagining a landscape is what enables the possibility
of acknowledging difference and building bridges to it, then turning this landscape into a sensuous reality is one more step toward allowing difference to*

emerge in our midst, not as the Other, but as a part of who we are as a collectivity.

Ever since the early 1990s, the fervor over Genoa's revitalization has spawned the creation of cultural festivals that, like the Festival of Poetry, the Festival of Science, and the Genova Film Festival, draw primarily on the initiative of visionary individuals who organize these events by harnessing local, national, and EU funding as well as private sponsorships. While previous chapters delved into the experiences and the biographies of the Genoese who contribute to their city's revitalization, this chapter focuses on some of the worlding practices through which these individuals seek to shape the urban everyday. Hence, in what follows I explore the utopian light cast on Genoa's diversity by organizers and participants of one of these festivals: the Suq. Broadly definable as a multicultural festival, the Suq takes place in Genoa every June under the direction of two Genoese women, Valentina Arcuri and Carla Peirolero, and with the participation of local small business owners such as ethnic artisans and restaurateurs, but also artists, intellectuals, city administrators, and representatives of local cultural and ethnic associations. In its attempt to prospect a spatiality where cultural hybridizations are a desirable and enjoyable outcome, the Suq is an example of what Foucault (1986) called heterotopias: it is an "other place" that condenses the qualities of different spatialities: the market, the agora, the theater, and an arena for learning experiences that pleasurably engage all the senses. By proposing an ideal model of peaceful and delectable integration, the Suq has a utopian quality to it; and yet, just like any heterotopia, it differs from utopias primarily due to its material, though temporary, existence. And just like any heterotopias, the spatiality of the Suq relates to other places (both physical and metaphorical) through a thick traffic of meanings and experiences as it compensates for what is present in, or absent from, the everyday that surrounds it.

As a sham for capitalism (Žižek 1997) and neoliberal governance (Hale 2005), multiculturalism has long been the object of scathing critiques that highlight its concealment of complex issues of inequality through the commoditization and celebration of expressive culture (Ameeriar 2012; Fish 1997; Moodley 1983; Rahier 2008). Multicultural festivals in particular have been denounced as opportunities for the consumption of "other" cultures that are added as commoditized and politically irrelevant "spices" to the otherwise seemingly bland everyday of mainstream groups (hooks 1992; Kirshenblatt-Gimblett 1991), or for boosting corporate revenues even as

Figure 12. The Suq. Photo by author.

they gesture toward inclusivity (Harvey 1990; Zukin 1996). Yet festivals are not entirely devoid of subversive potential even in the face of the many limitations imposed on them (Gotham 2005). They may, indeed, resort to turning identities into consumer products (Peterson 2010: 9); yet, by the same token, they may also become arenas where emergent moral communities (Peterson 2010) or communities of affect (Kapchan 2008) negotiate difference by proposing potentially alternative views on race, gender, class, ethnicity, nationhood, and history (Ballerino-Cohen 1998; Guss 2000; Ho 2000; Peterson 2010).

As I show in this chapter, some of the concerns raised about multicultural festivals are certainly applicable to the Suq as well, in that the latter enacts models of multiculturalism that range from facile anti-racism (Zinn 2002) and the consumption of a sanitized Other to Arab-face belly dance performances (Maira 2008). While acknowledging the orientalist dynamics embedded in the practice of displaying the Other at the Suq, however, this chapter contextualizes this festival within the broader politics of representing and consuming selves and others in contemporary Italy. In the same vein, it also provides an exploration of how the Suq articulates with dominant urban trends in the production of alluring "visitable" spatialities whose main purpose is to promote consumption (Dicks 2004) as well as specific forms of commerce. Due to its focus, the chapter privileges a sensuous approach to cultural analysis: instead of following the longstanding scholarly tradition of favoring vision and hearing over the "lower senses" (Howes 2003; Jackson 2007; Stoller 1976), it pays close attention to ways of presenting and manipulating multisensory objects as part of the Suq's attempt to penetrate the Italian sensorium—and with it the experiential foundations of a local and a national imaginary—for the sake of challenging dominant representations of culture, identity, belonging, and roots.

Welcome to the Suq

Installed at the heart of Genoa's Porto Antico marina, the Suq presents itself as a microcosm of colors, sounds, scents, shapes, and textures. Year after year, Suq visitors are welcome by a carpet of intricate Maghrebi pottery whose clay provides an earthy background to the red, green, blue, and yellow enamels glistening in the summer afternoon. The whiffs of incense and spices lead you further into a structure shaped after an exotic bazaar, with narrow alleys surmounted by ornate arcs and decorated with colorful banners. All the goods for sale stimulate the visitor's senses, providing a palette of aesthetic pleasures. Ecuadorian necklaces carved out of vegetal ivory surprise with their vibrant colors, their unusual shapes, and the unexpected lightness of the material. Indonesian cotton and silk clothes expand the scope of this chromatic experience, furnishing a soft background for the hard brightness of semi-precious stones imported from India. Embroidered and handmade leather shoes keep company with woven raffia purses, and carved African statues converse with the watercolor Golems painted by an Israeli artist. A few steps away, handmade herbal soaps catch the eye with their cool pastel colors, contrasting vividly with the soft mounds of yellow, orange, and red spices. And, as if the visual stimulations were not enough, the myriad scents from the Suq's food Babel keep visitors enthralled. Every few steps Indian, Ethiopian, Indonesian, African, Latin American, and Arab restaurants offer samples of couscous, tabbouleh, samosas, and kebab that compete for the visitor's olfactory sense and her taste.

At all times of the day and till late in the night, visitors walk around the Suq, gently stroking the soft silks and the crispy cottons, the prickly raffias and the smooth leathers. They smell the pungent spices and the flowery essential oils; they visually imbibe the earthy colors and the cool hues, the round and the edgy shapes of locally handmade crafts and imported objects. Periodically, the flow tends to coalesce around the central piazza of the Suq: a small stage where debates on serious issues such as homelessness, sustainability, and the rights of immigrants alternate with ethnic music performances and theatrical plays, and exotic cooking classes are followed by children entertainment and belly dance sessions. Listening to the pounding sound of Middle Eastern and African drums, visitors float around the booths, lightly brushing against each other and gently pushing away from the bodies that slowly move in all directions. Every now and then, the crowd is infused by a smattering of maroon as Buddhist monks from a Tuscan monastery join the festive crowds, or by the dark garments of the Catholic friars who hold evening spiritual retreats for the seekers. It is hard to assign provenance to all visitors: a kaleidoscope of languages, hairdos, and clothes points to North Africa, South and East Asia, the Sub-Saharan region, and Latin America. However, even more pervasive is the presence of Italians: some of them wearing colorful Indian shirts and embroidered purses, others sporting jeans and slacks, or, in a few cases, even office attire. Some of them are parading their "liberalmindedness" (Black 2012: 134); others, instead, are looking to spend a few hours in a different setting. Hailed as members of a moral community that promotes mutual understanding over xenophobia (Peterson 2010: 151), they expect to be entertained in novel ways while perhaps learning something new. Every year, the Suq attracts thousands of visitors (70,000 in 2013),[1] and its events receive daily coverage in the local media. Since 1999, the appeal of the Suq has spread beyond Genoa's confines: some of its shows travel all over Italy to promote the festival's multicultural tenets, and in 2013 the Suq earned the Italian government's Best Practice endorsement for fostering intercultural dialogue.[2]

Multicultural Festivals: A Genealogy

The Suq, I suggest, proposes a political pedagogy of Self and Otherness that is embedded in sensuous spatial experience (Mukerji 2012: 509); hence, its genealogy ideally begins with the World Fairs that were held in European capitals in the nineteenth century. The purpose of these events was to foster patriotic pride by situating the nation and its accomplishments in an international perspective. Such fairs were prominent stages whereby orientalist representations of non-Western peoples as alluring and visually intriguing but also disorganized and primitive stood in stark contrast to displays of Western rationality, science and technology (Mitchell 1989). Meant to educate and "enlighten" their visitors (Buchli 2002:6), World Fairs proposed representations of Otherness whose sensuous immediacy was regarded as the evidence of the cultural inferiority of non-European peoples (Mitchell 1989).

A more recent phenomenon, multicultural festivals as ostensible attempts at including and accepting difference in multiethnic societies claim to somewhat scramble the authorship of former top-down representations of alterity by allowing "ethnics" more power in representing themselves. Yet such events may not only contribute to reifying identities for the sake of a mindless consumption of subaltern cultures, but may also occult inequalities even as they preempt dissent (Staeheli, Mitchell, and Nagel 2009). Critics of multicultural performances are often accurate in their assessment of the role of orientalism as well as colonial and imperial ideology intrinsic to displaying the Other (Kirshenblatt-Gimblett 1991; hooks 1992). Some of the same objections apply to the Italian context, too: Italy's designation as a European country gives it access to a peripheral European-ness as well as a degree of reflected "imperial capital" (Parker 2000) that allow it to represent itself as the bearer of a superior whiteness. Hence, multicultural events in multiethnic Italy are frequently characterized by a "romantic anti-racism" in which immigrant communities are represented as living in harmony without trespassing their assigned cultural boundaries (Zinn 2002: 209–217).

Yet it also bears mentioning that, while orientalisms of the North Atlantic blend are predicated upon the juxtaposition of an allegedly disembodied Western rationality and Eastern sensuousness, the processes underlying the construction of Italian national identity posit a somewhat different scenario: one that cannot be adequately understood without taking into account the sensuous qualities through which, in the global economy of value (Herzfeld 2004), Italian nationhood is imagined, commoditized, and consumed both from within and from without. Current representations of Italian national identity popularized by the media as well as everyday discourse are frequently peppered with boisterous claims about Italy's superior artistic, historical, and cultural heritage. Moreover, as if the alleged supremacy of Italian heritage were not enough, popular quantifications disseminated in the Italian media attribute to this country 40 percent to 80 percent of the world's material heritage,[3] often suggesting that such historical and artistic wealth is not sufficiently treasured and valorized, but rather stashed away in museum basements. Not only does this polemic seek to instill the values of heritage-mediated patriotism (Anderson 2006) as a remedy to the common complaint that Italians lack a shared national identity—and with it, civic values (Koenig-Archibugi 2003; Putnam 1993)—but it also establishes an Italian primacy vis-à-vis the rest of the world, even in the face of what is perceived as this country's semi-peripheral status in terms of its spotty economic achievements and its disappointing political records.

Just as fundamental in the Italian national imaginary is the role of this country's design industry on a global scale—Italian fashion in the first place. Developed out of premodern Italy's myriad artisan traditions (Crane and Bovone 2006) and boosted by generous U.S. funds after the end of World War II (White 2000), Italy's fashion and design industry enjoys a worldwide popularity that, since the late twentieth century, has been studiously cultivated through large investments in international marketing and advertising (Crane and Bovone 2006). Within the confines of the country, this industry targets a proportionally large internal market of consumers who are particularly concerned with matters of style (Taplin 1989: 418), thus contributing to a national "aesthetic economy" (Crane and Bovone 2006) focused on the collective cultivation of a sensuous taste for colors, textures, shapes, proportions, patterns, and originality. Along with fashion and style, other consumable cultural forms are also nurtured to a fault: one of them is food, and especially "slow food" as a form of resistance against the top-down globalization brought about by food multinationals such as McDonald's, but also against culturally insensitive regulations and attempts at homogenizing local food traditions imposed by the European Union (Leitch 2003). In Italy, regional cuisines are thus undergoing a valorization that feeds local identities as part of a more complex discourse on national pride vis-à-vis foreign and global pressures (Helstosky 2006).

The question at hand, given such premises, is not whether the immigrant cultures that are often imagined through their artisanry and cuisines can add "spices" to an everyday that is hardly imagined as "bland" (hooks 1992); instead, it is the question of whether these spices will be accepted as worthy of a place among the many intense (and intensely self-absorbed) flavors of the Italian table, or the variegated nuances of its fashion and design productions. What is at stake, here, is a recognition of difference as the acknowledgment of the worth of immigrant cultures (Taylor 1994: 64) instead of their dismissal as inferior to the local and national cultures of the host country. While such recognition does not necessarily entail the de facto acceptance of immigrants and their ways of life, it may imply a step away from the "negative recognition of difference" (Grillo 2002: 10) that is so common in multiethnic Italy. This is precisely what Suq organizers seek to achieve by means of a "cultural work" that is implicitly or explicitly meant to "resist the stereotype, to challenge the insults, to lift the restrictions" (Appiah 2007: 161).

Politics by Another Means: Festivals and the Senses

The English word "festival" is only a partial translation for what the Suq really is. The Suq combines serious political and intellectual content with entertainment, food, and shopping. Aside from being a classroom and an agora for political debates, it is also a theater and above all a fair. In this respect, it closely resembles the genre of *sagre*: rural festivals in which villages and small towns celebrate local produce and traditional food types by offering producers and vendors an opportunity to promote and sell their goods to visitors gathered to sample local specialties even as they enjoy folkloric performances. Even though, ideally, sagre trace their ancestry to ancient Roman agricultural festivals, their tradition underwent a hefty reinvention under the twentieth-century Fascist regime (Cavazza 1997). Aside from striving to valorize agricultural production, Italian Fascism sought to regiment leisure through institutions that encouraged citizens to devote themselves to sports and a "culture" meant to instill patriotic sentiments into the Italian imaginary. Leisure, under Mussolini, was made public: highly visible, tightly controlled, and always again patriotic in its manipulation of individual feelings and experiences for the purposes of the regime (Falasca-Zamponi 1997). Combined with the Duce's emphasis on rurality as the essence and sustenance of Italian civilization, the anti-modern aesthetics of sagre valorized the products and pleasures of peasant life and ancient artisan traditions as opposed to the mass-produced industrial commodities that populated urban landscapes (Cavazza 1997). Not only did sagre inculcate folklore (Rockefeller 1999), but they also showcased the peasants and farmers who, up to that point, had been viewed with a degree of contempt by urbanites, and presented them as belonging with full dignity in Italy's composite national self. Often epitomes of invented traditions (Hobsbawm 1983), sagre kindled anti-modern nostalgia by embedding themselves in the modern context of a growing internal tourism (Cavazza 1997).

By the mid-twentieth century, Fascism had declined; however, nurtured by the rising tourist industry, the passion for sagre remained, with such festivals being celebrated year after year in towns and villages all over the country. At sagre, natives and tourists alike still expect to have all of their senses delighted through the experience of flavors, scents, sights, textures, and sounds that accompany the celebration of traditional dishes, local produce, or native flowers along with music and dance performances.[4] Sagre thus continue to be regarded as venues for enjoyable sensuous experiences and shopping, but also as educational folkloric events that boost local economies, especially during the high summer season. Most importantly, sagre bring people together in the name of a collective understanding of "culture": a representation that frequently mobilizes discourses about "identity" and "roots" grounded in local modes of production and reified through shared sensuous experiences. I suggest that such events are yet another example of politics by another means (Haraway 1989 in Mukerji 2012: 511), or even of affective politics (Massumi 2002) whereby the apparent immediacy of spatial and sensuous experiences in fact strive to shape one's view of the cultural, but also the social and the political world (Guano 2002; Mukerji 2012).

The role of festive public events in holding a sensuous mirror to shared imaginaries even as they help mold them in their complex articulations has been long known to sociologists and anthropologists. As "stor[ies people] tell themselves about themselves" (Geertz 1973: 448), festive public events are occasions in which members of a group create, display, and reflect upon their collective identities (Errington 1987: 654). They may do so by promoting an emotional sense of belonging (Durkheim 1915; Kapchan 2008) and by providing their participants with sensuous symbols invested with the power to support and loosely unify disparate perspectives (Turner 1967). Festivals, Barbara Kirshenblatt-Gimblett (1991: 416) argued, are "multisensory, multifocus events" that pursue "sensory saturation" in the face of elitist Western preferences for splitting up the senses and parceling them out "one by one, to the appropriate art form"; in so doing, festivals create a thick traffic of experiences and meaning between imaginaries and sensuous landscapes. And so does the Suq, as a multisensory story that its participants and its organizers, Valentina Arcuri and Carla Peirolero, tell the Genoese about themselves and their city—past, present, and hypothetical—as they engage and subvert dominant representations of local and national identity.

The Path to the Heart Is Through the Senses

As members of that Genoese creative class that draws on formal education as well as personal talents to craft public urban experiences, Carla Peirolero and Valentina Arcuri earned degrees in sociology and political science that got them thinking about important social and political issues. However, throughout their formative years they also kept cultivating their passion for theater as an expressive—and intrinsically political (Ingram 2011)—medium to reach out to broad audiences by engaging their intellect, their senses, and their emotions. As they first designed Genoa's Suq, Carla and Valentina were already explicit in their intent to utilize the theatrical and sensuous qualities of the festival to convey important social and political contents. For this purpose, they recruited a scenographer whose task was to design a Suq that, as Valentina Arcuri told me, has to be "so beautiful that when one walks in he goes 'oooh!' We wanted a stimulating scenography even though we weren't interested in the pursuit of authenticity. The basis of the Suq is the encounter between different cultures, but with the idea of finding a shared culture and to invent a new way of being together. . . . We wanted a beautiful space where we can all be comfortable, but where no individual style prevails." In the comfortably hybrid space of the Suq, visitors have to be exposed to scents, sights, sounds, textures, and flavors that do not necessary entail commercial transactions. In Arcuri's view, the Suq needs to entice "people to . . . spend the whole day here, looking at things, smelling them, and eating them," though for a purpose that is actually higher than mindless consumption. Such alluring experiences have to smuggle in, through a layer of sensuous pleasures and an animated format, deeper thoughts on important issues such as racism, xenophobia, and the rights of immigrants. This is why, as the bazaar of the Suq keeps visitors enthralled with its sensuous stimuli, many of the events taking place on the stage are, and have to be according to Arcuri, "serious, with a deep meaning."

Fascist sagre sought to use sensuous events to propose models of and for primordial Italianness and rural authenticity; by contrast, the goal of the Suq is to propose a hybrid model of society to be attained through what Arcuri calls a "stimulating scenography": though one that, unlike that of Fascist sagre, does not strive for authenticity. Implicitly sensing that the effort to establish "authenticity" is, after all, an attempt to dominate (see also Zukin 2010), Arcuri is adamant about the importance of finding a shared culture and of inventing a new way of being together. The pursuit of a beautiful space that makes you feel comfortable, but without having one specific cultural style prevail, establishes a cosmopolitan canopy (Anderson 2012): a "third place" (Oldenburg 1991) that allows for harmonious interactions between different ethnic groups or individuals who may otherwise fail to acknowledge each other (Mommaas 2009: 3 in Richards 2011: 1240).

This hybridity that "entertains difference without an assumed or imposed hierarchy" (Bhabha 1994: 4) reaches out to its publics in a Suq that functions as a communal "living room" where visitors can, in the words of Carla Peirolero and her team, "at any time sit down and enjoy not just some exotic dish that will contribute to making us feel closer to faraway peoples but also the chance to ponder the themes of a conference or a performance, thus initiating a dialogue between citizens and speakers or artists" (Peirolero et al. n.d.: 5). Such a space is also meant to "create opportunities for recognition and celebration for those who come back from distant countries where one was forced to migrate, and who can find in this 'mixing site' an affinity with her own human and professional journey" (Peirolero et al. n.d.: 6).

Genoa, for Peirolero, is an ideal location for such an endeavor in that "the strong essence of intersections and exchanges is intrinsic to the DNA of the port city; it can be observed in its urban texture but also in its language. [Local] art has frequently utilized to its fullest the strength of these crossings . . . , thus living the 'contamination' as a resource to be shared with the world, for the sake of communicating respect, love, and tolerance" (Peirolero et al. n.d.: 6).[5] "Contamination" (*contaminazione*) is a key word in the ideation of the Suq, which constantly attempts to identify the contaminated "roots" of Genoese culture as a model for an open society where ethnic groups can not only coexist peacefully, but also and above all mingle in mutual appreciation. Drawing on Barnor Hesse (2000: 17), I suggest that the intentional hybridity of the Suq creates a space for transruptions that cut across dominant discourses on "culture," "civilization," and the purity of "roots": a space that is hospitable to an emergent métissage concocted out of a continuous work of bricolage (Lionnet 1991: 8).

Often imagined as a discrete unit where change and hybridization are not possible (Zinn 2002), "culture" in contemporary Italy is the terrain of forms of racism whereby ethnic chauvinism asserts the incompatibility of the host culture with those of immigrants, or at the very least its undiscussed superiority (Cole 1997; Holmes 2000; Però 2007; Stolcke 1995). Ever since the early 2000s, much of Europe suffered a backlash against diversity (Grillo 2002, 2007; Vertovec and Wessendorf 2005). In Italy, the populist rhetoric on the "Judeo-Christian roots" of European—and hence Italian—"civilization" put forth by the Catholic Church and Italian conservatives began to posit a scenario whereby immigrants are expected at best to fully integrate in their host society, and at worst to steer clear of Italian shores. Liberals, instead, took to denouncing the threat posited to Italy's liberal democracy by Muslim immigrants' alleged propensity to have their faith interfere with their civic duties and responsibilities vis-à-vis their host country (see, e.g., Sartori 2000). In the face of a rising wave of xenophobia, the Suq strives to remind its visitors that the encounter among "cultures" need not be ridden with conflict—even though, at times, this message is still conveyed in a somewhat problematic fashion.

Food of the Other, Food of the Self

A walk through the Suq exposes visitors to the sights, scents, and flavors of a plethora of Asian, African, and Latin American tapas-sized portions of food, displayed in small booths by local ethnic restaurants and eateries. In many cases, the spiciness of these treats has been tamed down to accommodate the common Italian aversion to hot food; the small portions are meant to lure first-timers, encouraging them to deepen their experience through a visit to the actual restaurant. Although by now most Italian cities have an array of ethnic dining venues, the food business has been a comparatively challenging field for many immigrant communities. Most Italians are very aware of the worldwide recognition garnered not just by their artistic and historical heritage, but also by their foodways: an admiration that they mirror with a degree of national pride, even chauvinism. In the absence of political or economic accomplishments, Italy's alleged superiority in all things aesthetic and sensuous is the yardstick against which other nations— and, by extension, cultures—are frequently measured and found lacking. This explains at least in part why, in Italy, food has become a battlefield in the culture wars fought against immigrants. Racism, in a country where culinary traditions are the subject matter of identity, often manifests itself in the form of contempt for the foodways of foreigners. If many Italians display a degree of amused skepticism vis-à-vis the eating habits of their European neighbors, such culinary chauvinism may turn into an overt manifestation of disgust when confronted with the spicy fares of African, Asian, and Latin American immigrants (Maritano 2002: 69) and their failure to comply with—or, depending on viewpoints, measure up to—the Italian taste palette. This is why, all over Italy, many a culture war have been fought around the smells emanating from ethnic restaurants and even neighbors' kitchens, markers of a seemingly uncontainable foreign presence that causes anxiety and the compulsion for sanitation (Ameeriar 2012; Manalansan 2006; Ong 2003), while school cafeterias featuring ethnic dishes are often bombarded by Italian parents' complaints that their children are fed inappropriately. What is often forgotten, however, is that the cultural contempt also carries economic undertones: in Lucca, a small Tuscan town, kebab parlors and Chinese restaurants have been banned from the city center under the accusation of diluting local quality and tradition, but also for undermining a restoration industry that caters largely to tourists.

Unlike what happened in Great Britain, in Italy ethnic restaurateurs cannot claim an available niche: plenty of Italian businesses provide food on the go that is both cheap and tasty. These restaurateurs' hope, then, is to attain a degree of cultural recognition by inducing open-minded customers to explore an exotic culinary tradition that promises to offer a sensuous gratification hopefully not unlike the one brought about by the consumption of Italian regional foods—of course with no guarantees that this enjoyment will take on the form of a reflexive approach rather than that of a mindless consumption (Heldke 2003).[6] Ever since the 1980s, ethnic restaurants have become increasingly common in Italy. In Genoa, the sector was pioneered by the Chinese in the 1980s, followed in more recent years by a few Indians, Indonesians, Ethiopians, Arabs, and a smattering of

Latin Americans. Such food choices, however, are usually purged of the pungent spices that North Italian palates would find offensive; most importantly, the restoration sector is still dominated by Italian gastronomy, prepared by Italian chefs and served mainly (though certainly not exclusively) to Italian customers and tourists on their quest for authentic Italian experiences.

It is in the spirit of promoting gastronomic cosmopolitanism that every edition of the Suq features shows and initiatives by Chef Kumalè, an Italian cook and self-proclaimed "gastronomad" who, after claiming an Arabic-sounding name, has made a reputation for himself by offering incursions into the world cuisines represented among immigrant communities. In the attempt to expand local culinary horizons, Kumalè habitually offers classes showcasing exotic ingredients. In recent years, one of these has been *brick*, the thin wheat dough utilized in Tunisia as a wrap for mixes of tuna, ground meat, chicken, eggs, and spices.

Standing behind a table set with a white cloth, an array of ingredients, and an electrical wok, on one Sunday evening Kumalè began his cooking lesson by challenging a particularly crowded Suq to expand the dominant definition of Mediterranean cuisine:

> We need to talk about Mediterranean diet in its plural form, because Mediterranean cuisine does not entail only French, Italian, and Spanish cuisine on one hand, and Arabic cuisine on the other, as if the Mediterranean were split in two through a straight line: the Western Mediterranean on one side, and the Eastern Mediterranean on the other. As a matter of fact, in the Mediterranean area there are a plethora of cuisines, each of which is very different from the others. Most importantly, let's not forget that olive oil is hardly the only oil. There are a variety of oils and butters that are used all over the Mediterranean besides olive oil.

After decentering olive oil, Italy's most celebrated condiment, Kumalè moved on to introduce the ingredient of the day, the thin dough known in Tunisia as *feuille de brick*. He asked how many in the audience already knew it. As only a few raised their hand, he threw a few sheets into the crowd: the dough needs to be assayed through the senses even before it can be turned into a cultural category worth engaging. "Touch it!" was his injunction. "It's a versatile dough that lends itself to so many recipes." Not only that, but it is a cosmopolitan dough, too: "There are similar doughs all over the Mediterranean, for example the Greek *phyllo*, the Turkish *yufta*, the Moroccan *warka*, which are in turn related to our *lasagne*. . . . But I have also seen Chinese women work a similar dough exactly like women do it in Morocco. How did this dough make it from China to Morocco? Probably through Ibn Battuta, the explorer who preceded Marco Polo."

For Kumalè, Battuta's geographical feats are also responsible for the popularity of Chinese tea and vermicelli (which he calls *spaghetti cinesi*) in Moroccan cuisine. If Maghrebis can have such a close tie to the Far East, it is time for Italians, too, to expand their culinary horizons. Not to mention that, although the original Tunisian recipe calls for a tuna filling, the feuilles lend themselves to incursions into a variety of other cuisines: "If you stuff them with lentils you can turn them into Indian *samosas*, but you can also make a Greek stuffing with feta cheese, boiled potatoes and mint." Sensing he had grabbed the interest of his audience, Kumalè continued: "So, you may be wondering 'I want to try [the brick], but where do I find it?' The answer is 'right around the corner.'" Gesturing toward the nearby historic city center where, in the face of a partial gentrification many immigrants still live and work, he added, "You find the brick in any Islamic butchery, and it costs only one euro."

Sitting in the audience, I wondered if Kumalè was aware that a large number of his Italian spectators were likely not to have ever set foot into an Islamic butchery. In the eyes of many liberal Italians anything Islamic still carries a somewhat dangerous halo—not to mention that, in Genoa, Islamic butcheries are to be found in fairly degraded parts of the centro storico such as the notorious via Prè: a dark and narrow street that has traditionally hosted all sorts of illicit traffics and that, although it is located at a stone's throw from Porto Antico, is proactively avoided by most Genoese. With his exhortation, Kumalè encouraged cosmopolitan foodies not only to break culinary taboos, but also to penetrate the sociospatial boundaries that separate the Italian middle classes from immigrant communities, thus making a different use of the city and above all casting immigrants not as a threat but as a resource.

As Kumalè went on to expound on the versatility of the feuilles de brick, a middle-aged woman sitting in front of me asked her friend, "Why did he choose 'Kumalè' as his name? Is it from the Genoese [dialect] *'cumm'a l'è?'* [how is it?]?" Chuckling, her friend replied, "No, it's an Arabic name"; overhearing that, a woman to her right bent over to ask, "Is he an Arab?

Figure 13. Chef Kumalè at the Suq. Photo by author.

He looks Italian to me." "He is not an Arab; he is from Turin" was the answer. Visibly disappointed, the other woman blurted, "He is from *Turin*? Couldn't they find an *Arab* to do this show?"[7] While underscoring a concern with the Suq's intentional disavowal of authenticity, this reaction may have also potentially denoted disappointment at discovering that, even at such a cosmopolitan venue, the subaltern were still expected to speak through, and be represented by, a white male from the dominant ethnic group. After all, their "exotic" food types were being proposed for the culinary pleasures of a largely (though not exclusively) white middle class.

In her analysis of Kumalè's "ethnogastronomic tourism," Rachel Black (2012: 119, 136) recently objected that, in spite of his supposedly good intentions, the Turinese chef still promotes a mindless consumption of exotic food. Being disembedded from its social and cultural contexts, his gastronomic practice fails to promote a genuine understanding of difference. This argument echoes Daniel Miller's (2001: 145) concern that even well-meaning cosmopolitan foodies may, after all, be consuming the fare of exotic cultures in the sanitized privacy of their own home. If that is the case, he asks, "Are we really eating at the same table?" (Miller 2001: 145). Indeed, Black's and Miller's objections to the decontextualization and co-optation of foreign cuisines are legitimate; yet the practice of promoting exotic food at the Suq also must be analyzed in light of the multiple contexts surrounding the festival itself—namely, the politics of cultural recognition in contemporary Italy.

Writing about the frequently shoddy treatment meted out by British customers to Chinese takeout employees in the United Kingdom,' David Parker (2000) argued that the repositioning of Chinese and Indian food at the core of British national cuisine did not entail an improvement in the status of immigrants, nor did it imply a cultural acceptance. Instead, it simply cast them once again as providers of cheap goods and services. The Italian context, however, is quite different. For one, there is little in the way of a colonial memory among contemporary Italians;[8] convenient though it may be, this oblivion ensures that Italy does not have the same amount of "imperial capital" as Great Britain (Parker 2000). This certainly does not preclude Italians from enjoying and perpetuating the privileges of whiteness and a still contested Europeanness vis-à-vis those whom they call *extracomunitari* (non-EU immigrants). Yet Italy's own status in the Western world is semi-peripheral. The country is part of the West's own internal Orient: a large beachside historical theme park where one may satisfy one's desire for aesthetic and sensuous pleasures. To tourists from all over the world, Italy is a country to be explored, but also consumed, through the experience of its food, its beauty, its mild climate, and the allegedly passionate temperament of its residents. This representation is not just integral to Italy's popularity as a tourist destination, but also to the global imaginary that transpires through films such as *Eat Pray Love* (Murphy 2010), *Under the Tuscan Sun* (Wells 2003), and *Italian for Beginners* (Scherfig 2000), all of which feature narrations of Italian affects and sensuous pleasures (both real and imagined) that help shape the North Atlantic experience, even as they remind Italians of their country's place in the global tourist imaginary. If, at least since the time of the Grand Tour, the North Atlantic sensorium exercises taste, touch, and sight under the pretext of knowledge in its indulgent consumptions of Italy, Italians are also inclined toward using similar criteria in evaluating themselves—and, just as importantly, in approaching each other across regional lines.

Italy's internal tourism frequently involves traveling to different regions to experience local food types—be it cheeses, meats, fish, produce, pastas, breads, desserts, or wines—on a quest for local culinary traditions that, taken together, compose the larger and highly delectable national whole. The habit of exploring the country through its dishes and specialty foods is best exemplified by the popular food maps printed on posters and kitchen towels where each region of Italy is represented by a dish or a wine, or by films such as *Benvenuti al Sud* (Miniero 2010), where Northerners and Southerners overcome entrenched mutual stereotypes by, among others, finally agreeing to sample each other's regional cheeses. Learning to appreciate the food of the Others, in this perspective, is regarded as akin to accepting them as part of a shared national imaginary ready to be consumed by selves and others, from within and from without its national borders: a national foodscape (Appadurai 1988) that emerges through the glorification of the country's gastronomic traditions as worthy components of a variegated whole in which each region, be it Northern or Southern, finds its place.

Indeed, as a way of consuming alterity, Kumalè's gastronomadism is a manifestation of food colonialism (Heldke 2003). Yet dismissing Kumalè's practices as *simply* food colonialism would cause one to ignore the complex ways in which food participates in the negotiation of regional and national identities in the Italian context. If, on one hand, Kumalè's gastronomadism entails a degree of objectification and his shows are manifestations of a social tourism that contributes to fixing "the meanings of cultural difference" in Italy's cultural imaginary (Rahier 2008: 151), on the other hand his invitation to consume alterity can also be read as a first step toward a rapprochement with the culinary Other as a "culture" worthy of one's consideration. And so is visual pleasure and the admiration of the beauty that comes from elsewhere.

Disturbing the Mosaic

As a "fabrication of memory in which present individuality, collective belonging and home are established" (Kowalczyk and Popkewitz 2005: 424), multiculturalism often arranges "cultures" as discrete units (Eller 1997): compilations of things that can be sensed such as food choices, hairstyles, clothing, along with immaterial but undeniably real (especially when reified) objects such as languages, behaviors, and beliefs. Along these lines, multiculturalism is often imagined as the root of an Italian culture that is categorized as a *mosaico di culture*: an aesthetically pleasing if variegated mosaic of cultures assembled through an ancient history of ethnic connections and clashes. These include the alliances, wars, and migration and trade routes that crisscrossed the Mediterranean moving peoples, goods, and ideas in all directions. In the Italian imaginary, the phrase mosaico di culture emphasizes the visual dimension of multiculturalism, in that it evokes vivid images of ancient Roman artworks or of Ravenna's Byzantine masterpieces as epitomes of the encounter between Occident and Orient: works of stunning beauty that draw myriad visitors every year. Imagining Italy's cultural history as a "mosaic" posits some important signposts for envisioning today's multiethnic society.

For one, Italy's ancient mosaics may originate from an encounter between peoples and traditions from the East and from the West; however, their images are frozen in space and time as part of a now unchanging configuration to which nothing can be added. Furthermore, Italy's much-celebrated Byzantine mosaics are assembled of tiles whose translucent colors form flat and sharp images. By their nature, these tiles have edges that prevent the blurring of nuances and create a stark contrast to their background. When transposed to the multicultural metaphor, each tile joins in the production of a harmonious whole, though without ever changing its place or its essence. Not only does the mosaic of cultures metaphor cast "groups and cultures [that] are clearly delineated and identifiable entities that coexist, while maintaining firm boundaries, as would pieces of a mosaic" (Benhabib 2002: 8), but it also naturalizes and aestheticizes hierarchies by reminding its audiences of how brightly colored patterns naturally gain visual preeminence over their neutral backgrounds. While all tiles have a role to play, they are obviously not all equal in the way they attract and guide the gaze of their observers: the core images they compose are those of Catholic saints and emperors as emblems of the secular and religious powers that dominated ancient Italy and still play a paramount role in today's stratified society. Hence, the pretense of openness in the "mosaic of cultures" metaphor is, in fact, an indicator of not only how the "cultures" that are seen as comprising the whole are imagined as essential, discrete, and static units unable to change or hybridize (Zinn 2002), but also and most importantly of how they are expected to organize around a vertical, elitist, and Catholic core. To the contemporary viewer, the visual pleasure generated by the experience of Ravenna's mosaics may aestheticize ancient inequities. It is thus easy to see how the ubiquitous mosaic of cultures

metaphor may use the immediacy of sensuous aesthetic experience to legitimize a static and highly hierarchical representation of culture and society:
one where diversity is acceptable only if frozen in time and organized
around an undisputed center.

By proposing a radically hybrid model of culture, instead, the Suq's
organizers and many of its participants implicitly seek to disturb the immobility of the mosaic of cultures model to inject alternative representations
into the visitors' sensorium that complicate dominant notions of cultural
roots. One of these Suq participants is Stella, a young and dynamic Ecuadorian woman whose booth is easily identifiable by the thick crowds of
visitors it keeps attracting, year after year. Stella sells colorful jewelry that
Ecuadorian indigenous people carve out of vegetal ivory: a material that is
translucent like stone, but has a surprising feather-like lightness. Stella
moved to Genoa in the early 1990s, joining the largest immigrant Ecuadorian community in all of Italy. Like many of her female co-nationals, for a
while Stella worked as a caregiver for the elderly (*badante*); however, soon
enough she decided to break out of the mold of the immigrant domestic
worker and try something different.[9] Her inspiration was her passion for
beauty and her pride for her home country, whose peculiarities she sees
reflected in its folk art: "We [Ecuadorians] paint with bright true colors
because the equator runs through our country, and the sunrays hit the
ground perpendicularly. . . . We have a type of energy there that is very
different from that of other countries, and it is this energy that painters
illustrate with these colors." Stella's national imagination thus establishes a
sensuous chain connecting the landscapes of Ecuador, its equatorial location, the intensity and directness of the sunshine bathing it, its energy, and
the colors used by its painters and artisans. It is this multipronged fullness
of deeply emplaced sensuous and aesthetic experiences—which she com-
pares to her own enraptured joy of "smelling Ecuador's soil" each time she
goes back to her home country—that Stella seeks to pass on to her Genoese
customers. Moreover, as if the radiant energy of her rainbow-like jewelry
were not enough to mesmerize her customers, she generously regales them
with stories about each object they observe. Thus, as they admire her jewelry, visitors get to learn not only about the properties of vegetal ivory and
Ecuadorian crafts, but also about the artisans who made them: indigenous
people who deserve recognition for their talent as well as a fair compensa-
tion for their labor. Hence, Stella presents the act of perusing, purchasing,

and donning a piece of her jewelry as equivalent to capturing and experiencing a glimpse of Ecuador with all of its quintessential energy: its colors, its light, and the creativity of its *indigena*, who, due to their ancestral ties to the land, are best equipped to infuse their crafts with these qualities.

As she presents herself as an informal ambassador of Ecuadorian culture, Stella straddles the juxtaposition between her own urban upbringing, education, and cosmopolitan experience and the rooted tradition of indigenous artisans, whom she envisions as both closer to the timeless essence of her home country and as removed from the modernity of which she so easily partakes. Stella also presents her trade as a service to Italian culture as well. "There is no more artisanry in Europe, only mass-produced goods of low quality, all of them Chinese," she says. It is only through this infusion of Latin American crafts, she suggests, that Italians' longstanding hunger for artisan goods can be satiated even in the face of the global diffusion of disappointingly low-quality Chinese wares. In advancing this claim, Stella is fully aware of her role in "adding spices to a bland everyday" (Kirshenblatt-Gimblett 1991; hooks 1992); however, her representation of Ecuadorian heritage is both exoticizing and empowering (Bunten 2008), in that it utilizes essentialist tropes to pursue equal standing for her Ecuadorian heritage vis-à-vis Italian tradition.

In discussing the decline of Italian artisanry, Stella concedes that the influx of mass-produced cheap imports has not fully succeeded in erasing local aesthetic tradition. "I went to Florence and Venice," she says, "and I was stunned by the artwork there." Yet Ecuador, her home country, is just as beautiful: "Ecuador may be small, but we have all sorts of incredible landscapes." By creating an essential connection between Ecuador's landscape and its folk culture, she contends that this country is capable of generating the same sensuous cultural and aesthetic pleasures as Italy—an essential qualification of viable nationhood in the eyes of many Italians. On the same breath, Stella also proudly suggests that the beauty of Ecuadorian artisan production is on par with that of Italy's own heritage: "Going back to my home country I found just as much beauty there." The difference, she argues, is that "while beautiful things in Venice or Florence cost millions, in Ecuador things are much cheaper." Stella is right in identifying local artisanry as the root of Italian artistic and historical heritage: the beauty and renown of cities like Venice and Florence, but also the richness and the worldwide standing of contemporary Italian design stems historically from

the labor of small artisan *botteghe* (workshops) that provided local aristocrats with the paintings, statues, frescoes, tapestries, and furnishings but
also the fabrics, jewelry, and leathers they needed in order to impress their
rivals as well as their subjects, thus legitimizing their privilege. The jewelry
Stella sells is considerably more democratic, though. Even as she aims to
make sure that her artisans' work is paid properly, Stella wants her jewelry
to become available to Italians at accessible prices, thus catering to a dis-
cerning cosmopolitan taste that prizes exotic beauty and handcrafted originality over the cachet of famous brands and high prices. Not only does
Stella turn Ecuadorian "roots" into global "routes" (Storey 2003), but she
prospects the potential for Ecuadorian "routes" to become part of Italy's
own "roots." Her view of Ecuador's folk culture as the lymph that can
revitalize Italy's own ailing artisanry proposes a transnational revisitation
of the Romantic idea of the "folk" as a primordial and highly vital culture
that is not just rooted in local nature and buried deeply within its own
society (Eagleton 2000: 25), but is also, in Stella's model, available to be
transfused into another, less vital national milieu in need of rebuilding its
core.

Primordializing Hybridity

If talented Latin American indigenous people can be imagined as the "folk"
that can replenish Italy's dwindling artisanry, the task of repositioning
Islam at the core of the Italian mosaic of cultures is considerably more
challenging. In contemporary Italy, Latin American immigrants may be
marginal to dominant representations of European whiteness; Muslims,
however, are almost invariably envisioned as perpetuating backward lifeways that are downright antithetical to local culture (Sartori 2000). As elsewhere in the Western world, much of this hostility is due to post-9/11
anxieties (Triandafyllidou 2006). Yet in Italy this enmity goes back at least
a thousand years. Situated at the center of the Mediterranean, over the
centuries the Italian peninsula has been exposed to constant contacts—both
peaceful and belligerent—with Arabic and Turkish populations. Inevitably,
it is in the coastal cities like Genoa that the Muslim presence was felt the
most, with the latter alternating between the role of merchants and sailors
bringing in spices and exotic merchandise and that of marauding pirates.

Genoa's earliest experience with Muslims as the Enemy dates back to the time when, between 934 and 935 A.D., the city was looted and destroyed by Arabs who terrorized and displaced its inhabitants (Epstein 1996: 14). This first encounter set the tone for subsequent centuries of enmity, wars, and mutual piracy. However, even though throughout European history the struggles with Muslims of various provenances had frequent religious overtones, for Genoese merchants the desire to obtain access to spices, silks, and gems invariably trumped pious considerations. Hence, even as their devoted fellow citizens rushed to participate in their holy crusades, profit-oriented Genoese entrepreneurs had few qualms about trading with Arabs and Turks. And what could not be obtained from Muslim traders peacefully was often forcibly extracted from them by Genoese pirates (Epstein 1996). This is why, on some Mediterranean shores, the Genoese earned a dubious reputation comparable to that of Muslim pirates along Italy's coasts.

In the popular memory of many contemporary Genoese, however, the well-documented connections between their merchant ancestors and Muslim populations from across the Mediterranean have been erased along with the awareness of Genoa's own tradition of piracy. In vernacular retellings of medieval history, the trope of war often obscures that of commerce, and what remains after this distillation process is the memory of the Muslim Enemy—a memory that, since the 1980s, gained momentum through the rise of xenophobic sentiments against immigrants from Maghreb, Senegal, and Nigeria, and further intensified after 2001. This is when, bolstered by the Huntington-inspired language of Silvio Berlusconi's conservative government and his media empire, the dominant feeling became one of the impending threat to "Western civilization" and its "Judeo-Christian roots" allegedly posited by the Muslim presence.[10]

In today's Genoa, Moroccans, Tunisians, and the Senegalese form some of the largest immigrant communities (Erminio 2004: 57), living and working side by side with the Genoese as well as with Latin Americans, Asians, and other Africans. However, political propaganda keeps kindling anxieties about the Muslim danger. The ensuing phobia translates, among others, in the ongoing attempt to deny Muslim immigrants a place of their own in the city—for example, by consistently sabotaging all attempts to build a mosque. In recent years, plans to establish a worship center for local Muslims in the working-class Lagaccio neighborhood have been met with open hostility both by the right-wing and by part of the local (and traditionally left-wing) population, who vehemently invited the city's progressive elites to allot space for the mosque in their own posh neighborhoods. As Genoese Muslims continue to pray in garages and empty storage rooms, new plans are slowly developing for the creation of a mosque in the port area, where in centuries bygone one such building already existed. Yet few Genoese are aware of the historical existence of a mosque in their own city, and many continue to cultivate representations of the Muslim as the threat from elsewhere. Such imagery is supported, among others, by everyday retellings of stories about Muslim pirates as Genoa's longstanding nemesis: stories that are frequently prompted by architectural considerations whereby the built environment provides a sensuous support for a practice of remembering as a way of organizing and managing the past in light of the present (Storey 2003: 84).

As the story goes, the medieval vicoli of Genoa's centro storico are so narrow, dark, and damp because these qualities made it easier for residents to pour scorching hot oil on marauding Muslim pirates. Had it not been for these enemies, the city would have looked very different: more spacious, luminous, hygienic, and above all safer, thus cultivating an accessibility that would have preempted many of its problems in centuries to come. Spun around the cityscape, the exclusionary reading of Genoa's roots organizes righteous selves and dangerous others along the lines of a defensible space to be experienced on a daily basis: a phantomic space whose materiality contributes in the generation and transmission of affect (Navaro-Yashin 2012)—fear, in the first place. In narratives such as this, the cityscape serves as a material referent for an affective imaginary whereby the city is molded around the need to keep out the Muslim Enemy, and as it does so it has no option but to deny itself the modern qualities that would have made it more comfortable, sanitary, and safe for the ease of its contemporary residents.

In the face of much Genoese lore that posits Islam as the historical Other that has to be kept out of the city at all costs, the Suq installs a deeply hybrid version of an imaginary Moroccan bazaar right at the heart of Genoa's popular Porto Antico marina, just a few steps away from its centro storico and less than a mile from its modern, "European" downtown. In so doing, it interpellates local and national claims to Europeanness (Chambers 2008: 34), thus proposing an interpretive axis for Italian and Genoese culture that is deeply ensconced in the latter's Mediterranean milieu. This take is reinforced by frequent events that cast a different light on the cultures of Islam and their local connections. One such example was the talk delivered by Alireza Naser Eslami, an architectural historian who teaches at the local university. Eslami used the forum of the Suq to popularize notions that would have otherwise been confined almost exclusively to academic audiences, thus spinning an alternative narrative web around the cityscape of medieval Genoa: one whereby the Muslim presence in the centro storico is not that of an external enemy, but rather that of a co-creative inspiration.

Addressing an enraptured audience on a warm June afternoon, Eslami spoke about the extent to which the pristine layout of medieval Genoa is indebted to Arabic urban models. According to Eslami, this early connection is demonstrated by some of Genoa's most ancient typologies as well as toponyms: "A commercial space such as this souk belongs to Byzantine and Arabic areas. As a matter of fact, what we know as *bottega* (shop), *magazzino* (storehouse), and *fondaco* (warehouse) are all urban structures molded after an Eastern template. Even the words have an Eastern etymology, [as they derive] from the Byzantine *apotheke* and the Arabic *machsan* and *fondoq*." The etymological evidence was compelling: magazzino, fondaco, and bottega are common use Italian words that few would identify as foreign. Tracing an Eastern, let alone Arabic origin for them was an act that could not go unnoticed. Floating from booth to booth, many visitors began to trickle into the piazza where Eslami was speaking. Soon enough, all seats were taken. Standing onlookers crowded the space around the audience. Eslami continued: "There is a fourteenth-century Florentine merchant manual that lists all the trade locations around the Mediterranean. When it comes to Genoa, it mentions the *bazarrà arabo*, the Arabic bazaar. In the Islamic world, a market square where people sell but also socialize is known as *raiba*, and one of the few piazzas in Medieval Genoa is called Piazza Raibetta, which follows the typology of the Arabic market plaza." By then, the whole Suq had gone quiet. Nobody was paying attention to the colorful wares any longer; even the vendors had temporarily left their stalls to listen to his talk. Piazza Raibetta is only a few yards away from the location of the Suq; possibly, many visitors remembered crossing it on their way to the festival. Having caught the undivided attention of his audience, Eslami went on to dispel a well-known myth about Genoa: "Urban historians have been all too eager to brand Genoa as a city devoid of communal spaces. This is not true. It is true that, with a few exceptions, until the nineteenth century Genoa did not have the piazzas that are typical of other Italian cities. The lack of piazzas has generated this inaccurate categorization. However, Muslim cities have no plazas, either. Instead, they have blind alleys—just like Genoa. This is an urban planning culture with which the Genoese have had contacts since early on: in the year 1000, Genoese merchants are reported in Egyptian cities; the road between Costantinopolis and Tabriz was known as the Road of the Genoese. When they go back to their home city, these Genoese bring back with them the organization of urban space. The building of the Sottoripa arcades, for example, begins in 1133, and its model is the byzantine arcade. Even the structure of the Genoese port is Arabic and Byzantine, and the arsenal has an Arabic origin, just like the word that defines it." "Genoa," Eslami concluded, "is the end product of the sedimentation of different ideas about other cities"; in the specific case with these "other cities" being urban formations from all over the Southern and Eastern Mediterranean.

By intervening in the narratives surrounding Genoa's primordial encounters with the Eastern and the Southern Mediterranean, Eslami selected "trade" over "war," thus recrafting the centro storico's phantomic spatialities into architectural formations that emerged out of collaboration rather than conflict. Even Genoa's notorious lack of communal spaces, in his reading, was not a deficiency caused by a local character flaw (the alleged introversion of the Genoese), but rather the signal of a radical openness to the world, and the manifestation of a cultural difference endowed with its own dignity and reason to be. Furthermore, by demonstrating the Byzantine and Arabic influence on Genoa's primordial and yet still visible architecture and layout, Eslami provided his audiences with an alternative version of atavistic urban narratives: one whereby the roots of Genoa and its merchant culture are deeply intertwined with those of Middle Eastern and North African cities. The much-feared Other was repositioned at the core of the city's own highly recognizable everyday life—its streets, its arcades, even its businesses and storehouses; as the alien was found to be inextricable from the familiar, one could begin to question dominant dichotomies. Eslami's reading of ancient Genoa as a city modeled after Islamic templates was yet another transruption (Hesse 2000: 15) that challenged hegemonic claims about the essential purity of Italian civilization. Positioning Islamic culture not at the margins but rather inside the very core of Genoa's most ancient vestiges was an apt move in the attempt to turn the utopian hybridity of the Suq as a project for a future society into a *historical fact* supported by topographic and linguistic evidence, but also and above all a sensuous reality of which the Genoese are reminded on a daily basis by the physical immediacy of the built environment.

Figure 14. "Middle Eastern" Genoa: the Sottoripa arcade. Photo by author.

A Tradition Worth Saving

Consistent with its strategy of translating explicit political language into implicit sensuous experience, the 2002 edition of the Suq hosted a peculiar and all-Genoese character: a small farmer who, dressed in a medieval outfit, pushed a cart full of basil plants for sale, spreading the herb's tangy scent to all corners of the Suq. And when people stopped to peruse, smell, and purchase his basil, the "basil man" instructed them on the uniqueness of his herb—the only one that should ever be used for an authentic pesto sauce—and thanked them for supporting local small farmers. The basil in his cart was labeled "*basilico di Prà*": a local variety known for its peculiar aromatic qualities and for being an essential ingredient in the traditional recipe for pesto sauce, Genoa's flagship dish and the object of local celebrations such as the Pesto Olympiads. Leaving behind a trail of basil scent, the farmer's presence at the Suq was an unequivocally patriotic message to anyone who had been privy to the "pesto war" (*guerra del pesto*) which, at that time, was unfolding between food multinational Nestlè and Genoa's basil farmers, city administrators, business owners, consumers, and concerned citizens.

In May 2002, Nestlè had announced that it was going to commercialize a pesto sauce produced with foreign basil, which it would sell under the label of *pesto alla genovese*. This communiqué came as a slap in the face of Genoese basil producers and city administrators, who had engaged in a longstanding struggle with the European Union to pursue the D.O.P. (*Denominazione di Origine Protetta*, or Protected Origin Denomination) appellation for Genoa's Prà basil: a designation that would sanctify the connection between the local basil variety and its place of origin by making it impossible for basil producers located elsewhere to label their herbs "basilico di Prà." While the genuine Genoese pesto recipe calls for basil farmed on Genoa's Prà hill, Nestlè's industrial pesto contained German and French greenhouse varieties; to make things worse, the multinational had patented these two herbs with the very Ligurian names of "Sanremo," a well-known town in the Riviera, and "Pesto." Following a notoriously common corporate strategy (Black 2012: 147), Nestlè was attempting to create an imaginary association between its own pesto sauce and patented basil varieties and Ligurian flavors, toponyms, and soil, thus compounding the economic damage to local basil farmers and pesto producers with a challenge to local identity politics for which "authentic" pesto is both a deeply rooted cultural symbol and a culinary badge of honor.[11]

The backlash was immediate, and it was bipartisan. Conservative Liguria Region president Sandro Biagiotti declared a boycott against Nestlè products. COOP, Italy's foremost supermarket chain and a close ally of the Italian Left, announced it would pull all Nestlè basil products from its Ligurian stores. Genoese and Italian newspapers ran headlines on a pesto war where Genoese small farmers took on the role of a courageous David challenging a corporate Goliath. Faced with a reaction that threatened to tarnish its image and cut into its revenues, Nestlè backed off. In a full-page ad it published in the local newspaper *Il Secolo XIX*, the corporation announced it would change the names of its patented basil varieties to respect the sensibilities of Genoese consumers and to safeguard Ligurian basil producers. In 2005, Prà's basil finally obtained the D.O.P. appellation from the European Union, thus making it illegal for farmers utilizing different seed or growing their crops outside of Genoa to use this denomination.[12] As long as the pesto war raged, however, the act of wearing a medieval costume and selling Prà basil at the Suq was not just a shrewd marketing move by a small farmer. In this context, the basil man's medieval costume added value to the herbs he was selling by primordializing basil and connecting it to local history, in an implicitly polemic stance on the importance of local food in producing and consuming heritage in the face of the globalizing forces of corporate capitals (Leitch 2003).[13] With his peculiar costume and his fragrant plants, the basil man was an integral component of the "experience economy" (Richards 2011: 1228) that characterizes the Suq: one whereby goods and services are enriched by providing customers with sensuous experiences as well as an invitation to exercise political awareness. Furthermore, the basil man proposed an alternative model of local heritage. While his medieval costume evoked the notion of "tradition," he did not tap the popular conservative rhetoric that posits local lore as beleaguered by an increasingly multiethnic society (Dematteo 2011; Guano 2010a). The "cultural anxiety" he manifested did not target cultural pluralism, as it often happens (Grillo 2002); instead, it astutely isolated corporate globalization as the real source of uncertainty (Grillo 2002: 158). In his quest to raise awareness about the plight of Genoese farmers, the basil man quietly positioned his presence at the Suq as that of one tradition, one culture, and one small-scale business out of many—all of which were conjoined in the attempt to resist the onslaught of transnational corporations.

Alternative Consumptions

A common theme in urban studies is the concern regarding how corporations have inscribed onto cityscapes an alienated, top-down, and highly consumable version of "culture" that is meant to maximize profits even as it commercializes the everyday of residents and tourists alike (Dicks 2004; Zukin 1996; Richards 2011; Ritzer 2010). Multicultural festivals, in particular, have been found to feed into similar dynamics by proposing an aesthetically pleasurable performance of "difference" that, instead of facilitating a shift in political awareness, can be written off as a frivolous, ephemeral experience that commoditizes "culture" and reinforces existing stereotypes (Harvey 1988, 1990; hooks 1992; Staeheli, Mitchell, and Nagel 2009; Zukin 1996). In this chapter, however, I highlight some of the nuances that may complicate the boundary between commodification and acceptance, between stereotype and transgression, and between othering and acknowledging, as "culture" is put on display not only for public enjoyment and consumption but also for public recognition. I thus follow John and Jean Comaroff's (2009: 26) exhortation to appreciate the contradictions intrinsic to a marketing of ethnic identities whereby the Faustian bargain that may bring about alienation, stereotyping, and self-parody also carries the potential to "(re)fashion identity, to (re)animate cultural subjectivity, to (re)charge collective self-awareness, to forge new patterns of sociality, all within the marketplace." Just as importantly, I also argue that the reification and commodification of heritage at the hands of Suq organizers and participants is a strategy of resistance against forms of corporate commerce that are undermining the livelihood of large segments of the local population.

While analyzing the Suq against the backdrop of much social-scientific literature on urban spectacle, it bears remembering that the Suq is not the result of corporate choices; in fact, at its core its spatial and commercial typology stands in stark contrast to the globalized corporate spatialities that are sprouting all over Italy: shopping malls and outlets in the first place. As they take over Italy's dismissed industrial areas, these "cathedrals of consumption" (Ritzer 2010) herald the spread of a global economy whereby small businesses and local production are increasingly replaced by large franchises and their imported goods. Most importantly, the shopping malls that have become popular since the early 2000s have triggered important changes in Italian society as a whole. This is the case especially in cities like Genoa, where the deindustrialization that began in the late 1970s was somewhat buffered through the creation of a plethora of small businesses, mostly established by laid-off industrial workers with little hope of finding new employment. In recent years, Italy's small business owners have been crushed by taxation levels and a bureaucratic maze that have few matches in the rest of Europe (Guano 2010a), by stifling credit restrictions, and by a recession, often losing their livelihood to shopping malls and large stores that can afford to sell similar goods at lower prices even as they offer additional services such as free transportation and parking. The result is the rapid disappearance of family-owned stores, and the progressive impoverishment of what used to be a large sector of Italian society (Ginsborg 1990; Scarpellini 2001, 2007).

The spatiality of the Suq, I suggest, emerges as a polemic alternative against the backdrop of such transformations in the Italian economy and its urbanscapes. Since their creation in the early 2000s, for example, Genoa's shopping malls like Fiumara or the inland Serravalle Designer Outlet have captured the attention of a large number of consumers. Both spaces are examples of the non-places of super modernity (Augé 1995): captive spaces where consuming is the only possible activity (Goss 1993; Guano 2002). Carved out of a former industrial area in the city's western periphery, Fiumara is a mid-size shopping mall whose nondescript interior could be situated anywhere in the world; just like most malls, Fiumara hosts popular retail chains, a large grocery store, and multiple movie theaters, and has become a popular hangout for teenagers and families alike. The Serravalle Designer Outlet—Europe's largest and one of the first to materialize in Italy—is a quaint stucco replica of an Italian village. Its design is the result of complex workings of transnational imagination: with its plastic geranium plants, its fake balconies, and perfunctory Venetian bridges, it echoes the Italianate genre that is popular in north Atlantic countries (Goss 1993). Yet visitors to the Serravalle Outlet are not traveling to an imaginary Tuscany; on the contrary, they are being transported to a non-place (Augé 1995) from where they can experience a sanitized upscale Italianness as seen through a North Atlantic lens: an Italianness that is reinforced through the Prada, Armani, and Versace goods sold at bargain prices.[14]

What the Suq and Genoa's Outlet have in common is their nostalgic rendition of marketplaces from a different place and a different time (Goss 1993: 30). After all, the Suq, too, draws a fictional landscape into the globalized space of Genoa's Porto Antico waterfront, creating a hybrid orientalist bazaar where one can feast on pakoras, kebab, and tacos while listening to a debate on global warming. In this respect, both the Suq and Genoa's malls emerge from a reification of culture that is increasingly common in the

Figure 15. The Serravalle Designer Outlet. Photo by author.

insular, themed, and above all consumable spaces of "fantasy cities" around the world blending "edutainment" with "eatertainment" and "shoppertainment" (Hannigan 1998: 81). Indeed, the Suq sells "culture," too, in the form of sensuous experiences (Richards 2011) wrought around things that, in most cases, can be purchased. Yet what sets the Suq aside is its conspicuous opposition to corporate branding and the exclusionary dynamics of shopping malls, where no small—let alone ethnic—entrepreneur could ever afford to rent a venue. Against the global landscapes of consumption posited by shopping malls and outlets, the Suq proposes a model of retailing and consumption characterized by an "aesthetic economy" (Crane and Bovone 2006) from below whereby locally produced crafts and exotic imports sold by members of vulnerable sectors of local society such as small farmers, artisans, and immigrant entrepreneurs posit an alternative to the logos and the mass-produced brands of large retail chains.

An analysis of the messages disseminated by the Suq and its participants cannot but raise questions about how such spatiality mediates the delicate relationship between "commerce" and "culture." In a scholarship informed by Frankfurt school tenets, these are the frequently juxtaposed terms of a dichotomy that praises the aesthetic freedom of the latter while condemning the vulgar pursuit of profit of the former (Jackson 2002). Indeed, the Suq promotes commerce, too; however, it is hardly a corporate mall. Instead, it is an attempt to create an enjoyably hybrid and inclusive "third place" (Oldenburg 1991) where people from different ethnic groups can pursue cultural recognition even as they get a chance to support their small businesses under a welcoming cosmopolitan canopy (Anderson 2012). Undeniably, the Suq falls under the purview of the production of urban visitability, in that it utilizes a sensuous multiculturalism for the sake of offering consumable experiences to its visitors (Staeheli, Mitchell, and Nagel 2009; Dicks 2004). The model it follows, however, is one of ethical shopping (Miller 2001) whereby commerce supports, rather than overwhelms, opportunities for cultural and political change, even as it offers an alternative to dominant forms of consumption.

Strategic Orientalism and Subversive Hybridity

In her assessment of multicultural festivals, Barbara Kirshenblatt-Gimblett (1991: 428) warned against aestheticized representations of difference.[15] She argued that, since spectacle displaces analysis and occults issues of conflict and marginalization, the act of creating appealing displays of culture at festivals aestheticizes marginality even as it triggers orientalistic voyeurism. Cast in the static light of a perennial holiday (Kirshenblatt-Gimblett 1991: 420), the ethnic groups on display are caught in a "banality of difference" that glosses over important issues, making them inconsequential (Kirshenblatt-Gimblett 1991: 433). Writing more recently about the compartmentalized sensoria of multicultural Canada, Lalaie Ameeriar (2012) argued that the acceptance of exotic food at festivals does not translate in their integration into a more inclusive citizenship. Indeed, as a multicultural festival, the Suq, too, provides aestheticized renditions of difference with its multisensory attempts to catch its visitors' attention. In doing so, however, it utilizes a format for cultural recognition that, consistent with dominant ways of evaluating selves and others on the basis of delectability, utilizes the senses in assessing the worth of difference vis-à-vis local sensorial preferences and aesthetic identifications. Its purpose is to show that, when it comes to food and artisanry, immigrant cultures are on par with Italy's own national and regional heritage, and are thus worthy not just of positive recognition but also of a place of their own in an updated and dynamically hybrid version of this country's mosaic of cultures.

By utilizing the pedagogical format of the sensuous display (Buchli 2002: 6; Howes 2003: 52; Mukerji 2012: 509), the Suq traces its imaginary genealogy to Italian rural fairs whose festive dimension has a broad folksy appeal, even as the events strategically inculcate their attendees with sensuous pleasures along with appreciation and pride for local culture as part of a pedagogy of national cohesion. Just like rural fairs, the Suq is meant to support segments of Italian society that are increasingly at risk of being squashed by corporate commerce: from ethnic artisans and small-business owners to Italian small farmers. As it does so, the Suq implements a sui generis strategic orientalism (Scherer 2001) that exploits the practice of consuming alterity as a platform for the creation of a hybrid imaginary that disturbs dominant cultural hierarchies. Not only do the alternative forms of consumption encouraged by the Suq support small businesses in the face of corporate behemoths, but they also provide an arena from which it becomes possible to imagine new configurations of selves and others in the face of rampant cultural essentialisms (Grillo 2002). At the Suq, vibrant indigenous folk cultures from Latin America can be imagined as coming to the aid of Italy's ailing artisanry, the medieval core of an all-Italian city reveals its pristine Muslim soul, and food grammars are scrambled to give way to cosmopolitan recipes where culinary traditions from overseas are presented not as static alien objects, but rather as dynamic sensuous trajectories toward a renewed and more inclusive self. As roots blend with routes, cultural pasts, presents, and futures can be reorganized along the lines of a radical hybridization project that, while providing no guarantees on how it will be received, may become all the more possible in that it can not only be imagined, but also and above all experienced in the sensuous here-and-now.

Conclusion

> When consulted about Marozia's destiny, an oracle said: "I see two
> cities, one of the mouse, one of the swallow." Thus was the oracle
> interpreted: today Marozia is a city where everybody runs through
> tunnels of lead like packs of mice stealing from each other's mouth
> the leftovers fallen from the teeth of more threatening mice; however,
> a new century is about to begin during which everybody in Marozia
> will fly like swallows in the summer sky, playfully calling each other.
> Their wings stretched out wide, they will spin around proudly,
> cleaning up the air from mosquitos and fruit flies. "It is time for the
> century of the mouse to end and for that of the swallow to begin,"
> said the most resolute ones.
> —Italo Calvino (1972)

The professional trajectory of environmentally minded poet, festival organizer, and Suq presenter Massimo Morasso epitomizes the challenges
encountered by the creative Genoese who, inspired by Genoa's revitalization, have contributed their talents and efforts to transforming the public
image of the city and establishing its culture industry. As far as he can
remember, Massimo always had a strong interest in poetry as well as environmental issues. Years later, he still tells of how he managed to pursue his
dreams even though the odds were stacked against him. For one, his family
had none of the connections that are necessary to launch a career in Genoa's cultural sector; furthermore, Massimo had no interest in pursuing a
job as a high school teacher like most Italian poets do. Even had he wanted
to, a saturated teaching job market would have been a powerful deterrent

anyway. At that time, Massimo did what was expected of any sensible young adult: with the help of a relative, he obtained stable white-collar employment in the shipping sector. Yet, even though this was a well-paid job, it definitely did not match his talents and aspirations. Ten years later Massimo persuaded an engineering cooperative to develop an environmental communication division and hire him as a consultant. This was a fortunate move: within a couple of years, Massimo's team was awarded a large European Union grant for the creation of an environmental science museum. In 2000, he and his team opened a science center in a seaside village that had suffered from the devastating impact of a shipwreck. In his capacity as the museum director, Massimo established a reputation for himself; most importantly, he built a network that, when funding for the museum ran out in 2002, helped him land a managerial position at the first edition of Genoa's prestigious Science Festival. The latter position kept being renewed year after year, thus allowing him the time to write and publish his poems and essays even as he pursued his activist goals as an environmentalist. Like most Genoese initiatives, however, even the Festival della Scienza was affected from the downturn in the global and the local economy, and after 2008 its budget thinned out considerably. To make things worse, Massimo's project for another science center collapsed in 2014 after the death of its main sponsor. The bills kept coming, though; when I met him again in 2015, Massimo informed me that he had had no choice but to extend the scope of his activities as event organizer to more highly visible cities. He was now taking frequent trips to Venice and Monaco—two cities from where it is easier to attract national and international sponsors. "For all its hopes, Genoa is still a marginal city. Here, the creative offer significantly outweighs the city's actual possibilities," he told me with a nonchalant smile and just a hint of sadness.

The undulating line drawn by Massimo's biography reproduces the alternating cycles of hope and disappointment in the lives of those who believed that Genoa's conversion to an economy of culture could solve all of this city's problems. After the crisis of the 1970s and the struggles of the 1980s, the promise of revitalization kindled the belief that a solution to this city's woes was near, and that times were ripe to initiate forms of small-scale entrepreneurship in line with Genoa's presumably luminous destiny as a cultural tourism destination. In the face of the city's ongoing deindustrialization, a sequence of great events (the Expo of 1992, the Group of Eight summit of 2001, and the Capital of European Culture program of

2004) brought about waves of hopefulness that went along with the deep changes in the built environment. Historical buildings were renovated, and forty-two of them obtained UNESCO World Heritage status; plazas were repaved and pedestrianized, and the centro storico was repopulated and reintegrated into the city's everyday even as it retained its great diversity and some of its dubious reputation. Furthermore, the Porto Antico waterfront reestablished the long-severed connection between downtown Genoa and the sea; once restored, the majestic Palazzo Ducale began hosting art exhibitions that attracted large publics and developed a thick agenda of public symposia. This is the setting against which, with the help of talented individuals like Massimo, a variety of festivals proliferated in downtown Genoa, and the Suq became a popular yearly recurrence. As the promise of cultural tourism seemed to gain momentum, hope kept rising among segments of Genoa's under- and unemployed intellectual workforce. Mostly children of working- and middle-class families, the latter were often bereft of the patronage and the kinship ties that, in a city tightly controlled by a close-knit oligarchy of bourgeois families and political parties, were needed to secure the kind of employment that would match their aspirations and skills. Many of these individuals were women: a social category that had traditionally been kept at the margins of the job market even in more financially secure times, and that, when the local student population shrank due to the demographic crisis, lost access to its traditional source of employment in the local school system.

Prodded by the salvific underpinnings of neoliberal urbanism (Anderson and Holden 2008), in the 1980s a new urban imaginary emerged that cast consumable versions of "culture" at the forefront of a promise of collective progress and a general improvement of the conditions of life. After more than a decade of diffuse blight, by the late 1990s many Genoese were willing to trust that Genoa could finally recover its economic prowess as one of Italy's most important cities. The lingering tightness of the job market required inventiveness and flexibility; hence, new professional and self-employment niches emerged that pivoted on Genoa's rising economy of culture. Among these were the walking-tour guides, the street antique dealers, the event organizers, the artisans, and the small business owners who are among the protagonists of this book—and are all somewhat unusual subjects for an urban ethnography.

Taking on an explicitly Marxist approach, much research in urban anthropology has historically focused on poverty and social exclusion, thus highlighting a type of agency that almost inevitably rhymes with resistance. In this book, however, I diverged from this well-trodden path to shift my attention to middle-class individuals as members of a still relatively under-studied social sector that nonetheless plays an important role in city life. While much urban studies literature casts middle-class subjects exclusively as consumers (see, e.g., Ley 1996; Featherstone 2007; Smith 1996; Zukin 1989, 1991, 1996), I explored how the latter may instead become producers and purveyors of symbolic goods and cultural services. I also argued that the protagonists of this ethnography exercised their agency by contributing to the substantial makeover of Genoa's public image through practices set against the backdrop of large-scale revitalization processes. My goal was to show how members of these middling urban sectors were able to take advantage of some of the ongoing social, cultural, and economic transformations that fall under the rubric of neoliberalism: after all, as Carla Freeman (2014) observed, the latter has a degree of geographical and cultural malleability that, under some circumstances, may be productively exploited even by middle classes. Recent anthropological research showed this to be the case especially for the rising middling sectors of emergent economies (Freeman 2014; Hoffman 2010; Leshkowich 2014; Liechty 2003; O'Dougherty 2002; Srivastava 2014; Zhang 2010); however, the fate of older middle classes is considerably more varie-gated. By the late twentieth and the early twenty-first century, some of the latter were experiencing a decline that matched that of the state-run industri-alization projects that had brought them into existence in the first place (Guano 2002; Heiman 2015; Heiman, Liechty, and Freeman 2010; Newman 1999; Patico 2008). Genoa's middle classes certainly belong to this category. However, as I sought to demonstrate in this book, their attempts to latch on to the new market for cultural and symbolic goods and services also bore fruits—at least for some, and at least for a time.

Small-scale entrepreneurialism has a long-standing tradition in Italy (Blim 2001; Ginsborg 1990, 2003; Scarpellini 2001, 2007; Yanagisako 2002). In the Genoa of the twentieth century, the creation of a small business owned and staffed by an individual or at most by a handful of family mem-bers was a viable alternative to salaried labor, especially in times of penury. This trend intensified when, with the onset of deindustrialization in the early 1970s, much of Genoa's workforce had to deal with rising unemploy-ment rates; at that time, it was not uncommon for laid-off blue-collar workers to open small shops selling dairy, newspapers, or cigarettes, or to become electricians, plumbers, or repair people. Unemployed middle-class individuals instead often opted for selling goods with a symbolic aura, such as apparel, accessories, and home decor. Twenty years later, the trend toward small-scale entrepreneurship took on a new turn when, spurred by an infusion of hope, some middle-class Genoese began to utilize the circumstances of their city's revitalization to create professional and business opportunities for themselves. As they supported the passionate urbanity that characterizes the public life of Italian cities, the renovations, pedestrianizations, and overall architectural transformations that unfolded in downtown Genoa helped generate venues of creative self-employment as a largely immaterial labor infused with symbolic and affective connotations (Freeman 2014; Hardt and Negri 2000, 2004; Heiman, Liechty, and Freeman 2010; Hochschild 1983). Drawing on classed and, at times, gendered skills and knowledge types, a new cohort of street antique dealers, walking-tour guides, artisans, and small business owners began crafting and commercializing symbolic goods and services to be consumed as part of an aestheticized urban everyday. The city they brought into being is a multifarious and exciting trove of "hidden" treasures waiting to be discovered. These are characterized by the authoritative facets of history and high culture and the nostalgic ones of folklore, by the sensory lures of crafts and the reassuring aura of "made in Italy" goods, by layers of exoticism and antiquity, and by an intricate tapestry of diversity and tradition. What Genoa's revitalization gave these individuals was not just a chance to earn a living in an economy where other employment opportunities were denied to them, but also and most importantly the option to do so in a way they found both meaningful and rewarding.

As the protagonists of Genoa's newly found tourism vocation, the walking-tour guides, event organizers, street antique dealers, artisans, and small business owners described in this ethnography formed a sui generis "creative class" (Florida 2012): one that contributed to remaking the city from the bottom up by cultivating its economy of culture. However, unlike that of Florida's highly mobile yuppies, the vocation of Genoa's talents was born out of the impossibility or unwillingness to relocate. Most importantly, if compared to Florida's "talents" (2012), Genoa's creative classes were quite vulnerable. Their professions were often a result of the precarity (Butler 2009) that began in the Italy of the early 1970s and pushed Genoa's working and middle classes into a state of redundancy. They were also a product of deeply ingrained social inequities reproduced through exclusionary dynamics that co-opt access to jobs and resources (Guano 2010b;

Zinn 2001). Hence, none of the stories I told in this book are of the rags-to-riches kind. In fact, by 2015 most of my ethnographic subjects were living hand-to-mouth, and this struggle did not spare even those whose talents and professionalism would have fetched, at a different time and in a different society, a more comfortable livelihood.[1] Yet in spite of all the difficulties they encountered, the protagonists of my ethnographies managed to support themselves in ways they enjoyed by drawing on their talents and sensibilities. None of them escaped precariousness; however, in an exploitative neoliberal labor market, being one's own boss and controlling not just how one works, but also and most importantly how one feels about her work, is a privilege in its own right (Freeman 2014: 210). Precarious though it may have been, this empowerment underscores a fundamental difference between the cottage-scale and independent quality of a segment of Genoa's culture industry on one hand, and the exploitation of service sector labor reported in revitalized "global" cities on the other (see, e.g., Crick 1989; Dicks 2004; Nash and Smith 1991; Zukin 1996). Hence, the role of small-scale cultural entrepreneurship in Genoa's revitalization highlights the importance of a more nuanced approach to the study of urban processes that do not necessarily follow the blueprint of North Atlantic cities.

Even though this book advocates paying closer attention to specific social, cultural, and historical settings of urban revitalization, it is by no means a global defense of its potential ramifications. Revitalization processes are unquestionably dominated by financial and political interests that extend well above the reach of most city residents. Hence, the agendas of great events may overwhelm the official promise of improving lives, thus causing hurts that are hard to heal, and the financial interests driving the aestheticization of a cityscape may contribute to the marginalization of less powerful urban actors. While Genoa's refurbished cityscape may have provided the protagonists of this ethnography with the hope they needed to find a stimulating way to earn a living, many of the choices and policies implemented over the same years at the local as well as the European level have done just as much to undermine these very same efforts and pursuits. Rapidly expanding corporate commerce has had a negative impact on small businesses as well as entire neighborhoods: since their appearance, Genoa's shopping malls and its big-box stores have ignited the decline of what, until the early 2000s, had been this city's thick web of family-owned businesses.[2] In July 2014, Genoa's storekeepers were relieved to see their municipal council vote down the project of installing yet another shopping mall within walking distance from this city's downtown; yet more shopping centers are already planned for the years to come. The recession that began in 2008 and deepened in 2011 also contributed to undermining the livelihood of Genoa's small-scale entrepreneurs: if brick-and-mortar stores have lost revenues, the business volume of the street antique dealers featured in this ethnography continues to be alarmingly low, too. In summer 2015, local newspapers reported a 23 percent growth in the number of tourists visiting Genoa.[3] Possibly caused by the proximity of Milan's World Fair, this increase did not benefit all sector operators equally. As walking-tour guides lament, new directives have granted all EU guides permission to lead tours wherever they wish without first obtaining a local license, as formerly required by the Italian law. Hence, leading groups of foreign visitors on walking tours of the city—a necessity to complement revenues from local tourism—has become increasingly difficult for Genoese guides. Furthermore, if in 2015 employment grew by 3 percent in Genoa's restoration sector, these were mostly low-paying and highly precarious contract jobs for waiting and kitchen staff.[4]

Yet, even though the wealth produced by the increased tourist flows is not evenly distributed, the news is not all grim. While some small business sectors seem to have bottomed out, others are climbing back up, catering to middle-class tastes and needs that have shifted during the recession. As they wait for the Italian government to pass a law restoring their exclusive right to lead tours in the city for which they hold a license, Genoa's guides are beginning to tap the growing tourist flows from India and China. Furthermore, working together with local small businesses, several of them are now offering tours that include a broader variety of experiential options such as cooking classes and the sampling of local wines and food specialties. As crowds of visitors finally swarm through the city, the creative resilience of members of Genoa's middle classes begins to be stirred by a cautious optimism; new small businesses are appearing in this city's centro storico, and some of the older ones are undergoing a makeover. At the time of writing these words in the fall of 2015, the recession is said to be approaching its end: speaking through the media controlled by yet another controversial government,[5] Italy's oracle has announced that the century of the swallow is about to begin. Not everyone in Genoa is ready to agree; for some, however, hope is timidly growing. A few voices are rising to claim that, if the crisis represented a temporary setback, after all these years Genoa may be finally back on its track to a luminous future.

Notes

Introduction

1. For the anthropological analysis of how urban elites contribute to shaping the city and the experiences of those who live in it, see McDonogh (1991) and Rotenberg (1995).

2. Notable exceptions include Freeman (2014), Ho (2009), and Leshkowich (2014).

3. For a discussion of performativity and non-verbal communication in the public realm, see Sennett (1977).

4. The public practice of heteronormative patriarchal desire is also the underpinning of a sexual harassment that is meant to keep women in their place (Guano 2007).

5. The stimuli of flânerie have often been described as predominantly visual (Tester 1994); however, the urban experience relies just as heavily on sound, smell, touch, and taste (Featherstone 1998; Guano 2003b; Hall 1966; Howes 2003; Rodaway 1994) along with more esoteric sensations such as ambient light and even face vision as the pressure that distant objects seem to exercise on one's body (Rodaway 1994: 49).

6. At that time, Genoese society already comprised a considerable network of family-owned businesses (Scarpellini 2007) whose status ranged from working-class to bourgeois depending not just on size and revenues, but also on the symbolic value of the goods they sold.

7. By offering a quality of education that in many cases outperformed that of private schools, Italy's public school system somewhat fostered cross-class relations by allowing working-class students to take classes along with wealthier ones.

8. Starting with the economic miracle of the 1960s, much of Genoa's working class comprised immigrants from the south of the country, who thus became targets for composite blends of ethnic and class stereotypes.

9. As Italy's largest port and one of its industrial hubs, during World War II Genoa was devastated by allied forces' bombardments.

10. http://www.creativecitiesproject.eu/en/pp/it/comunediGenova-it, accessed June 15, 2014.

11. http://www.tuttitalia.it/liguria/45-genova/statistiche/popolazione-andamento-demografico/, accessed July 10, 2015.

12. Several of my subjects asked me explicitly not to discuss their financial woes in this book. Out of respect for their privacy and the discomfort they feel at not keeping up with middle-class material standards (see also Patico 2008), I have complied with their requests.

13. To date, more Italians are alleged to live in Australia, the Americas, and Northern Europe than in Italy itself. Even though for much of the nineteenth and twentieth centuries Italians migrated to the rest of the world mainly as manual labor, the diaspora that began in the late 1900s and continues to date mainly comprises academics, professionals, and entrepreneurs who are unable or unwilling to carve a place for themselves in the clientelistic networks that control access to jobs and resources in Italian society (Gabaccia 2000).

Chapter 1

1. As of 2015, heroin is allegedly spreading again in Genoese society.

2. A television series broadcast on Italian public television channel Rai1 proposed an alternative label for this decade: *Gli anni spezzati: The Broken Years* (Diana 2013).

3. http://genova.mentelocale.it/55512-genova-genova-anni-70-movimento-pas sione/, accessed on December 17, 2013.

4. In Italy, the study of foreign languages is a gendered practice that is regarded as appropriate for women.

5. This representation was most often applied to Genoa's port workers: a "blue collar aristocracy" that, unlike other workers, enjoyed great independence in managing their own work schedule and had salaries that were considerably higher than the norm (Arvati 1994: 859).

6. The role of clientelism and nepotism in the process of assigning jobs and positions in the local public sector—from the university to the administration—is camouflaged through the rational-bureaucratic practice of holding *concorsi*: national contests where applicants are selected through allegedly objective and impersonal criteria. The latter, however, invariably allow ample room for collusion and influence peddling.

7. This shift is reflected in the rapid rise in the 1980s of the Lega Nord (Northern League) party: a revanchist North Italian party that blamed "corrupt" Southern Italian mores for all the ills in the country, and, appealing largely to small business owners from Northern Italy, pursued the secession from Rome's government and posited a "Northern" ethos of hard work and productivity (Dematteo 2011).

8. On the issue of rapidly declining fertility rates in twentieth-century Italy, see Krause (2004, 2009).

9. http://www.tuttitalia.it/liguria/45-genova/statistiche/censimenti-popolazione/, accessed on March 12, 2014.

10. Between the mid-1990s and the early 2000s, the strategy of utilizing great events to bring visibility to Genoa spawned the creation of a series of smaller events at the national and the local scale, such as the Festival of Science, the Festival of Poetry, and the Suq multicultural festival discussed in Chapter 6. These smaller events often

drew on the initiative of local "talents" who succeeded in harnessing funding from the municipality, the central government, and local and national sponsors.

11. Conducted against a contemporary art museum in Milan, the Renaissance Uffizi Gallery in Florence, and San Giorgio in Velabro and San Giovanni in Laterano, two of Rome's most famous churches, for the sake of destroying places that represent Italy's cultural and artistic legacy, the mafia bombings of 1993 underscored the role of heritage in the Italian national imaginary even as they issued their violent warning against the Italian state.

12. As of 2015, the Erzelli project is still incomplete.

13. http://www.lastampa.it/2012/07/28/economia/sos-della-cgia-centocinquanta mila-negozi-a-rischio-chiusura-nel-3WlvWypWBEcMnyCRWFx1AK/pagina.html? exp = 1, accessed on June 12, 2014.

14. The Ecuadorian immigration that began in the mid- to late 1990s was spearheaded by women who moved to Italy to sell their services as *badanti*: caregivers for a rapidly aging population. As their employment situation in the host country stabilized, Ecuadorian women began to have their children and husbands join them. Yet, while employment is relatively easy to come through for women in the domestic sector, the same is not the case for adult men. Some of the latter become construction workers (Queirolo Palmas 2005); others, instead, find themselves chronically marginalized in their host country; a few react by turning to alcoholism and anti-social behaviors. In no cases do the immigrants' educational achievements and their professional background receive any recognition in Italy. Ecuadorian children are not allowed to attend classes consistent with their age and education; lacking an adequate proficiency in Italian and in the local educational curriculum, they are often forced to attend lower grades where they do not bond with younger non-Ecuadorian children. Even if they pursue employment, they often find themselves excluded from a tenuous job market (Queirolo Palmas 2005). Several of these youth end up joining the ranks of those who are locally known, with an English acronym, as NEET: Not in Education, Employment, or Training. As a representative of the local Ecuadorian community told me, "[State bureaucracies] are blocking everything.These kids will never achieve a real qualification; they can acquire technical skills for example as artisans, but it's impossible [for them] to obtain a high school or college degree. It's absurd, because in ten years this country will depend on these kids." Given this scenario, pandillas help Ecuadorian teenagers alleviate their isolation and establish a sense of identity and belonging (Queirolo Palma 2005).

15. On the other hand, it bears mentioning that, in recent years, local newspaper *Il Secolo XIX* has started featuring articles in Spanish on issues relevant to the local Latin American community.

16. http://www.tuttitalia.it/liguria/45-genova/statistiche/popolazione-andamento -demografico/, accessed on July 10, 2015.

17. http://www.regione.liguria.it/argomenti/media-e-notizie/archivio-comunicati -stampa-della-giunta/item/35316-annuario-statistico-regionale-diminuisce-la-popo

lazione-genova-sotto-la-soglia-dei-seicentomila-abitanti-assessore-rossetti-in-aumen
to-le-famiglie-single-servono-politiche-di-sostegno-alle-donne.html, accessed on
March 12, 2014; http://www.gruppocarige.it/gruppo/html/ita/arte-cultura/la-casana/
2007_1/pdf/28_33.pdf, accessed on March 12, 2014.

Chapter 2

1. Unless otherwise noted, the reports and testimonials used in this chapter are
drawn from ethnographic interviews conducted from 2002 through 2010 with individuals who resided or worked inside the Red Zone.

2. Berlusconi's request did not sit well with many Genoese, who reacted to this
imposition by hanging underwear from their window lines for the duration of the
summit.

3. Genoa's restorations before the event cost 70 billion lire: approximately 35
billion euros (Chiesa 2001: 6). Its reconstruction after the end of the summit cost
another 8 million euros (Della Porta and Reiter 2003: 5).

4. The event was entirely managed by the national government, which marginalized Genoa's municipal administration for the duration of the summit.

5. In the days preceding the summit, electrical consumption and waste disposal
reportedly dropped by 40 percent (Della Porta and Reiter 2003: 3).

6. Continuous coverage at the local level was offered by the Genoese television
station PrimoCanale. Broadcasts on the event were provided by Italy's three public
(RAI) television channels along with Berlusconi's own Canale 5, Rete 4, and Italia
Uno. While RAI 1 and RAI 2 were tightly controlled by Berlusconi's government, RAI
3 is traditionally closer to the Italian Left. At that time, however, the latter was still
critical of the Genoa Social Forum.

7. As prospected by Jürgen Habermas in his 1989 theorization of an ideally democratic public sphere as one comprising face-to-face dialogic engagements among members of culture-debating publics (Habermas 1989), contemporary television and print
media are, indeed, characterized by a lack of participation in the process of opinion
formation. And yet, this monologic quality does not have to be an insurmountable
obstacle to democracy—provided that the pluralism and the accountability of information channels are guaranteed (Thompson 1994: 27–49). Unfortunately, both of
these conditions were denied in the organization and official coverage of the 2001 G8
summit.

8. The movements were critical of neoliberal and corporate globalization rather
than globalization as a whole (Della Porta 2006: 12).

9. For the GSF map of Genoa's red and yellow zones, see http://www.processig8
.org/GSF/redz.htm.

10. http://www.struggle.ws/global/about/yabasta.html, accessed on June 12, 2010.

11. http://struggle.ws/global/genoa/ramor.html, accessed on June 12, 2010.

12. http://www.lamiaterraan.it/pdf/ng27_05_01c.pdf, accessed on February 14,
2011.

13. http://struggle.ws/global/genoa/ramor.html, accessed on June 11, 2010.

14. As Mike Zajko and Daniel Béland (2008: 719–735) point out, the role of the police at recent international summits has increasingly become that of enforcing a territorial form of state power that is asserted through the creation of no-protest zones.

15. http://struggle.ws/global/genoa/ramor.html, accessed on June 10, 2010.

16. On July 20, Carlo Giuliani had joined the White Overalls march toward the Red Zone. In the clashes that ensued after the police had attacked the White Overalls, an army Land Rover Defender was cornered in nearby Piazza Alimonda. Carlo approached the jeep holding a fire extinguisher in his hands. From inside the jeep, carabiniere conscript Mario Placanica fired two shots, one of which hit Giuliani in the head and killed him (GSF 2001: 80–91). In the ensuing trial, Placanica claimed he had acted in self-defense; he also argued that he had aimed in the air, but a falling stone had deflected the bullet, causing it to hit Giuliani. Placanica's line of defense was accepted, and his acquittal drew much discontent from the GSF and Giuliani's parents. By then, however, Giuliani had become an icon of the movement. In 2006, a room of the Italian Parliament was dedicated to his memory. On July 20, 2011, a memorial stele was erected on the site where Carlo had been killed.

17. This is what happened, among others, to Rete Lilliput movements (mainly pacifists and feminists) assaulted by the police in Piazza Manin on July 20, as well as to the protesters who were attacked in the Foce neighborhood on July 21 (Chiesa 2001; Juris 2006).

18. As Juris (2006: 8) pointed out, small-pack actions are synonymous with a commitment to "diversity, de-centralization, and self-management."

19. If, as posited by David Waddington (2008: 675–687), violent acts committed by protesting crowds are typically guided by a rationality of their own, the question of how Black Bloc selected the targets of their attacks contributes to raising issues about this group's real affiliation and purposes.

20. http://www.struggle.ws/freeearth/genoa.html, accessed on June 12, 2010.

21. Not to be confused with the contemporary definition of "sacred" as "holy," the sacredness of tricksters is akin to the condition of those ancient Romans who, after committing a forbidden act, were deprived of their rights and could be killed by anyone (Agamben 1988: 82–84).

22. Also drawing on Taussig (1987), in his ethnography of anti-capitalist global movements Juris called Genoa in its entirety a "space of terror" brought about by "blurring the line between law and violence, order and chaos" (Juris 2006: 167–168). While I agree with Juris's argument about the liminality that emerged within this city's boundaries during the July 2001 events, here I prefer to maintain Taussig's (1987: 4) definition of "space of death in the world of the living" for the sake of emphasizing the victims' experience of the disconnect between what was happening to them and the discourse of legality and rights that continued to regulate to varying degrees the "world of the living" (Taussig 1987: 4) just a short distance away, both within and without the city limits. It is important to note that the repression peaked at specific

locations, and not all of Genoa was directly and homogeneously subjected to the terror of police violence.

23. Italian police and carabinieri officers are not required to wear visible identification.

24. On the sartorial politics of social movements and the officialdom, see Graeber (2007: 329).

25. Historically, the practice of violently suppressing public protests culminated with mid-twentieth-century *scelbismo* (named after Christian Democratic President of the Council of Ministers Mario Scelba) and became considerably less prevalent in the late 1900s (Della Porta and Reiter 2003).

26. Police officers also complained that during the summit they had to serve consecutive shifts; instead of being given time to decompress, they were fed more coffee and were sent back to confront the protesters. This supposedly led to reactions and behaviors that would not have been possible under normal circumstances.

27. It bears mentioning that not all the police officers and soldiers deployed in the G8 summit participated in the repression (Nativi 2001). In fact, throughout the battle of Genoa there were several outstanding cases of officers who succored the victims of their own colleagues' brutality (GSF 2001).

28. Ceremonies, as Victor Turner (1980) suggested, have illustrative purposes; rituals, instead, have transformative effects.

29. Here I draw on Michel Foucault's (1998) notion of heterotopia as an "other" place: that is, a segregated spatiality that helps compensate for a society's needs, crises, and desires.

30. Aside from beating whomever they encountered, the police who irrupted into the Diaz school also destroyed all of the Indymedia computers, camcorders, and equipment that contained images and testimonials of the abuses perpetrated throughout the summit, a behavior that critics interpreted as the attempt to eliminate evidence of state repression (Della Porta and Reiter 2003: 113).

31. Carlo Giuliani went on to become a controversial icon in Italy's political discourse. If the social movements and segments of the Italian Left hailed him as a hero, conservatives accused him of being a thug and attempting to attack the carabiniere who shot him in self-defense.

32. Berlusconi served a third term as President of the Council of Ministers from 2008 to 2011.

33. The Black Bloc remained just as elusive, and only ten convictions were issued to protesters found to have played a role in the destructions.

Chapter 3

The epigraph to this chapter can be found at http://genova.mentelocale.it/19073 -pettinotti-vi-racconto-i-miei-caruggi/, accessed on December 19, 2015.

1. This complexity is aptly exemplified by Michael Herzfeld's (2009) analysis of how the residents of a Roman neighborhood that is squashed between a greedy Church and an indifferent state tackle the threat of gentrification.

2. Italian laws tend to protect tenants over property owners; for example, it is extremely difficult for the latter to evict a delinquent tenant. This difficulty accounts at least in part for the remarkably high number of empty apartments scattered all over the country: some owners prefer to let their property go vacant rather than risk leasing it to a potentially delinquent tenant. According to the Italian Bureau of Statistics (ISTAT), in 2011 the percentage of unoccupied homes was at 22 percent; see http://dati-censimentopopolazione.istat.it/Index.aspx?DataSetCode = DICA_ABIT_PR_COM, accessed on August 4, 2015.

3. For a description of the woes of a former centro storico resident who lost all her social contacts after being forcibly moved to Begato, see the documentary film *Iolandia*, available at http://vimeo.com/15867688, accessed on July 20, 2014.

4. According to ISTAT, Italy has some of the highest rates of home ownership in the whole European Union. In 1999, home ownership in Italy was at 72 percent; in 2013, it reached 73.4 percent in spite of the crisis. In the same year, the percentage of leased properties was at 16.7 percent—down from 16.9 percent in 2012 and 18 percent in 2011 (http://www.istat.it/it/archivio/127996, accessed on August 5, 2015).

5. As of 2006, the centro storico hosted both the highest percentage of college graduates and the highest percentage of illiterate individuals of all Genoa; furthermore, 21.7 percent of the foreign immigrants living in Genoa resided in the centro storico, versus an average of 5.7 percent in the rest of the city (Leone 2010: 46–47).

6. http://genova.mentelocale.it/19073-pettinotti-vi-racconto-i-miei-caruggi/, accessed on September 4, 2013.

7. On the issue of fiscal receipts, see Guano 2010a.

8. For this information I am indebted to Antida Gazzola, the urban sociologist of the School of Architecture who participated in this decision.

9. In 1984, the municipality launched an initiative named Vivi il Centro Storico, which featured street theater, dance, and music performances in the caruggi. The initiative, which took place in the early summer, showcased this neighborhood's charms to adventurous local visitors.

10. "A crisis in Italy? That cannot be," Berlusconi notoriously blurted at the 2011 Group of 20 summit. "Restaurants are always full!" See http://www.lastampa.it/2011/11/05/italia/politica/berlusconi-crisi-da-noi-ma-se-i-ristoranti-sono-pieni-nDGdFNhvbgwZt7tBu2vAYM/pagina.html, accessed on March 20, 2014.

11. The Chinese migration to Italy began in the early 1980s (Ceccagno 2003). This is when the first Chinese restaurants appeared all over Genoa. Soon enough, however, Chinese business expanded into other sectors, especially leather and garment manufacturing. Like elsewhere in Europe (Pieke 2004), in Italy Chinese immigrants established themselves as "ethnic entrepreneurs" who prefer self-employment over working for Italian employers—and, in some cases, achieve a remarkable upward mobility (Ceccagno 2003). Soon enough, Chinese families began to populate Genoa's street markets as the traditional venues for frugal shoppers. The most successful among them opened stores not only in the centro storico, but also in very central, and

expensive, streets. Usually referred to by locals as *i cinesi*, such stores are characterized by a vast assortment of clothes and accessories. Some of these goods are produced in local, Chinese-owned and Chinese-operated, sweatshops; others are imported from China. All of them, however, have very competitive prices that exert a powerful draw on the general public. Yet, even though they fulfill a growing demand for affordable garments, the success of Chinese entrepreneurs has caused a degree of discontent in the host society. Unlike other ethnic groups, which may be disparaged by conservatives and Lega Nord atavists but are eagerly defended—at least in theory—by politically correct leftists, Chinese entrepreneurs and their goods encounter hostility both on the right and the left end of the Italian political spectrum.

On one hand, for sophisticated consumers boycotting Chinese goods is a matter of taste, and derogatory comments are frequently made about those who choose to wear cheap clothes that look like *roba dei cinesi* (Chinese stuff). As highbrow critics never fail to point out, the quality of Chinese garments often falls short of local tastes for textiles such as pure cotton, wool, and leather, as well as dominant standards for safety, design, and manufacturing. On the other hand, while the Italian Right has made no mystery of its xenophobic attitudes toward immigrants, the Left has been traditionally more cautious in its expressions of racism, which it frequently modulates with a façade of political correctness (Però 2007). Yet, in the eyes of their left-leaning critics, not only are Chinese businesses guilty of neglecting the fair labor relations and the laws that regulate European employment and of undermining Italy's apparel sector as a whole, but they are also suspected of customarily committing fiscal fraud: an allegation that, in contemporary Italy, is bound to generate much discontent especially among honest taxpayers and the salaried (Guano 2010a). Most importantly, Chinese businesses posit a remarkable threat to local stores, which, in the face of a declining economy and the growing impoverishment of their customers, are unable to compete with their pricing strategies. Hence, many small shopkeepers dread the appearance of a Chinese store next to their own—not just as a trigger to the depreciation of their own business, but also and most importantly as a formidable competitor.

In recent years, Genoa's left-wing mayors have put their already dwindling reputation at stake to engage in a most unpopular battle to build a mosque in low-income neighborhoods—a battle that, to date, has produced no results. No one, however, has thus far spent a word to support the small Chinese entrepreneurs who are increasingly populating the city, and who are the target of much resentment. While, as the crisis deepens, Chinese businesses hardly lack customers, politically correct leftist shoppers refuse to patronize Chinese stores. In such a stance, the desire to protect other ethnic entrepreneurs as well as Italian artisans and shopkeepers, the commitment to uphold workers' rights, and, often, a class-based appreciation for quality goods go hand in hand with an ethnic dislike that, for once, can be voiced safely.

Chapter 4

1. As of 2012, women had founded and were running 25 percent of all Italian firms (CENSIS 2013: 17).

2. Since the conservative turn of the 1980s, the hegemonic perception has been that women have achieved full parity, thus making feminist struggles redundant (Valentini 1997). Hence, the word *femminista* has taken on a negative connotation: one that conjures the ghosts of bra-burning, man-bashing fanaticism. Feminism, to most Italian women and men, has become the female equivalent of *maschilismo* (masculinism): a philosophy of prevarication grounded in gender supremacy.

3. This claim was almost as frequently bounced around by women in my parents' generation ("My husband says I don't need to work") and by my girlfriends ("Dad says Mom doesn't need to work"), thus choreographing a dance of mirrors in which man's will and his decisional power as the head of the family were the only images worth reflecting.

4. Working-class women who held jobs, instead, were relatively more likely to receive praise for "helping" their exploited husbands.

5. The longstanding tradition of Italian women's "double presence" at the workplace and at home still continues, with employed women still putting in about five and a half hours daily of domestic labor against the forty-eight minutes contributed by their husbands (Balbo 1978; Valentini 1997; Blim 2001; Neve 2002; see also Couniham 2004).

6. Questions like "Are you married?" and "Do you have children?" are customary during job interviews, and many young women resort to lying about their marital status for the sake of securing the position. Women may also be asked to sign a blank sheet that will be turned into their resignation letter should they ever get pregnant (see also Molé 2011).

7. On how capitalist discourse casts women in the role of shoppers, see also Gibson-Graham (1996).

8. As conservative President of the Council of Ministers Silvio Berlusconi frequently boasted, nowadays Italy has one of the most flexible labor laws in the entire European Union, making it much easier for companies to hire low-paid contract workers.

9. After all, as Lefebvre (1991) suggested, social space is produced out of the tension between conceptual space—space as it is conceived by planners and architects—on one hand, and perceptual space and spatial practice (space as it is perceived and utilized by its users in their daily life), on the other.

10. For the analysis of a similar dynamic in British society, see McDowell (1997).

11. Still in 2001, the unemployment rate for Italian women ages fifteen to sixty-four was 13 percent, ranking only behind Spain in the European Union. In contrast, the unemployment rate for men in Italy was 7.3 percent. The data about employment opportunities for women with university degrees are not more encouraging: in 2001, only 3.8 percent of men with college degrees had not found a job yet, whereas 7.2 percent of highly educated women were unemployed—a figure that did not include the scores of women who, upon failing to secure employment, are systematically classified as "homemakers," thus disappearing from the unemployment statistics (CENSIS

2002: 234–241). By 2011, the number of unemployed women had dropped to 9.6 percent, while that of men had risen to 7.6 percent. Rather than indexing an improvement in women's condition, however, these numbers are largely due to women's flexibility and their willingness to accept precarious employment as well as the expansion of low-paid employment opportunities in the caregiving sector due to Italy's rapidly aging population and the lack of adequate infrastructures; see Osservatorio Abi-Censis sulla società italiana 2/le donne italiane per la ripresa, http://www.censis.it, accessed on March 18, 2014.

12. On women as the bearers of their families' cultural identity, see also Domosh and Sedger (2001: 73).

13. Whereas antique and artisan fairs are a relative novelty in Genoa, their presence is customary in many other Italian cities, especially those that have been part of older and better-established tourist circuits.

14. When brick-and-mortar antique stores held the monopoly of the trade, their customer base used to comprise wealthy collectors almost exclusively. Street markets, however, attracted the attention of middle-class publics. Many of the new collectors were educated young couples and college students who had little expendable income to decorate their homes, but who, for reasons of taste as well as political inclination, were wary of the mass- (and sweatshop-) produced items sold in the discount superstores and shopping malls in the periphery of the city. The demand combined with the offer to create a new, and more affordable, category of antiques: *modernariato* (modern antiques). While valuable *alto antiquariato* eighteenth-century items were most likely to still be found in the protected environment of a store, modernariato accounted for a large share of the items circulating in the fairs.

15. As Jennifer Scanlon (2000: 201) pointed out, much of the literature on gender and consumer capitalism tends to depict women exclusively in the role of passive consumer, without paying due attention to women's agentive roles in generating consumer culture.

16. On the other hand, as several of my informants suggested, women antique dealers who go to private homes to purchase items are often seen as more trustworthy than men, and hence, if they are careful not to bargain too hard, they are more likely to secure a good deal.

17. On the politics of gender, class, and respectability in Italian society, see Guano (2007).

18. Only single women did so; however, at that time they were an underrepresented group in the street antique business.

Chapter 5

1. As one of Italy's powerful maritime. republics, for centuries Genoa was known as "La Superba."

2. http://www.itineraliguria.it/index.php?option = com_content&view = article& id = 80&Itemid = 90&lang = it, accessed on June 12, 2013.

3. Several of their biographies follow the same template: after earning a college degree in the humanities—and hence often having a strong background in local art history—these women took the *patentino* (tourist guide board license) exam while scouting the job market for any available opportunity, but especially for teaching positions or even an academic career. After being added to the roster of local licensed guides, though, several of these women were contacted by a municipal office or a tourist agency and were asked to lead a tour. For them, what had been at first an expedient turned into a source of livelihood and a professional identity. At first reluctant, they eventually realized that this was their best opportunity for earning an income.

4. http://ricerca.repubblica.it/repubblica/archivio/repubblica/2008/12/30/capita le-degli-scippi-altra-faccia-della.html, accessed on August 22, 2013.

5. A similar struggle over historical authority has been observed by Paula Mota Santos (2012) in her ethnography of walking tours in Porto. For another example of amateur historians walking the streets of their city in their quest for a peculiar spatial experience that may restore their sense of self, see Richardson (2008: 167). On amateur history as a field whose actors vie for legitimacy, see Stewart (2003).

6. Due to the growing competition among walking-tour guides, eventually ghost tours have made their appearance even in Rome, Venice, and Florence.

Chapter 6

1. http://suqfestival.wordpress.com/, accessed on August 14, 2013.

2. http://www.suqgenova.it/index.php?id = 106, accessed on August 14, 2013.

3. See, e.g., http://archiviostorico.corriere.it/2011/marzo/24/quei_Numeri_che_ Non_Tornano_co_9_110324068.shtml; http://giovanipace.sermig.org/index.php?op tion = com_content&view = article&id = 11773%3Afratelli-ditalia-litalia-se-desta& catid = 163%3Aarticoli&Itemid = 255&lang = pt; https://twitter.com/AndCappe/status /331144508093902849; http://www.onlineviaggi.it/case-vacanza/363-residence-cala -di-mola.html?format = pdf, accessed on May 10, 2013.

4. In some cases, however, sagre celebrate food types that have little to do with local production. This is the case, for example, of the *sagre della nutella* (an industrial product) that are ubiquitous on Italian territory.

5. http://www.suqgenova.it/fileadmin/progetti/Progetto_di_riqualificazione_Me rcato_del_Carmine.pdf, accessed on June 20, 2012.

6. The popularization of international travel since the 1980s has done much to promote the appreciation of "other" cuisines in Italy. Nowadays many well-traveled and highly educated middle-class Italians feel compelled to express a cosmopolitan appreciation of the gastronomic opportunities offered by a multicultural society (see also Black 2012: 130).

7. In her ethnography of Turin's Porta Palazzo produce market, Rachel Black (2012: 120) suggests that Kumalè's name derives, in fact, from the Piedmontese expression *"cum'a l'è,"* "how is it going?"

8. This oblivion also hindered the onset of a critical debate on Italian colonialism (Grillo 2002: 12), and it supports the common belief that Italians are *brava gente* (good people) and hence supposedly incapable of racism and other heinous practices.

9. In positing herself as a cultural ambassador for Ecuador, Stella implicitly questions a number of stereotypes about people from her home country. For one, she breaks the cliché that casts all Ecuadorian women as *badanti*: home caregivers for the elderly. Furthermore, she challenges dominant cultural hierarchies that position Ecuador at the margins of the civilized world. Genoa has one of the largest Ecuadorian communities in Italy; at first, this immigration, which began in 1999, was welcome for many reasons: Ecuadorians are mostly Catholic, and the first immigration waves almost exclusively comprised women who entered the domestic service sector, providing local women with the support they never received from the state (Guano 2010a) and from their male family members. Family reunions that began shortly thereafter, however, brought in Ecuadorian men and children who were not quite as welcome in their new host society. Many of the men had trouble finding employment in a country where unemployment rates are chronically high, and eventually found work in the construction sector—hardly the kind of upward mobility many of them had hoped to attain. The children began attending the local schools, often disappointed at the few opportunities that Italian society offered them in comparison to what they had expected (Queirolo-Palmas 2005; Torre 2005). While Ecuadorian women retain a steady presence in the domestic service sector, soon enough men and teenagers began being cast as a "problem." The men are blamed for the drunken brawls in the streets of the Sampierdarena neighborhood, which keep residents awake until the wee hours and leave sidewalks plastered with broken beer bottles. Ecuadorian youth, instead, are blamed for the proliferation of street gangs such as the Latin Kings, the Vatos Locos, the Manhattan, and the Los Diamantes, which terrorize Genoa's residents regardless of ethnic affiliation. In recent years, the whole Ecuadorian community has come to be branded as undesirable—that is, lacking the culture required for it to be perceived as on equal footing with its host society.

10. Berlusconi's speechwriters were known for drawing heavily on the polarizing language of U.S. conservatives (Shin and Agnew 2008). This included Samuel P. Huntington's (1996) inflammatory rhetoric on the "clash of civilizations".

11. Liguria is the region of which Genoa is *capoluogo* (administrative center).

12. As of 2015, Genoa is pursuing the status of UNESCO Intangible Cultural Heritage for its pesto.

13. Years later, Chef Kumalè was put in charge of hybridizing basil by giving culinary demonstrations of how this herb is a valued ingredient of many cuisines from the global South.

14. The Serravalle Designer Outlet was built in 2000 by the McArthurGlen international corporation, which still owns it.

Conclusion

1. Out of respect for my subjects' sensibilities, I decided not to provide any details about the extent of their financial difficulties.

2. For the impact of twentieth-century department stores on Italy's small businesses, see Scarpellini (2001, 2007).

3. At least some of this increase was most likely caused by a redirection of tourist flows due to terrorist threats to North African seaside resorts. See http://genova.repub blica.it/cronaca/2015/08/01/news/turismo_la_rivoluzione_industriale_a_genova_po sti_di_lavoro_in_crescita-120223348/, accessed on August 20, 2015.

4. http://genova.repubblica.it/cronaca/2015/08/01/news/turismo_la_rivoluzione _industriale_a_genova_posti_di_lavoro_in_crescita-120223348/, accessed on August 20, 2015.

5. At the time of writing in 2015, Italy's President of the Council of Ministers is Matteo Renzi, who replaced Enrico Letta in 2014. Presiding over a government that comprised both center-left and center-right representatives, neither Renzi nor Letta was elected; instead, they were appointed by President Giorgio Napolitano after the 2011 electoral gridlock. Even though he is a leader of Italy's center-left Democratic Party (PD), Renzi has drawn much criticism for his neoliberal policies, such as the Jobs Act labor reform of 2015.

Bibliography

Accornero, Aris. 1979. Il lavoro come ideologia. Bologna: Il Mulino.

Agamben, Giorgio. 2007. Il regno e la gloria. Per una genealogia teologica dell'economia e del governo. Homo Sacer II, 2. Vicenza: Neri Pozza.

———. 2005. State of Exception. Chicago: University of Chicago Press.

———. 1988. Homo Sacer: Sovereign Power and Bare Life. Stanford, CA: Stanford University Press.

Ahearn, Laura M. 2001. Language and Agency. Annual Review of Anthropology 30:109–137.

Ahmed, Sara. 2010. The Promise of Happiness. Durham, NC: Duke University Press.

Aiello, Giorgia. 2011. From Wound to Enclave: The Visual-Material Performance of Urban Renewal in Bologna's Manifattura delle Arti. Western Journal of Communication 75(4):341–366.

Ameeriar, Lalaie. 2012. The Sanitized Sensorium. American Anthropologist 114(3):509–520.

Anderson, Benedict. 2006. Imagined Communities: Reflections on the Origin and Spread of Nationalism. London: Verso.

Anderson, Elijah. 2012. The Cosmopolitan Canopy: Race and Civility in Everyday Life. New York: W. W. Norton and Company.

Anderson, Ben, and Jill Fenton. 2008. Spaces of Hope. Space and Culture 11(2):76–80.

Anderson, Ben, and Adam Holden. 2008. Affective Urbanism and the Event of Hope. Space and Culture 11(2):142–159.

Appadurai, Arjun. 2013. The Future as Cultural Fact: Essays on the Global Condition. London: Verso.

———. 2006. Fear of Small Numbers: An Essay on the Geography of Anger. Durham, NC: Duke University Press.

————. 1988. How to Make a National Cuisine: Cookbooks in Contemporary India. Comparative Studies in Society and History 30(1):3–24.

————. 1986. Introduction: Commodities and the Politics of Value. In The Social Life of Things: Commodities in Cultural Perspective. Arjun Appadurai, ed. Pp. 3–63. Cambridge: Cambridge University Press.

Appiah, Kwame Anthony. 2007. Cosmopolitanism: Ethics in a World of Strangers. New York: W.W. Norton and Company.

Aretxaga, Begonia. 2003. Maddening States: On the Imaginary of Politics. Annual Review of Anthropology 32:393–410.

Arvati, Paolo. n.d. Demografia: Il caso genovese. Genova: Gruppo Banca Carige. https://www.gruppocarige.it/gruppo/html/ita/arte-cultura/la-casana/2007_1/pdf/28_33.pdf, accessed on September 12, 2014.

————. 1994. Classi e organizzazioni operaie. In Storia d'Italia: Le regioni dallUnità a oggi. La Liguria. Antonio Gibelli and Paride Rugafiori, eds. Pp. 845–884. Turin: Giulio Einaudi Editore.

————. 1988. Oltre la città divisa. Gli anni della ristrutturazione a Genova. Genoa: Sagep.

Augé, Marc. 1995. Non-Places: An Introduction to an Anthropology of Supermodernity. Brooklyn: Verso.

Avery-Natale, Edward. 2010. "We're Here, We're Queer, We're Anarchists": The Nature of Identification and Subjectivity Among Black Blocs. Anarchist Developments in Cultural Studies 1(1):95–115.

Avico, Ustik, T. Macchia, A. Dell'Utri, and R. Mancinelli. 1992. Droga e tossicodipendenze: Aspetti normativi, sociali, diagnostici e epidemiologici. Brescia: Class International.

Avila, Eric. 2014. The Folklore of the Freeway: Race and Revolt in the Modernist City. Minneapolis: University of Minnesota Press.

Babcock-Abrahams, Barbara. 1975. A Tolerated Margin of Mess: A Trickster and His Tales Reconsidered. Journal of Folklore Institute 11(3):147–186.

Bakhtin, M. 1982. The Dialogic Imagination: Four Essays. Caryl Emerson and Michael Holquist, trans. Austin: University of Texas Press.

Balbo, Laura. 1978. La doppia presenza. Inchiesta 32(1):3–6.

Baldassar, Loretta. 2001. Visits Home: Migration Experiences Between Italy and Australia. Melbourne: Melbourne University Press.

Balestrini, Nanni, and Primo Moroni. 1988. L'orda d'oro. 1968–1977: La grande ondata rivoluzionaria e creativa, politica ed esistenziale. Milan: Sugarco.

Ballerino-Cohen, Colleen. 1998. "This Is De Test": Festival and Cultural Politics of Nation Building in the British Virgin Islands. American Ethnologist 25(2):189–214.

Barbagli, Marzio. 1974. Disoccupazione intellettuale e sistema scolastico in Italia. Bologna: Il Mulino.

————. 1969. Le vestali della classe media. Bologna: Il Mulino.

Baudelaire, Charles. 1964. The Painter of Modern Life and Other Essays. London: Phaidon

Baudrillard, Jean. 2001. Selected Writings. Redwood City, CA: Stanford University Press.

Beauregard, Robert A. 1993. Representing Urban Decline. Urban Affairs Quarterly 29(2):187–202.

———. 1986. The Chaos and Complexity of Gentrification. In Gentrification of the City. Neil Smith and Peter Williams, eds. Pp. 35–55. New York: Routledge.

Beck, Ulrich. 1997. The Reinvention of Politics. Stafford: Polity.

Bender, Thomas. 2010. Reassembling the City: Networks and Urban Imaginaries. In Urban Assemblages: How Actor-Network Theory Changes Urban Studies. Ignacio Farías and Thomas Bender, eds. Pp. 303–323. London: Routledge.

———. 2007. The Unfinished City: New York and Metropolitan Area. New York: New York University Press.

Benhabib, Seyla. 2002. The Claims of Culture: Equality and Diversity in the Global Era. Princeton, NJ: Princeton University Press.

Benjamin, Walter. 1986. Reflections: Essays, Aphorisms, Autobiographical Writings. Ed. Peter Demetz. New York: Schocken.

———. 1973. Illuminations. London: HarperCollins.

Benson, Peter. 2005. Rooting Culture: Nostalgia, Urban Revitalization, and the Ambivalence of Community at the Ballpark. City & Society (17)1:93–125.

Berlant, Lauren. 2011. Cruel Optimism. Durham, NC: Duke University Press.

Berry, B. J. L. 1985. Islands of Renewal in Seas of Decay: Housing Policy and the Resurgence of Gentrification. Housing Policy Debate 10(4):711–771.

Bertora, Marco, and Carla Grippa. 2011. Per vie traverse. Racconti dal ghetto di Croce Bianca, videorecording.

Bhabha, Homi K. 1994. The Location of Culture. London: Routledge.

Black, Rachel. 2012. Porta Palazzo: The Anthropology of an Italian Market. Philadelphia: University of Pennsylvania Press.

Blaser, Mario. 2013. Ontological Conflicts and the Stories of Peoples in Spite of Europe. Current Anthropology 54(5):547–559.

Blim, Michael L. 2001. Italian Women After Development: Employment, Entrepreneurship, and Domestic Work in the Third Italy. History of the Family 6(2): 257–270.

———. 1990. Made in Italy: Small-Scale Industrialization and Its Consequences. Westport, CT: Greenwood.

Bloch, Ernest. 1998. Literary Essays. Andrew Joron, trans. Redwood City, CA: Stanford University Press.

———. 1986. The Principle of Hope. Neville Plaice, Stephen Plaice, and Paul Knight, trans. Cambridge, MA: MIT Press.

Boal, I., T. J. Clar, J. Matthews, and M. Watts. 2005. Afflicted Powers: Capital and Spectacle in a New Age of War. London: Verso.

Bourdieu, Pierre. 1993. The Field of Cultural Production. Cambridge: Polity.

———. 1984. Distinction: A Social Critique of Judgment of Taste. Cambridge, MA: Harvard University Press.

———. 1977. Outline of a Theory of Practice. Cambridge: Cambridge University Press.

Bourdieu, Pierre, and Jean Claud Passeron. 1990. Reproduction in Education, Society and Culture. Thousand Oaks, CA: Sage Publications.

Bourgois, Philippe, and Jeffrey Schonberg. 2009. Righteous Dopefiend. Berkeley: University of California Press.

Bourguignon, Erika. 1996. Vienna and Memory: Anthropology and Experience. Ethos 24(2):374–387.

Bovone, Laura, Antonietta Mazzette, and Giancarlo Rovati. 2005. Effervescenze urbane: Quartieri creativi a Milano, Genova e Sassari. Milan: Franco Angeli Editore.

Brash, Julian. 2011. Bloomberg's New York: Class and Governance in the Luxury City. Athens: University of Georgia Press.

Bromley, Rosemary, A. Tallon, and C. J. Thomas. 2003. Disaggregating the Space-Time Layers of City-Centre Activities and Their Users. Environment and Planning A 35(10):131–185.

Brown-Saracino, Japonica. 2009. A Neighborhood That Never Changes: Gentrification, Social Preservation, and the Search for Authenticity. Chicago: University of Chicago Press.

———. 2004. Social Preservationists and the Quest for Authentic Community. City & Community 3(2):135–156.

Buchli, Victor. 2002. Introduction. In The Material Culture Reader. Victor Buchli, ed. Pp. 1–22. Oxford: Berg.

Buck-Morss, Susan. 2002. Dreamworld and Catastrophe: The Passing of Mass Utopia in East and West. Cambridge, MA: MIT Press.

Bunten, Celeste Alexis. 2008. Sharing Culture or Selling Out? Developing the Commodified Persona in the Heritage Industry. American Ethnologist 35(3):380–395.

Butler, Judith. 2009. Performativity, Precarity, and Sexual Politics. Revista de Antropología Iberoamericana 4(1):i–xiii.

———. 2006. Precarious Life: The Powers of Mourning and Violence. London: Verso.

Caldeira, Teresa. 2001. City of Walls: Crime, Segregation, and Citizenship in São Paulo. Berkeley: University of California Press.

Calhoun, Craig, Richard Sennett, and Hariel Shapira. 2013. Poiesis Means Making. Journal of Public Culture 25(2):195–200.

Callinicos, Alex. 2003. The Anti-Capitalist Movement After Genoa and New York. In Implicating Empire: Globalization and Resistance in the 21st Century World Order. S. Aronowitz and H. Gautney, eds. Pp. 133–150. New York: Basic Books.

Calvino, Italo. 1972. Le città invisibili. Turin: Giulio Einaudi Editore.

Caracciolo, Luciano. 2001. Editoriale: Da Marx a Matrix. Limes 4(1):7–14.

Cassaniti, Julia. 2012. Agency and the Other: The Roles of Agency for the Importance of Belief in Buddhist and Christian Traditions. Ethos: The Journal of Psychological Anthropology 40(3):297–316.

Castelli, Lorenzo, and Antonio Gozzi. 1994. Un'economia in declino. In Storia d'Italia: Le regioni dall'Unità a oggi. La Liguria. Antonio Gibelli and Paride Rugafiori, eds. Pp. 885–905. Turin: Einaudi Editore.

Caulfield, Jon. 1989. Gentrification and Desire. Canadian Review of Sociology 26(4): 617–632.

Cavalli, Luciano. 1960. La città divisa. Sociologia del consenso e del conflitto in un ambiente urbano. Milan: Giuffrè.

Cavanaugh, Jillian, 2009. Living Memory: The Social Aesthetics of Language in a Northern Italian Town. Oxford: Wiley Blackwell.

Cavazza, Andrea. 2013. Gli imprendibili. Storia della colonna simbolo delle Brigate Rosse. Rome: Deriveapprodi.

Cavazza, Stefano. 1997. Piccole patrie. Feste popolari tra regione e nazione durante il fascismo. Bologna: Il Mulino.

Ceccagno, Antonella. 2003. New Chinese Migrants in Italy. International Migration 41(3):187–213.

CENSIS 2013. 47mo rapporto sulla situazione sociale del Paese. Rome: Franco Angeli.

———. 2004. 38mo rapporto sulla situazione sociale del Paese. Rome: Franco Angeli.

———. 2002. 36mo rapporto sulla situazione sociale del Paese. Rome: Franco Angeli.

Chambers, Iain. 2008. Mediterranean Crossings: The Politics of an Interrupted Modernity. Durham, NC: Duke University Press.

Chernoff, Michael. 1980. Social Displacement in a Renovating Neighborhood's Commercial District. In Back to the City: Issues in Neighborhood Renovations. S. Laska and D. Spain, eds. Pp. 208–218. New York: Pergamon.

Chesters, Graeme, and Ian Welsh. 2006. Complexity and Social Movement: Multitudes at the Edge of Chaos. London: Routledge.

———. 2004. Rebel Colours: "Framing" in Global Social Movements. Sociological Review 52(3):314–335.

Chiesa, Mario. 2001. G8/Genova. Turin: Einaudi.

Cinar, Alev, and Tomans Bender. 2007. The City: Imagination and Experience. In Urban Imaginaries: Locating the Modern City. Alev Cinar and Thomas Bender, eds. Pp. xi–xxvi. Minneapolis: University of Minnesota Press.

Clay, Phillip L. 1979. Neighborhood Renewal. Lanham, MD: Lexington Books.

Cole, Jeffrey. 1997. The New Racism in Europe: A Sicilian Ethnography. Cambridge: Cambridge University Press.

Collier, Stephen J., and Aihwa Ong. 2005. Global Assemblages, Anthropological Problems. In Global Assemblages: Technology, Politics, and Ethics as Anthropological Problems. Aihwa Ong and Stephen J. Collier, eds. Pp. 3–21. Oxford: Wiley Blackwell.

Colombi, Matteo. 2001. L'Italia intravista dagli Usa: Piuttosto illiberale e totalmente ininfluente. Limes (4):99–106.

Colombo, Andrea. 2002. Storia politica di un disastro. Il caso Genova: da piazza Alimonda alla scuola Diaz. Rome: Manifestolibri.

Comaroff, Jean, and John L. Comaroff. 2009. Ethnicity, Inc.. Chicago: University of Chicago Press.

———. 2000. Millennial Capitalism: First Thoughts on a Second Coming. Public Culture 12(2):291–343.

Coole, Diana. 2000. Cartographic Convulsions: Public and Private Reconsidered. Political Theory: 28(3):337–354.

Copeland, Tim. 2010. Site Seeing: Street Walking Through a Low-Visibility Landscape. In Culture, Heritage and Representation: Perspectives on Visuality and the Past. Emma Waterton and Steve Watson, eds. Pp. 229–248. Farnham: Ashgate.

Couniham, Carole. 2004. Around the Tuscan Table: Food, Family, and Gender in Twentieth-Century Florence. New York: Routledge.

Crane, Diane, and Laura Bovone. 2006. Approaches to Material Culture: The Sociology of Fashion and Clothing. Poetics 34:319–333.

Crapanzano, Vincent. 2003. Reflections of Hope as a Category of Social and Psychological Analysis. Cultural Anthropology 18(1):3–32.

Cresswell, Tim. 1996. In Place/Out of Place: Geography, Ideology, and Transgression. Minneapolis: University of Minnesota Press.

Crick, Malcolm. 1989. Representations of International Tourism in the Social Sciences: Sun, Sex, Sights, Savings, and Servility. Annual Review of Anthropology 18: 307–344.

Cristante, Stefano. 2003. Violenza mediata. Il ruolo dell'informazione nel G8 di Genoa. Rome: Editori Riuniti.

Debord, Guy. 1984. Society of the Spectacle. Detroit: Black & Red Books.

De Certeau, Michel. 1984. The Practice of Everyday Life. Berkeley: University of California Press.

de Koning, Anouk. 2009. Global Dreams: Class, Gender, and Public Space in Cosmopolitan Cairo. Cairo: American University in Cairo Press.

Della Porta, Donatella, Massimiliano Andretta, Lorenzo Mosca, and Herbert Reiter. 2006. Globalization from Below: Transnational Activists and Protest Networks. Minneapolis: University of Minnesota Press.

Della Porta, Donatella, and Herbert Reiter. 2003. Polizia e protesta: L'ordine pubblico dalla Liberazione ai "no global." Bologna: Il Mulino.

Della Porta, Donatella, and Alberto Vannucci. 1999. Corrupt Exchanges: Actors, Resources, and Mechanisms of Political Corruption. New York: Aldine de Gruyter.

Del Negro, Giovanna. 2004. The Passeggiata and Popular Culture in an Italian Town: Folklore and the Performance of Modernity. Montreal: McGill-Queen's University Press.

Dematteo, Lynda. 2011. L'idiota in politica. Antropologia della Lega Nord. Milan: Feltrinelli.

De Vogli, Roberto, M. Marmot, and D. Stucker. 2013. Strong Evidence That the Economic Crisis Caused a Rise in Suicides in Europe: The Case for Social Protection. Journal of Epidemiology and Community Health 67(4):298.

Diana, Graziano. 2013. Gli anni spezzati. Rai Fiction. Television series.

Dickey, Sarah. 2012. The Pleasures and Anxieties of Being in the Middle: Emerging Middle Class Identities in Urban South India. Modern Asian Studies 46(3): 559–599.

Dicks, Bella. 2004. Culture on Display: The Production of Contemporary Visitability. London: Open University Press.

Di Leonardo, Micaela. 1985. Women's Work, Work Culture, and Consciousness. Feminist Studies 11(3):491–495.

Dines, Nick. 2012. Tuff City: Urban Change and Contested Space in Central Naples. New York: Berghahn.

Dogliotti, Chiara. 2004. La colonna genovese delle Brigate Rosse. Studi Storici 45(4):1151–1177.

Domosh, Mona, and Joni Sedger. 2001. Putting Women in Place: Feminist Geographers Make Sense of the World. New York: Guilford Press.

Doria, Giorgio. 1969. Investimenti e sviluppo economico a Genova alla vigilia della prima guerra mondiale. Milan: Giuffrè Editore.

Douglas, Mary. 1966. Purity and Danger. New York: Routledge.

Durkheim, Émile. 1915. The Elementary Forms of Religious Life. London: Unwin and Allen.

Eagleton, Terry. 2000. The Idea of Culture. Hoboken, NJ: Wiley.

Eller, Jack David. 1997. Anti-Anti Multiculturalism. American Anthropologist 99(2):249–260.

Ellis, Carolyn. 2004. The Ethnographic I: A Methodological Novel About Autoethnography. Walnut Creek, CA : AltaMira Press.

Epstein, Steven. 1996. Genoa and the Genoese, 958–1528. Chapel Hill: University of North Carolina Press.

Erminio, Deborah. 2004. Il profilo socio-demografico: Chi sono gli immigrati. In Primo rapporto sull'immigrazione a Genova. Maurizio Ambrosini, Deborah Erminio, and Adrea Ravecca, eds. Pp. 41–106. Genoa: Fratelli Frilli Editori.

Errington, Frederick. 1987. Reflexivity Deflected: The Festival of Nations as an American Cultural Performance. American Ethnologist 14(4):654–667.

Eyerman, Ron. 2008. The Assassination of Theo Van Gogh: From Social Drama to Cultural Trauma. Durham, NC: Duke University Press.

Fabian, Johannes. 2002. Time and the Other: How Anthropology Makes Its Object. New York: Columbia University Press.

Falasca-Zamponi, Simonetta. 1997. Fascist Spectacle: The Aesthetics of Power in Mussolini's Italy. Berkeley: University of California Press.

Farías, Ignacio. 2011. The Politics of Urban Assemblages. City 15(3–4):365–373.

———. 2010. Introduction: Decentering the Object of Urban Studies. *In* Urban Assemblages: How Actor-Network Theory Changes Urban Studies. Ignacio Farías and Thomas Bender, eds. Pp. 2–24. London: Routledge.

Featherstone, Mike. 2007. Consumer Culture and Postmodernism. Thousand Oaks, CA: Sage Publications.

———. 1998. The Flâneur, The City and Virtual Public Life. Urban Studies 35(5–6):909–925.

Ferguson, James. 1999. Expectations of Modernity. Berkeley: University of California Press.

Ferraris, Maurizio. 2001. I silenzi della zona rossa. G8 e dintorni. Genoa: Fratelli Frilli Editori.

Ferrera, Maurizio. 1996. The "Southern Model" of Welfare in Social Europe. Journal of European Social Policy 6(1):17–37.

Fish, Stanley. 1997. Boutique Multiculturalism, or Why Liberals Are Incapable of Thinking About Hate Speech. Critical Inquiry 23(2):78–395.

Flores, Patricia, and Valencia León. 2007. Recorrendo los espacios urbanos. *In* Entre inclusión y exclusión. Francesca Lagomarsino and Andrea Torre, eds. Pp. 183–206. Quito: Abya-Yala.

Florida, Richard. 2012 [2002]. The Rise of the Creative Class, Revisited: Tenth Anniversary Edition. New York: Basic Books.

Foot, John. 2001. Milan Since the Miracle: City, Culture, and Identity. New York: Bloomsbury.

Foucault, Michel. 1986. Of Other Spaces. Diacritics 16(1):22–27.

Freeman, Carla. 2014. Entrepreneurial Selves: Neoliberal Respectability and the Making of a Caribbean Middle Class. Durham, NC: Duke University Press.

———. 2000. High Tech and High Heels in the Global Economy: Women, Work and Pink-Collar Identities in the Caribbean. Durham, NC: Duke University Press.

Friedberg, Anne. 1993. Window Shopping: Cinema and the Postmodern. Berkeley: University of California Press.

Fubini, Federico. 2001. Il prezzo di Genoa lo stiamo pagando anzitutto in Europa. Limes 4(1):85–99.

Fusero, Paolo, Bruno Gabrielli, Antida Gazzola, and Loredana Seassaro. 1991. Il Centro Storico di Genova. Archivio di Studi Urbani e Regionali 40:85–107.

Gabaccia, Donna. 2000. Italy's Many Diasporas. Seattle: University of Washington Press.

Gabrielli, Bruno. 1999. Il centro storico di Genova: Da freno a opportunità. La Nuova Cittá, 5/6:107–112.

Gal, Susan. 2002. A Semiotics of the Private/Public Distinction. Differences: A Journal of Feminist Cultural Studies 13(1):77–95.

Gale, Dennis. 1980. Neighborhood Resettlement: Washington, DC. *In* Back to the City: Issues in Neighborhood Renovation. Shirley Bradway Laska and Daphne Spain, eds. Pp. 95–115. Oxford: Pergamon Press.

Gamst, Frederick C. 1995. Introduction. *In* Meanings of Work: Considerations for the Twenty-First Century. Frederik C. Gamst, ed. Pp. xi–xxii. Albany: State University of New York Press.

Gardner, Carol B. 1995. Passing By: Gender and Public Harassment. Berkeley: University of California Press.

Garibbo, Luciana. 2000. Politica, amministrazione e interessi a Genova (1815–1940). Milan: Franco Angeli.

Gastaldi, Francesco. 2003. Processi di gentrification nel centro storico di Genova. Archivio di studi urbani e regionali 77:135–149.

Gazzola, Antida. 2013. Genova: Il Porto Antico. *In* Pratiche sociali di città pubblica. A. Mazzette, ed. Pp. 112–134. Rome-Bari: Laterza.

———. 2003. Trasformazioni urbane. Società e spazi di Genova. Genova: Liguori Editore.

Gazzola, Antida, Roberta Prampolini, and Daniela Rimondi. 2014. Negli spazi pubblici. Utilizzatori temporanei e pratiche sociali a Genova. Milan: Franco Angeli.

Geertz, Clifford. 1973. The Interpretation of Cultures. New York: Basic Books.

Genoa Social Forum. 2001. Genova. Il libro bianco. Milan: Nuova Iniziativa Editoriale.

Gibson-Graham, J. K. 1996. The End of Capitalism (As We Knew It): A Feminist Critique of Political Economy. Cambridge, MA: Basil Blackwell.

Giddens, Anthony. 1991. Modernity and Self-Identity: Self and Society in the Later Modern Age. Redwood City, CA: Stanford University Press.

Ginsborg, Paul. 2003. Italy and Its Discontents: Family, Civil Society, State. New York: Palgrave Macmillan.

———. 1990. A History of Contemporary Italy: Society and Politics 1943–1988. London: Penguin.

Gornostaeva, Galina, and Noel Campbell. 2012. The Creative Underclass in the Production of Place: Example of Camden Town in London. Journal of Urban Affairs 34(2):169–188.

Goss, Jon. 1993. The "Magic of the Mall": An Analysis of Form, Function, and Meaning in the Contemporary Retail Built Environment. Annals of the Association of American Geographers 83(1):18–74.

Gotham, Kevin Fox. 2005. Theorizing Urban Spectacles: Festivals, Tourism and the Transformation of Urban Space. City 9(2):225–246.

Gottfried, Heidi. 2002. Compromising Positions: Emergent Neo-Fordisms and Embedded Gender Contracts. British Journal of Sociology 51(2):235–259.

Graeber, David. 2007. Possibilities: Essays on Hierarchy, Rebellion, and Desire. Oakland: AK Press.

Greene, Solomon J. n.d. Staged Cities: Mega-events, Slum Clearance, and Global Capital. The Yale Human Rights and Development Law Journal, vol. 6. http://www.law.yale.edu/documents/pdf/LawJournals/greene.pdf, accessed on September 29, 2015.

Grillo, Ralph. 2007. An Excess of Alterity? Debating Difference in a Multicultural Society. Ethnic and Racial Studies 30(6):979–998.

———. 2002. The Politics of Recognizing Difference: Multiculturalism Italian-Style. Surrey: Ashgate.

Guano, Emanuela. 2010a. Taxpayers, Thieves, and the State: Fiscal Citizenship in Contemporary Italy. Ethos 74(4):471–495.

———. 2010b. Social Immobility and the Poetics of Contentment in Paolo Virzi's Caterina in the Big City. Studies in European Cinema 7(2):149–161.

———. 2007. Respectable Ladies and Uncouth Men: The Performative Politics of Class and Gender in the Public Realm of an Italian City. Journal of American Folklore 120(475):48–72.

———. 2004. The Denial of Citizenship: "Barbaric" Buenos Aires and the Middle-Class Imaginary. City and Society 1:69–97.

———. 2003a. A Color for the Modern Nation: The Discourse on Class, Race, and Education in the Porteño Opposition to Neoliberalism. Journal of Latin American Anthropology 8(1):148–171.

———. 2003b. A Stroll Through la Boca: The Politics and Poetics of Spatial Experience in a Buenos Aires Neighborhood. Space and Culture: International Journal of Social Spaces 6:356–376.

———. 2002. Spectacles of Modernity: Transnational Imagination and Local Hegemonies in Neoliberal Buenos Aires. Cultural Anthropology 17(2):181–209.

Guccini, Francesco. 2004. Piazza Alimonda. Song.

Gullí, Bruno. 2003. Beyond Good and Evil: A Contribution to the Analysis of the War Against Terrorism. In Implicating Empire: Globalization and Resistance in the 21st Century World. S. Aronowitz and H. Gautney, eds. Pp. 83–94. New York: Basic Books.

Guss, David M. 2000. The Festive State: Race, Ethnicity, and Nationalism as Cultural Performance. Berkeley: University of California Press.

Gustinchic, Franz. 2001. Anatomia del Black Bloc (con una scheda di Emmanuela C. Del Re-Facciamo che io ero un antiglobalizzatore violento). Limes 4(1):41–50.

Habermas, Jürgen. 1989. The Structural Transformation of the Public Sphere: An Inquiry into a Category of Bourgeois Society. Cambridge, MA: MIT Press.

Hackworth, Jason, and Neil Smith. 2001. The Changing State of Gentrification. Tijdschrift voor Economischer en Sociale Geografie 92(4):464–477.

Hale, Charles. 2005. Neoliberal Multiculturalism: The Remaking of Cultural Rights and Racial Dominance in Central America. PoLAR 28(10):10–28.

Hall, Peter. 1966. The World Cities. London: World University Library.

Hannigan, John. 1998. Fantasy City: Pleasure and Profit in the Postmodern Metropolis. New York: Routledge.

Haraway, Donna. 1989. Primate Visions: Gender, Race, and Nature in the World of Modern Science. New York: Routledge.

Hardt, Michael, and Antonio Negri. 2004. Multitude: War and Democracy in the Age of Empire. London: Penguin.

———. 2000. Empire. Cambridge, MA: Harvard University Press.

Harvey, David. 2005. A Brief History of Neoliberalism. New York: Oxford University Press.

———. 2001. Globalization and the Spatial Fix. Geographische Revue 2:23–30.

———. 2000. Spaces of Hope. Berkeley: University of California Press.

———. 1990. The Condition of Postmodernity: An Inquiry into the Origins of Cultural Change. Cambridge, MA: Basil Blackwell.

———. 1988. Voodoo Cities. New Statesman and Society 30(9):88.

Heiman, Rachel. 2015. Driving After Class: Anxious Times in an American Suburb. Berkeley: California University Press.

Heiman, Rachel, Mark Liechty, and Carla Freeman. 2010. Introduction: Charting an Anthropology of the Middle Classes. In The Global Middle Classes: Theorizing Through Ethnography. Rachel Heiman, Carla Freeman, and Mark Liechty, eds. Pp. 1–30. Santa Fe: School of Advanced Research Press.

Heldke, Lisa M. 2003. Exotic Appetites: Ruminations of a Food Adventurer. New York: Routledge.

Helstosky, Carol. 2006. Garlic and Oil: Politics and Food in Italy. Oxford: Berg.

Herzfeld, Michael. 2009. Evicted from Eternity: The Restructuring of Modern Rome. Chicago: University of Chicago Press.

———. 2004. The Body Impolitic: Artisans and Artifice in the Global Hierarchy of Value. Chicago: University of Chicago Press.

Hesse, Barnor. 2000. Unsettled Multiculturalisms. London: Zed Books.

Hillman, Felicitas. 2008. Big Ships on the Horizon and Growing Fragmentation at Home: Genoa's Transformation of the Urban Landscape. Erdkunde 62(4): 301–316.

Ho, Christine G. T. 2000. Popular Culture and the Aestheticization of Politics: Hegemonic Struggle and Postcolonial Nationalism in the Trinidad Carnival. Transforming Anthropology 9(1):3–18.

Ho, Karen. 2009. Liquidated: An Ethnography of Wall Street. Durham, NC: Duke University Press.

Hobsbawm, Eric. 1983. Mass-producing Traditions: Europe, 1870–1914. The Invention of Tradition 263(1):279–280.

Hochschild, Arlie Russell. 1983. The Managed Heart: The Commercialization of Human Feeling. Berkeley: University of California Press.

Hoffman, Lisa M. 2010. Patriotic Professionalism in Urban China: Fostering Talent. Philadelphia: Temple University Press.

Holmes, David. 2000. Integral Europe: Fast Capitalism, Multiculturalism, Neofascism. Princeton, NJ: Princeton University Press.

Holston, James. 1989. The Modernist City: An Anthropological Critique of Brasilia. Chicago: University of Chicago Press.

hooks, bell. 1992. Black Looks: Race and Representation. Boston: South End Press.

Howes, David. 2003. Sensual Relations: Engaging the Senses in Cultural Social Theory. Ann Arbor: University of Michigan Press.

Huizinga, Johan. 1955. Homo Ludens: A Study of the Play-Element in Culture. Boston: Beacon Press.

Huntington, Samuel P. 1996. The Clash of Civilizations and the Remaking of World Order. New York: Simon & Schuster.

Hynes, William J. 1997a. Mapping the Characteristics of Mythic Tricksters: A Heuristic Guide. In Mythical Trickster Figures. William J. Hynes and William G. Doty, eds. Pp. 33–45. Tuscaloosa: University of Alabama Press.

———. 1997b. Inconclusive Inconclusions: Tricksters as Metaplayers and Revealers. In Mythical Trickster Figures. William J. Hynes and William G. Doty, eds. Pp. 202–217. Tuscaloosa: University of Alabama Press.

Ingram, Mark. 2011. Rites of the Republic: Citizens' Theatre and the Politics of Culture in Southern France. Toronto: University of Toronto Press.

Isnenghi, Mario. 2004. L'Italia in Piazza. I luoghi della vita pubblica dal 1848. ai giorni nostri. Bologna: Il Mulino.

Iveson, Kurt. 2007. Publics and the City. New York: Wiley Blackwell.

Jackson, Michael. 2007. Excursions. Durham, NC: Duke University Press.

Jackson, Peter. 2002. Commercial Cultures: Transcending the Cultural and the Economic. Progress in Human Geography 26(1):3–18.

Jacobs, Jane M. 1969. The Economy of Cities. New York: Random House.

———. 1961. The Death and Life of Great American Cities. New York: Random House.

Jacquot, Sébastien. 2011. Plurality of the Production of Secured Spaces in Genoa's Historic Centre. Security Practices in Cities 4. http://www.jssj.org/article/pluralite-des-modalites-de-la-securisation-du-centre-historique-de-genes/, accessed on August 12, 2014.

Jager, Michael. 1986. Class Definition and the Esthetics of Gentrification: Victoriana in Melbourne. In Gentrification of the City. Neil Smith and Peter Williams, eds. Pp. 78–79. New York: Routledge.

Jameson, Fredric. 1991. Postmodernism, or, The Cultural Logic of Late Capitalism. Durham, NC: Duke University Press.

Jansen, Stef. 2001. The Streets of Beograd. Urban Space and Protest Identities in Serbia. Political Geography 20(1):35–55.

Johnson, Andrew Allen. 2013. Progress and Its Ruins: Ghosts, Migrants and the Uncanny in Thailand. Cultural Anthropology 28(2):299–319.

Juris, Jeffrey S. 2008. Performing Politics: Image, Embodiment, and Affective Solidarity During Anti-Corporate Globalization Protests. Ethnography 9(1):61–97.

———. 2006. Networking Futures: The Movements Against Corporate Globalization. Durham, NC: Duke University Press.

————. 2005. Violence Performed and Imagined: Militant Action, the Black Bloc and the Mass Media in Genoa. Critique of Anthropology 25(4):413–432.

————. 2003. Networked Social Movements: Global Movements for Global Justice. *In* The Network Society: A Cross-Cultural Perspective. Manuel Castells, ed. Pp. 341–362. Cheltenham: Edward Elgar.

Kane, Stephanie. 2012. Where Rivers Meet the Sea: The Political Ecology of Water. Philadelphia: Temple University Press.

Kapchan, Deborah A. 2008. The Promise of Sonic Translation: Performing the Festive Sacred in Morocco. American Anthropologist 110(4):467–483.

Keith, Michael, and Steve Pile. 1993. Place and the Politics of Identity. London: Routledge.

Kertzer, David. 1998. Politics and Symbols: The Italian Communist Party and the Fall of Communism. New Haven, CT: Yale University Press.

Kilgo, James. 1988. Deep Enough for Ivorybills. Athens: University of Georgia Press.

Kirshenblatt-Gimblett, Barbara. 1991. Objects of Ethnography. *In* Exhibiting Cultures: The Poetics and Politics of Museum Display. Ivan Karp and Steven Lavine, eds. Pp. 386–443. Washington, DC: Smithsonian Institution Press.

Koenig-Archibugi, Mathias. 2003. National and European Citizenship: The Italian Case in Historical Perspective. Citizenship Studies 7(1):85–109.

Kowalczyk, Jamie, and Thomas S. Popkewitz. 2005. Multiculturalism, Recognition and Abjection: (re) Mapping Italian Identity. Policy Futures in Education 3(4): 423–435.

Kramer, Kathryn, and Rennie Short. 2011. Flânerie and the Globalizing City. City: Analysis of Urban Trends, Culture, Theory, Policy, Action 15(3–4):322–342.

Krause, Elizabeth L. 2009. Unraveled: A Weaver's Tale of Life Gone Modern. Berkeley: University of California Press.

————. 2004. A Crisis of Births: Population Politics and Family-Making in Italy. Boston: Wadsworth.

Krause, Monika. 2013. The Ruralization of the World. Journal of Public Culture 25(2):233–248.

La Francesca, Sofia. 2003. Il turismo in Italia. Florence: Le Monnier.

Lash, Scott, and John Urry. 1987. The End of Organized Capitalism. Cambridge: Polity Press.

Lashaw, Amanda. 2008. Experiencing Imminent Justice: The Presence of Hope in a Movement for Equitable Schooling. Space and Culture 11(2):109–124.

Lefebvre, Henri. 1996. Writings on Cities. Oxford: Basil Blackwell.

————. 1991. The Production of Space. Oxford: Basil Blackwell.

————. 1978. La vita quotidiana nel mondo moderno (a cura di Paolo Jedlowski e Amedeo Vigorelli). Milan: Il Saggiatore.

Leitch, Alison. 2003. Slow Food and the Politics of Pork Fat: Italian Food and European Identity. Ethnos 68:437–362.

Lengkeek, Jaap. 2001. Leisure Experience and Imagination: Rethinking Cohen's Modes of Tourist Experience. International Sociology 16(2):173–184.

Leone, Marco. 2010. La leggenda dei vicoli. Analisi documentaria di una rappresentazione sociale del centro antico di Genova. Milan: Franco Angeli.

Leontidou, Lila. 1990. The Mediterranean City in Transition: Social Change and Urban Development. Cambridge: Cambridge University Press.

Ley, David. 1996. The New Middle Class and the Remaking of the Central City. Oxford: Oxford University Press.

———. 1994. Gentrification and the Politics of the New Middle Class. Environment and Planning D (12):53–74.

Leshkowich, Ann Marie. 2014. Essential Trade: Vietnamese Women in a Changing Marketplace. Honolulu: University of Hawai'i Press.

Liechty, Mark. 2003. Suitably Modern: Making Middle-Class Culture in a New Consumer Society. Princeton, NJ: Princeton University Press.

Lionnet, Françoise. 1991. Autobiographical Voices: Race, Gender, Self-Portraiture. Ithaca, NY: Cornell University Press.

Low, Setha. 2003. Behind the Gates: Life, Security, and the Pursuit of Happiness in Fortress America. New York: Routledge.

———. 2000. On the Plaza: The Politics of Public Space and Culture. Austin: University of Texas Press.

Lowenthal, David. 1985. The Past Is a Foreign Country. Cambridge: Cambridge University Press.

MacCannell, Dean. 1976. The Tourist: A Net Theory of the Leisure Class. Berkeley: University of California Press.

Maggiani, Maurizio. 2007. Mi sono perso a Genova. Milan: Giangiacomo Feltrinelli Editore.

Mahmood, Saba. 2005. Politics of Piety: The Islamic Revival and the Feminist Subject. Princeton, NJ: Princeton University Press.

Mains, Daniel. 2012. Hope Is Cut: Youth, Unemployment and the Future in Urban Ethiopia. Philadelphia: Temple University Press.

Maira, Sunaina. 2008. Belly Dancing: Arab-Face, Orientalist Feminism, and U.S. Empire. American Quarterly 60(2):317–345.

Makarius, Laura Levi. 1974. Les sacré et la violation des interdits. Paris: Payot.

Malpas, Jeff E. 1999. Place and Experience: A Philosophical Topography. Cambridge: Cambridge University Press.

Manalansan, Martin F. 2006. Queer Intersections: Sexuality and Gender in Migration Studies. International Migration Review 40(1):224–249.

Maritano, Laura. 2002. An Obsession with Cultural Difference: Representations of Immigrants in Turin. In The Politics of Recognizing Difference: Multiculturalism Italian-style. Ralph Grillo and Jeff Pratt, eds. Pp. 59–76. Aldershot: Ashgate.

Marcus, George. 1998. Ethnography Through Thick and Thin. Princeton, NJ: Princeton University Press.

————. 1995. Ethnography in/of the World System: The Emergence of Multi-Sited Ethnography. Annual Review of Anthropology 24(1):95–117.

Markusen, Ann. 2006. Urban Development and the Politics of a Creative Class: Evidence from the Study of Artists. Environment and Planning A 38(10):1921–1940.

Martin, Bill. 1998. Knowledge, Identity and the Middle Class: From Collective to Individualised Class Formation? Sociological Review 46(4):653–686.

————. n.d. Transforming the Contemporary "New Middle-Class": From Professionals and Managers to "Bricoleurs"? In Szelényi 60, http://hi.rutgers.edu/szelenyi60.martin.html, accessed on March 20, 2004.

Massey, Doreen. 1994. Space, Place, and Gender. Minneapolis: University of Minnesota Press.

Massumi, Brian. 2002. Navigating Movements. In Hope: New Philosophies for Change. Mary Zournazi, ed. Pp. 210–233. New York: Routledge.

Mastropiero, Eleonora. 2007. I grandi eventi come occasione di riqualificazione urbana. Il caso di Genova. ACME: Annali della Facoltà di lettere e Filosofia dell'Università degli Studi di Milano. 60(1):169–207.

Mattingly, Cheryl. 2008. Reading Minds and Telling Tales in a Cultural Borderland. Ethos 36(1):136–154.

Mayr, Ernst. 1992. The Idea of Teleology. Journal of the History of Ideas 53(1):117–135.

McCracken, Grant David. 1990. Culture and Consumption: New Approaches to the Symbolic Character of Consumer Goods and Activities. Bloomington: Indiana University Press.

McDonogh, Gary W. 2007. Mediterranean Cities. South European Society and Politics 5(1):143–155.

————. 1991. Culture and Categorization in a Turn-of-the-Century Barcelona Elite. Cultural Anthropology 6(3):323–345.

————. 1987. The Geography of Evil: Barcelona's Barrio Chino. Anthropological Quarterly 60(4):174–184.

McDonogh, Gary, and Marina Peterson. 2012. Introduction: Globalizing Downtown. In Global Downtowns. Marina Peterson and Gary McDonogh, eds. Pp. 1–26. Philadelphia: University of Pennsylvania Press.

McDowell, Linda. 1997. Capital Culture: Gender at Work in the City. Malden, MA: Basil Blackwell.

Mehta, Anna, and Lis Bondi. 1999. Embodied Discourse: On Gender and Fear of Violence. Gender, Place & Culture: A Journal of Feminist Geography 6(7):67–85.

Miller, Daniel. 2001. The Dialectics of Shopping. Chicago: University of Chicago Press.

Minnella, Maurizio Fantoni. 2014. Genova: Ritratto di una città. Genoa: Odoya.

Miniero, Luca. 2010. Benvenuti al Sud. Medusa Film. Film.

Mirzoeff, Nicholas. 2014. Visualizing the Anthropocene. Journal of Public Culture 26(2):212–232.

Mitchell, Don. 2003. The Right to the City: Social Justice and Public Space. New York: Guilford Press.

Mitchell, Timothy. 1989. The World as Exhibition. Comparative Studies in Society and History (31)2:217–236.

Miyazaki, Hirokazu. 2013. Arbitraging Japan: Dreams of Capitalism at the End of Finance. Berkeley: University of California Press.

———. 2006. Economy of Dreams: Hope in Global Capitalism and Its Critiques. Cultural Anthropology 21(2):147–172.

———. 2004. The Method of Hope: Anthropology, Philosophy, and Fijian Knowledge. Redwood City, CA: Stanford University Press.

Molé, Noelle. 2011. Labor Disorders in Neoliberal Italy: Mobbing, Well-Being, and the Workplace. Bloomington: Indiana University Press.

Mommaas, Hans. 2009. Spaces of Culture and Economy: Mapping the Cultural-Creative Cluster Landscape. In Creative Economies, Creative Cities. Lily Kong and Justin O'Connor, eds. Pp. 45–59. Heidelberg: Springer.

Moodley, Kogila. 1983. Canadian Multiculturalism as Ideology. Ethnic and Racial Studies 6(3):320–331.

Moore, Henrietta. 1994. A Passion for Difference. Bloomington: Indiana University Press.

Mordue, Tom. 2010. Time Machines and Space Craft: Navigating the Spaces of Heritage Tourism Performance. In Culture, Heritage, and Representation: Perspectives on Visuality and the Past. Emma Waterton and Steve Watson, eds. Pp. 173–194. Surrey: Ashgate.

Moretti, Cristina. 2015. Milanese Encounters: Public Space and Vision in Contemporary Urban Italy. Toronto: University of Toronto Press.

———. 2008. Places and Stages: Narrating and Performing the City in Milan, Italy. Liminalities: A Journal of Performance Studies 4(1):1–46.

Morris, Maeghan. 1993. Things to Do with Shopping Centres. In The Cultural Studies Reader. S. During, ed. Pp. 295–316. London: Routledge.

Muehlebach, Andrea. 2012. The Moral Neoliberal: Welfare and Citizenship in Italy. Chicago: University of Chicago Press.

Mukerji, Chandra. 2012. Space and Political Pedagogy at the Gardens of Versailles. Public Culture 24(3):509–534.

Mullin, Molly. 2001. Culture in the Marketplace: Gender, Art, and Value in the American Southwest. Durham, NC: Duke University Press.

Munt, Ian. 1994. "The Other" Postmodern Tourism: Culture, Travel and the New Middle Classes. Theory, Culture & Society 11(1):101–123.

Murphy, Ryan. 2010. Eat Pray Love. Columbia Pictures. Film.

Nash, Dennison, and Valene L. Smith. 1991. Anthropology and Tourism. Annals of Tourism Research 18:12–25.

Nativi, Andrea. 2001. Militari e poliziotti: Le lezioni da imparare. Limes 4(1):51–58.

Navaro-Yashin, Yael. 2012. The Make-Believe Space: Affective Geography in a Postwar Polity. Durham, NC: Duke University Press.

Neve, Elisabetta. 2002. Donne in difficoltá. *In* Cittadini invisibili: Rapporto 2002. su esclusione sociale e diritti di cittadinanza. Caritas Italiana, ed. Pp. 97–164. Milan: Feltrinelli Editore.

Newman, Katherine S. 1999. Falling from Grace: Downward Mobility in the Age of Affluence. Berkeley: University of California Press.

Nocerino, Alberto. 2013. Dino Campana, per Genova. Percorso Poetico. Genoa: Liberodiscrivere Edizioni.

Notarangelo, Cristina. 2011. Tra il Maghreb e i carruggi. Giovani marocchini di seconda generazione. Rome: CISU.

O'Dougherty, Maureen. 2002. Consumption Intensified: The Politics of Middle-Class Daily Life in Brazil. Durham, NC: Duke University Press.

Oldenburg, Ray. 1991. The Great Good Place: Cafés, Coffee Shops, Community Centers, Beauty Parlors, General Stores, Bars, Hangouts, and How They Get You Through the Day. St. Paul, MN: Paragon House.

Ong, Aihwa. 2011. Worlding Cities, or the Art of Being Global. *In* Worlding Cities: Asian Experiments and the Art of Being Global. Ananya Roy and Aihwa Ong, eds. Pp. 1–26. Oxford: Basil Blackwell.

———. 2006. Neoliberalism as Exception: Mutations in Citizenship and Sovereignty. Durham, NC: Duke University Press.

———. 2003. Buddha Is Hiding: Refugees, Citizenship, the New America. Berkeley: University of California Press.

Ortner, Sherry B. 2006. Anthropological Theory and Social Theory: Culture, People, and the Acting Subject. Durham, NC: Duke University Press.

———. 2003. New Jersey Dreaming: Capital, Culture, and the Class of '58. Durham, NC: Duke University Press.

Palumbo, Mauro. 1994. Il mutamento sociale. *In* Gibelli, Storia d'Italia: Le regioni dall'Unità a oggi. La Liguria. Antonio Gibelli and Paride Rugafiori, eds. Pp. 917–972. Turin: Giulio Einaudi Editore.

Parker, David. 2000. The Chinese Takeaway and the Diasporic Habitus: Space, Time and Power Geometries. *In* Un/settled Multiculturalism: Diasporas, Entanglements. Barnor Hesse, ed. Pp. 73–94. Transruptions. London: Zed Books.

Pateman, Carole. 1987. Feminist Critiques of the Public/Private Dichotomy. *In* Feminism and Equality. Anne Phillips, ed. Pp. 103–125. Oxford: Basil Blackwell.

Patico, Jennifer. 2008. Consumption and Social Change in a Post-Soviet Middle Class. Redwood City, CA: Stanford University Press.

Peck, Jamie. 2005. Struggling with the Creative Class. International Journal of Urban and Regional Research 29(4):740–770.

Peirolero, Carla, Ombretta Ricci, and Davide Viziano. n.d. Mercato del Carmine—Genova; Un'idea per la riqualificazione. http://www.suqgenova.it/fileadmin/pro

getti/Progetto_di_riqualificazione_Mercato_del_Carmine.pdf, accessed on September 21, 2014.

Perlmutter, David, and Gretchen L. Wagner. 2004. The Anatomy of a Photojournalistic Icon: Marginalization of Dissent in the Selection and Framing of "A Death in Genoa." Visual Communication 3(1):91–108.

Però, David. 2007. Inclusionary Rhetoric/Exclusionary Practices: Left-Wing Politics and Migrants in Italy. New York: Berghahn.

Peterson, Marina. 2010. Sound, Space and the City: Civic Performance in Downtown Los Angeles. Philadelphia: University of Pennsylvania Press.

Pieke, Frank. 2004. Chinese Globalization ad Migration to Europe. Working Papers, Center for Comparative Immigration Studies. San Diego: University of California.

Pipan, Tatiana. 1989. Sciopero contro l'utente. La metamorfosi del conflitto industriale. Turin: Bollati Boringhieri.

Pipyrou, Stavroula. 2014. Cutting Bella Figura: Irony, Crisis and Secondhand Clothes in South Italy. American Ethnologist 41(3):532–546.

Pitkin, Donald S. 1993. Italian Urbanscape: Intersection of Private and Public. In The Cultural Meanings of Urban Space. Gary McDonogh and Robert Rotenberg, eds. Pp. 96–101. Westport, CT: Bergin & Garvey.

Poria, Yaniv. 2010. The Story Behind the Picture: Preferences for the Visual Display at Heritage Sites. In Culture, Heritage and Representation: Perspectives on Visuality and the Past. Emma Waterton and Steve Watson, eds. Pp. 217–228. Farnham: Ashgate.

Putnam, Robert D. 1993. Making Democracy Work: Civic Traditions in Modern Italy. Princeton, NJ: Princeton University Press.

Queirolo-Palmas, Luca. 2005. Verso dove? Voci e pratiche giovanili tra stigmatizzazione, cittadinanza e rifiuto dell'integrazione subalterna. In Il fantasma delle bande. Genova e i latinos. Luca Queirolo-Palmas and Andrea T. Torre, eds. Pp. 279–328. Genoa: Fratelli Frilli Editori.

Rahier, Jean Muteba. 2008. Globalization and Race: Transformation in the Cultural Production of Blackness. Journal of Latin American and Caribbean Anthropology 13(2):471–473.

Reed, Adam. 2002. City of Details: Interpreting the Personality of London. Journal of the Royal Anthropological Institute 8(1):127–141.

Reed-Danahay, Deborah. 1997. Auto/ethnography: Rewriting the Self and the Social. Oxford: Berg.

Reyneri, Emilio. 1997. Occupati e disoccupati in Italia. Bologna: Il Mulino.

Richards, Greg. 2011. Creativity and Tourism: The State of the Art. Annals of Tourism Research 38(4):1225–1253.

———. 2006. Cultural Tourism: Global and Local Perspectives. London: Routledge.

———. 1996. Introduction. In Cultural Tourism in Europe. Greg Richards, ed. Pp. 3–17. Oxon: CAB International.

Richards, Greg, and Julie Wilson. 2006. Developing Creativity in Tourist Experiences: A Solution to the Serial Reproduction of Culture? Tourism Management 27(6):1209–1223.

Richards, Greg, and Robert Palmer. 2010. Eventful Cities: Cultural Management and Urban Revitalization. Oxford: Elsevier.

Richardson, Tanya. 2008. Kaleidoscopic Odessa: History and Place in Contemporary Ukraine. Anthropological Horizons. Toronto: University of Toronto Press.

Ritzer, George. 2010. Enchanting a Disenchanted World: Continuity and Change in the Cathedrals of Consumption. Thousand Oaks, CA: Sage Publications.

Rockefeller, Stuart Alexander. 1999. "There Is a Culture Here": Spectacle and the Inculcation of Folklore in Highland Bolivia. Journal of Latin American Anthropology 3(2):118–149.

Rodaway, Paul. 1994. Sensuous Geographies: Body, Sense, and Place. London: Routledge.

Rofe, Matthew. 2003. I Want to Be Global: Theorizing the Gentrifying Class as an Emergent Elite Global Community. Urban Studies 40(1):2511–2526.

Rorty, Richard. 1999. Philosophy and Social Hope. London: Penguin.

Rose, Damaris. 1984. Rethinking Gentrification: Beyond the Uneven Development of Marxist Urban Theory. Environment and Planning D: Society and Space 2(1):47–74.

Rotenberg, Robert. 2014. Material Agency in the Urban Material Culture Initiative. Museum Anthropology 37(1):36–45.

———. 1995. Landscape and Power in Vienna. Baltimore: Johns Hopkins University Press.

Routledge, Paul. 1996. Critical Geopolitics and Terrains of Resistance. Political Geography 15(6/7):505–531.

Roy, Ananya. 2011. Conclusion: Postcolonial Urbanism: Speed, Hysteria, Mass Dreams. In Worlding Cities: Asian Experiments and the Art of Being Global. Ananya Roy and Aihwa Ong, eds. Pp. 307–335. Oxford: Wiley Blackwell.

Rutheiser, Charles. 1996. Imagineering Atlanta: The Politics of Place in the City of Dreams. London: Verso.

Salerno, Irene. 2010. La gentrification come strumento per la rivitalizzazione economica e sociale delle aree urbane: il Raval di Barcellona e il Centro Storico di Genova. PhD dissertation, University of Bologna.

Santos, Paula Mota. 2012. The Power of Knowledge: Tourism and the Production of Heritage in Porto's Old City. International Journal of Heritage Studies 18(5): 444–458.

Sartori, Giovanni. 2000. Pluralismo, multiculturalismo e estranei. Saggio sulla società multietnica. Milan: Rizzoli.

Scanlon, Jennifer. 2000. Advertising Women: The J. Walter Thompson Company Women's Advertising Department. In The Gender and Consumer Culture Reader. Jennifer Scanlon, ed. Pp. 201–255. New York: New York University Press.

Scarpellini, Emanuela. 2007. La spesa è uguale per tutti. L'avventura dei supermercati in Italia. Venice: Marsilio.

———. 2001. Comprare all'americana: le origini della rivoluzione commerciale in Italia, 1945–1971. Bologna: Il Mulino.

Scheper-Hughes, Nancy. 1995. The Primacy of the Ethical: Propositions for a Militant Anthropology. Current Anthropology 36(3):409–440.

Scherer, Frank. 2001. Sanfancón: Orientalism, Confucianism and the Construction of Chineseness in Cuba, 1847–1997. In Nation Dance: Religion, Identity and Cultural Difference in the Caribbean. Patrick Taylor, ed. Pp. 153–170. Bloomington: Indiana University Press.

Scherfig, Lone. 2000. Italian for Beginners. Tardini. Film.

Schneider, Jane. 1971. Of Vigilance and Virgins: Honor, Shame and Access to Resources in Mediterranean Societies. Ethnology 10(1):1–24.

Sema, Antonio. 2001. Limoni e sangue: a che servivano gli scontri di Genova. Limes 4(1):17–28.

Sennett, Richard. 1977. The Fall of Public Man. New York: Knopf.

Sassen, Saskia. 1991. The Global City: New York, London, Tokyo. Princeton, NJ: Princeton University Press.

Shin, Michael E., and John Agnew. 2008. Berlusconi's Italy: Mapping Contemporary Italian Politics. Philadelphia: Temple University Press.

Signorelli, Amalia. 1990. L'incertezza del diritto. Clientelismo politico e innovazione nel mezzogiorno degli anni '80. In Modernizzazione? Industrialismo, innovazione e rapporti di classe. P. Adler, ed. Pp. 256–272. Milan: Franco Angeli.

Simmel, Georg. 2002 [1903]. The Metropolis and Mental Life. In The Blackwell City Reader. Gary Bridge and Sophie Watson, eds. Pp. 11–19. Oxford: Wiley Blackwell.

Smith, Andrew. 2012. Events and Urban Regeneration: The Strategic Use of Events to Revitalise Cities. London: Routledge.

Smith, Darren. 2002. Extending the Temporal and Spatial Limits of Gentrification: A Research Agenda for Population Geographers. International Journal of Population Geography 8(1):358–394.

Smith, Darren, and Louise Holt. 2005. Studentification and Apprentice Gentrifiers Within Britain's Provincial Towns and Cities: Extending the Meaning of Gentrification. Environment and Planning A 39(1):142–161.

Smith, Neil. 2002. New Globalism, New Urbanism: Gentrification as a Global Urban Strategy. In Space of Neoliberalism: Urban Restructuring in North America and Western Europe. Neil Brenner and Nik Theodore, eds. Pp. 80–103. Malden, MA: Basil Blackwell.

———. 1996. The New Urban Frontier: Gentrification and the Revanchist City. London: Routledge.

———. 1979. Toward a Theory of Gentrification: A Back to the City Movement by Capital, Not People. Journal of the American Planning Association 45(4):538–548.

Snow, Nancy. 2003. Framing Globalization and Media Strategies for Global Change. *In* Representing Resistance: Media, Civil Disobedience, and the Global Justice Movement. Andy Opel and Donnalyn Pompper, eds. Pp. 109–114. Westport, CT: Praeger.

Soja, Edward. 1996. Thirdspace: Journeys to Los Angeles and Other Real-and-Imagined Places. Oxford: Basil Blackwell.

Somers, Margaret R. 1994. The Narrative Constitution of Identity: A Relational and Network Approach. Theory and Society 23(1):605–649.

Srivastava, Sanjay. 2014. Entangled Urbanism: Slum, Gated Community and Shopping Mall in Delhi and Gurgaon. Oxford: Oxford University Press.

Staeheli, Lynn, Don Mitchell, and Caroline Nagel. 2009. Making Publics: Immigrants, Regimes of Publicity and Entry to "the Public." Environment and Planning D: Society and Space 27(4):633–648.

Stewart, Charles. 2003. Dreams of Treasure: Temporality, Historicization, and the Unconscious. Anthropological Theory 3(4):481–500.

Stolcke, Verena. 1995. Talking Culture: New Boundaries, New Rhetorics of Exclusion in Europe. Current Anthropology 36(1):1–24.

Stoller, Paul. 1976. Sensuous Scholarship. Philadelphia: University of Pennsylvania Press.

Storey, John. 2003. Inventing Popular Culture. London: Basil Blackwell.

Swyngedow, Erik, Frank Moulaert, and Arantxa Rodriguez. 2002. Neoliberal Urbanization in Europe: Large-Scale Urban Development Projects and the New Urban Policy. *In* Spaces of Neoliberalism. N. Brenner and N. Theodore, eds. Oxford: Basil Blackwell.

Tabucchi, Antonio. 1986. Il filo dell'orizzonte. Milan: Feltrinelli.

Taplin, Ian M. 1989. Segmentation and the Organization of Work in the Italian Apparel Industry. Social Science Quarterly 70(2):408–424.

Taussig, Michael. 1991. Tactility and Distraction. Cultural Anthropology 6(2):147–153.

———. 1987. Shamanism, Colonialism, and the Wild Man: A Study in Terror and Healing. Chicago: University of Chicago Press.

Taylor, Charles. 1994. The Politics of Recognition. *In* Multiculturalism: Examining the Politics of Recognition. Charles Taylor, ed. Pp. 25–74. Princeton, NJ: Princeton University Press.

Tester, Keith. 1994. Introduction. *In* The Flâneur. Keith Tester, ed. Pp. 1–21. London: Routledge.

Thomas, Colin, and Rosemary Bromley. 2000. City-Centre Revitalisation: Problems of Fragmentation and Fear in the Evening and Night-Time City. Urban Studies 37(8):1403–1429.

Thompson, J. B. 1994. Social Theory and the Media. *In* Communication Theory Today. David Crowley and D. Mitchell, eds. Pp. 27–49. Stanford, CA: Stanford University Press.

Torre, Andrea T. 2005. La presenza urbana. L'immigrazione a Genova (1985–2004): Un breve excursus. *In* Il fantasma delle Bande. Genova e i latinos. Luca Queirolo-Palmas and Andrea T. Torre, eds. Pp. 31–54. Genoa: Fratelli Frilli Editore.

Triandafyllidou, Anna. 2006. Religious Diversity and Multiculturalism in Southern Europe: The Italian Mosque Debate. *In* Multiculturalism, Muslims and Citizenship: A European Approach. Tariq Modood, Anna Triandafyllidou, and Richard Zapata-Barrero, eds. Pp. 117–142. New York: Routledge.

Tsing, Anna L. 2004. Friction: An Ethnography of Global Connection. Princeton, NJ: Princeton University Press.

Turner, Victor. 1980. Social Drama and Stories About Them. Critical Inquiry 7(1):141–168.

———. 1974. Dramas, Fields, and Metaphors: Symbolic Action in Human Society. Ithaca, NY: Cornell University Press.

———. 1967. The Forest of Symbols: Aspects of Ndembu Ritual. Ithaca, NY: Cornell University Press.

Twain, Mark. 2010. The Innocents Abroad. Ware: Wordsworth Editions.

Urry, John. 2002. The Tourist Gaze. 2nd ed. London: Sage Publications.

Valentini, Chiara. 1997. Le donne fanno paura. Milan: Il Saggiatore.

Van Criekingen, Mathieu, and Jean-Michel Decroly. 2001. Revisiting the Diversity of Gentrification: Neighborhood Renewal Processes in Brussels and Montreal. Urban Studies 40(12):2451–2468.

Van der Berg, Marguerite. 2012. Femininity as a City Marketing Strategy: Gender Bending Rotterdam. Urban Studies 49(1):153–168.

Vanderford, Emily. 2003. Ya Basta!—A Mountain of Bodies That Advances, Seeking the Least Harm Possible to Itself. *In* Representing Resistance: Media, Civil Disobedience, and the Global Justice Movement. Andy Opel and Donnalyn Pompper, eds. Pp. 16–26. Westport, CT: Praeger.

Vertovec, Steven, and Susanna Wessendorf. 2005. Migration and Cultural, Religious and Linguistic Diversity in Europe: An Overview of Issues and Trends. Oxford: Oxford University Press.

Vitali, Francesco. 2001. La rete della sconfitta. Limes 1(4):67–70.

Waddington, David. 2008. The Madness of the Mob? Explaining the "Irrationality" and Destructiveness of Crowd Violence. Sociology Compass 2(1):675–687.

Wagner-Pacifici, Robin. 2000. Theorizing the Standoff: Contingency in Action. Cambridge: Cambridge University Press.

———. 1986. The Moro Morality Play: Terrorism as Social Drama. Chicago: University of Chicago Press.

Watson, Steve. 2010. Constructing Rhodes: Heritage Tourism and Visuality. *In* Culture, Heritage and Representation: Perspectives on Visuality and the Past. Emma Waterton and Steve Watson, eds. Pp. 249–270. Farnham: Ashgate.

Watson, Steve, and Emma Waterton. 2010. Introduction: A Visual Heritage. *In* Culture, Heritage and Representation: Perspectives on Visuality and the Past. Emma Waterton and Steve Watson, eds. Pp. 1–18. Farnham: Ashgate.

Weber, Max. 1965. Politics as a Vocation. Minneapolis: Fortress Press.

Wells, Audrey. 2003. Under the Tuscan Sun. Film.

Welsch, Wolfgang. 1998. Undoing Aesthetics. Thousand Oaks, CA: Sage Publications.

Wertsch, James. 2008. The Narrative Organization of Collective Memory. Ethos 36(1):120–135.

White, Nicola. 2000. Reconstructing Italian Fashion: America and the Development of the Italian Fashion Industry. Oxford: Berg.

Win, Thet Shein. 2014. Marketing the Entrepreneurial Artist in the Innovation Age: Aesthetic Labor, Artistic Subjectivity, and the Creative Industries. Anthropology of Work Review 35(1):2–13.

Wolf, Eric R. 1982. Europe and the People Without History. Berkeley: University of California Press.

Wright, Erik Olin. 1989. A General Framework for the Analysis of Class Structure. The Debate on Classes. Erik Olin Wright, ed. Pp. 3–43. New York: Verso.

Wynn, Johnson. 2005. Guiding Practices: Storytelling Tricks for Reproducing the Urban Landscape. Qualitative Sociology 28(4):397–415.

Yanagisako, Sylvia. 2013. Transnational Family Capitalism: Producing "Made in Italy" in China. In Vital Relations: Modernity and the Persistent Life of Kinship. Susan McKinnon and Fenella Cannell, eds. Pp. 63–84. Santa Fe: School for Advanced Research Press.

———. 2002. Producing Culture and Capital: Family Firms in Italy. Princeton, NJ: Princeton University Press.

Young, Iris. 1990. Throwing like a Girl and Other Essays in Feminist Philosophy and Social Theory. Bloomington: Indiana University Press.

Zajko, Mike, and Daniel Béland. 2008. Space and Protest Policing at International Summits. Environment and Planning D: Society and Space 26(1):719–735.

Zhang, Li. 2010. In Search for Paradise: Middle Class Living in a Chinese Metropolis. Ithaca, NY: Cornell University Press.

Zinn, Dorothy Louise. 2002. Pacem in Terris: Problems in Reading a "Multiethnic" Television Variety Show. In The Politics of Recognizing Difference: Multiculturalism Italian Style. R. D. Grillo and Jeff Pratt, eds. Pp. 197–218. Surrey: Ashgate.

———. 2001. La raccomandazione. Clientelismo vecchio e nuovo. Milan: Donzelli.

Žižek, Slavoj. 1997. Multiculturalism, or the Cultural Logic of Multinational Capitalism. New Left Review 225(2):28–51.

Zukin, Sharon. 2010. Naked City: The Death and Life of Authentic Urban Places. Oxford: Oxford University Press.

———. 1996. The Culture of Cities. Oxford: Basil Blackwell.

———. 1991. Landscapes of Power: From Detroit to Disney World. Berkeley: University of California Press.

———. 1989. Loft Living: Culture and Capital in Urban Change. Baltimore: Johns Hopkins University Press.

Index

Acknowledgments

The first time I heard about Romer's rule was fifteen years ago. Paleontologist Alfred Romer, my colleague Kathryn Kozaitis informed me, had discovered how animals living in pools of water that periodically dry up evolve legs: it is by walking on land that they can look for water elsewhere whenever their pool evaporates. "We diasporic people are like that, too," my Greek-born friend told me. "We grow legs to get out of our home pool when it gets dry, but we also grow them to get back to it later in life." Kathryn was right. This book bears witness to how, after allowing me to leave an inhospitable home pool, my newly evolved legs also took me back to it years later—though, this time around, out of choice rather than necessity.

The early stages of my Genoese ethnography began in 2002. The project soon turned out to be a deeply rewarding endeavor because of the enthusiastic support I received from many of my old and new friends. My gratitude goes to Michela Ceccarini, Simone Gatto, Alberto Nocerino, Franca Scotto, Patrizia Ponte, Stefania Zanelli, Massimo Morasso, and Silvia Perrone, as well as the many other Genoese—walking-tour guides, antique dealers, festival organizers and participants, city administrators, museum curators as well as centro storico artisans, small business owners, and residents—who spent time with me, patiently answered all of my questions, and introduced me to their friends and colleagues. Without them, this book would not have been possible. I am also thankful for the feedback a host of reviewers and colleagues volunteered on this manuscript at various stages of its development. I am particularly indebted to Gary McDonogh for his support and his astute reviews, as well as to Kathryn Kozaitis, Jennifer Patico, Faidra Papavasiliou, Megan Sinnott, and Katherine Hankins for their comments. The extended gestation of this book was made bearable by the encouragement I received from my husband Sandeep as well as from my friends

Cristina Cinti, Karen Hannah, Goran Matkovic, Carla Roncoli, and Emanuela Floris. I also thank Caterina Ghinazzi for providing loving sustenance during my stays in Genoa and heartfelt prayers when I was away, and above all my mother Maria Serena for her unwavering support. It is to her that this book is dedicated.

*   *   *

Earlier versions of Chapters 2 and 4 were published, respectively, in Arijit Sen and Lisa D. Silverman (eds.), Making Place: Space and Embodiment in the City (Bloomington: Indiana University Press, 2014), 69–94, and Gender, Place and Culture: A Journal of Feminist Geography 13(1) (2006): 105–122. A modified version of Chapter 5 appeared in City & Society 27(2) (2015): 160–182.